ABUSIR XX

LESSER LATE PERIOD TOMBS AT ABUSIR

THE TOMB OF PADIHOR
AND THE ANONYMOUS TOMB R3

Excavations of the Czech Institute of Egyptology

ABUSIR XX

LESSER LATE PERIOD TOMBS AT ABUSIR

THE TOMB OF PADIHOR AND THE ANONYMOUS TOMB R3

Filip Coppens – Květa Smoláriková

with a preface by **Ladislav Bareš**
and a contribution by **František Ondráš** and **Eugen Strouhal**

Czech Institute of Egyptology
Faculty of Arts, Charles University in Prague
Prague 2009

The book was published from the financial means allocated for the research project of the Ministry of Education, Grant No. MSM 0021620826 ('The Exploration of the Civilisation of Ancient Egypt').

Reviewed by Petr Charvát and Marie Dufková

Text: Ladislav Bareš, Filip Coppens, František Ondráš, Květa Smoláriková and Eugen Strouhal
Photographs: Archive of the Czech Institute of Egyptology (CIE), Filip Coppens (FC), Květa Smoláriková (KS) and Kamil Voděra (KV).
Figures and plans: Květa Smoláriková, Filip Coppens, Petra Maříková Vlčková and Lucie Vařeková.

Type-setting layout: AGAMA® poly-grafický ateliér, s.r.o.

ISBN 978-80-7308-295-6

Contents

Acknowledgements

We would like to express our gratitude to Prof. Ladislav Bareš, director of the Czech Institute of Egyptology, Charles University in Prague and field director of the Czech excavations in the Saite-Persian shaft tomb necropolis at Abusir, for entrusting us with the publication of the burial complex of Padihor and the anonymous tomb R3 and for the numerous helpful remarks and observations made during the work on this book. Our thanks also go to Petra Maříková Vlčková for her part in the documentary work of the architecture of Padihor's tomb carried out during the spring season of 2001, and to team members Martin Dvořák and Michael Balík for their assistance during the excavations of both burial complexes.

We acknowledge with gratitude the support and cooperation of the officials of the Supreme Council of Antiquities, in particular the Permanent Secretary Dr. Zahi Hawass and his predecessor Prof. Gaballa A. Gaballa, and the General Director of the Saqqara Antiquities Zone Mr. Usama es-Shimi and his predecessor Mr. Adel Hussein. We would also like to thank the inspectors Nasir Ramadan and Mustafa Zaki Taha, present during the excavation and documentation works in the tombs of Padihor and R3 (2001-2002 and 2008). In Abusir, the workmen were as always expertly headed by the *reisin* Muhammad Talaal el-Kerety and Ahmed el-Kerety.

We would like to thank our colleagues Petr Charvát (Centre for Near Eastern Studies, University of West Bohemia, Pilsen), Marie Dufková (Department of Classical Archaeology, National Museum – Historical Museum, Prague) and Jiří Janák (Czech Institute of Egyptology, Charles University in Prague), who took the time to carefully read the original manuscript and made many helpful remarks in the process. We are very grateful to Ramadan B. Hussein (Director of the Documentation Centre of the Egyptian Supreme Council of Antiquities) for providing us with his not yet published PhD thesis, *The Saite Pyramid Text Copies in the Memphite and Heliopolitan Shaft-Tombs: A Study of their Selection and Layout* (Brown University 2009). Numerous other colleagues provided support in many different ways during the writing of this volume. We would like to single out Katarína Arias, Marek Dospěl, Veronika Dulíková, Lucie Jirásková, Miroslav Ottmar and Lenka Suková of the Czech Institute of Egyptology, Charles University in Prague, for their help during the work with the plans, foils, photos and plates of both burial complexes, and Lucie Vařeková for producing all line-drawings for this volume. The photographs were taken by Kamil Voděra (now a part of the photographic archive of the Czech Institute of Egyptology, Charles University in Prague) and the authors. Kateřina Honskusová is heartily thanked for her expert help in correcting the English of this study. The staff at Agama, in particular Irena Macháčková, Ivana Heranová and Jiří Macháček, were as always of great assistance in preparing the manuscript for the printers.

The publication of this book was financed from a grant of the Ministry of Education within the research plan of the Czech Institute of Egyptology, Charles University in Prague: 'The Exploration of the Civilisation of Ancient Egypt' (Grant No. MSM 0021620826).

Filip Coppens and Květa Smoláriková

List of Illustrations

(Figs. 1 – 30 line drawings, plates 1-25 photographs)

Figures

Photographs

Abbreviations

ÄA	Ägyptologische Abhandlungen, Wiesbaden.
ÄAT	Ägypten und Altes Testament, Wiesbaden.
ADAIK	Abhandlungen des Deutschen Archäologischen Instituts, Abteilung Kairo, Glückstadt.
ÄF	Ägyptologische Forschungen, Glückstadt.
AJPA	American Journal of Physical Anthropology, Baltimore.
ASAE	Annales du Service des Antiquités de l'Egypte, Cairo.
AV	Archäologische Veröffentlichungen des Deutschen Archäologischen Instituts, Abteilung Kairo, Mainz am Rhein.
BACE	Bulletin of the Australian Centre for Egyptology, Sydney.
BASOR	Bulletin of the American Schools of Oriental Research, Winona Lake, Indiana.
BdE	Bibliothèque d'Etude, Cairo.
Beiträge Bf	Beiträge zur ägyptischen Bauforschung und Altertumskunde, Zürich–Wiesbaden.
BIFAO	Bulletin de l'Institut français d'archéologie orientale, Cairo.
BiGen	Bibliothèque Générale, Cairo
CASAE	Annales du Service des Antiquités de l'Egypte. Cahier, Cairo.
CCE	Cahiers de la céramique égyptienne, Cairo.
CdE	Chronique d'Egypte, Bruxelles.
CRAIBL	Comptes-rendus des séances de l'Académie des Inscriptions et Belles-Lettres, Paris.
DÖAW	Denkschriften der Österreichischen Akademie der Wissenschaften, Philosophisch–historische Klasse, Wien.
EA	Egyptian Archaeology: The Bulletin of the Egypt Exploration Society, London.
EVO	Egitto e Vicino Oriente, Pisa.
GM	Göttinger Miszellen, Göttingen.
GOF	Göttinger Orientforschungen. Veröffentlichungen des Sonderforschungsbereiches Orientalistik an der Georg-August-Universität Göttingen. IV. Reihe: Ägypten, Wiesbaden.
JARCE	Journal of the American Research Center in Egypt, New York.
JEA	The Journal of Egyptian Archaeology, London.
JEOL	Jaarbericht van het Vooraziatisch Egyptisch Genootschap 'Ex Oriente Lux', Leiden.
JNES	Journal of Near Eastern Studies, Chicago.
JSSEA	Journal of the Society of the Study of Egyptian Antiquities, Toronto.
LAPO	Littératures anciennes du Proche–Orient, Paris.
MÄS	Münchener ägyptologische Studien, München–Berlin.
MDAIK	Mitteilungen des Deutschen Archäologischen Instituts, Abteilung Kairo, Berlin–Wiesbaden–Mainz.
MIFAO	Mémoires de l'Institut français d'archéologie orientale, Cairo.
MVAG	Mitteilungen der Vorderasiatisch–Ägyptischen Gesellschaft, Leipzig.
OIMP	Oriental Institute Museum Publications, Chicago.
OLA	Orientalia Lovaniensia Analecta, Leuven.
OLP	Orientalia Lovaniensia Periodica, Leuven.
PdÄ	Probleme der Ägyptologie, Leiden.
PM	B. Porter – R.L.B. Moss, *Topographical Bibliography of Ancient Egyptian Hieroglyphic Texts, Reliefs and Paintings* I–II, Oxford 1960–1964 (2nd revised edition); B. Porter – R.L.B. Moss, *Topographical Bibliography of Ancient Egyptian Hieroglyphic Texts, Reliefs and Paintings* III (edited, revised and

	augmented by J. Malek), Oxford 1978–1981; B. Porter – R.L.B. Moss, *Topographical Bibliography of Ancient Egyptian Hieroglyphic Texts, Reliefs and Paintings* IV–VII, Oxford 1934–1951; J. Malek – D. Magee – E. Miles, *Topographical Bibliography of Ancient Egyptian Hieroglyphic Texts, Reliefs and Paintings* VIII, Oxford 1999.
RdE	Revue d'Egyptologie, Cairo–Paris.
RT	Recueil de Travaux Rélatifs à la Philologie et à l'Archéologie Egyptiennes et Assyriennes, Paris.
SAGA	Studien zur Archäologie und Geschichte Altägyptens, Heidelberg.
SAK	Studien zur altägyptischen Kultur, Hamburg.
SAOC	Studies in Ancient Oriental Civilizations, Chicago.
SAT	Studien zum Altägyptischen Totenbuch, Wiesbaden.
SDAIK	Sonderschrift des Deutschen Archäologischen Instituts, Abteilung Kairo, Mainz.
YES	Yale Egyptological Studies, New Haven.
ZÄS	Zeitschrift für Ägyptische Sprache und Altertumskunde, Leipzig–Berlin.
ZDMG	Zeitschrift der Deutschen Morgenländischen Gesellschaft, Leipzig.

Bibliography

Abubakr, Abd el Monem Joussef, *Untersuchungen über die ägyptischen Kronen*, Hamburg – Glückstadt – New York: Verlag J.J. Augustin 1937.

Allen, T.G., *Occurrences of Pyramid Texts with Cross Indexes of Those and Other Egyptian Mortuary Texts*, (SAOC 27), Chicago: Oriental Institute 1950.

Allen, J.P., 'The Cosmology of the Pyramid Texts', in J.P. Allen – J. Assmann – A.B. Lloyd – R.K. Ritner – D.P. Silverman (eds.), *Religion and Philosophy in Ancient Egypt* (YES 3), New Haven 1989, pp. 1-28.

Allen, J.P., *The Ancient Egyptian Pyramid Texts*, (Writings from the Ancient World 23), Atlanta: Society of Biblical Literature 2005.

Altenmüller, B., *Synkretismus in den Sargtexten*, (GOF IV/7), Wiesbaden: Harrassowitz 1975.

Altenmüller, H. 'Bemerkungen zur frühen und späten Bauphase des Djoserbezirkes in Saqqara', *MDAIK* 28 (1972), pp. 1-12.

Anthes, R., *Mit Rahineh 1956*, Philadelphia: The University of Pennsylvania Museum 1965.

Arnold, Di., *Building in Egypt. Pharaonic Stone Masonry*, New York – Oxford: Oxford University Press 1991.

Arnold, Di., 'The Late Period Tombs of Hor-khebit, Wennefer and Wereshnefer at Saqqara', in C. Berger – B. Mathieu (eds.), *Etudes sur l'Ancien Empire et la nécropole de Saqqara dédiées à Jean-Philippe Lauer*, (Orientalia Monspeliensia IX), Montpellier: Université Paul Valéry – Montpellier III 1997, pp. 31-54.

Arnold, Di., *Temples of the Last Pharaohs*, New York – Oxford: Oxford University Press 1999.

Arnold, Di., *The Encyclopaedia of Ancient Egyptian Architecture*, London – New York: I.B. Tauris 2003.

Assmann, J., 'Death and Initiation in the Funerary Religion of Ancient Egypt', in J.P. Allen – J. Assmann – A.B. Lloyd – R.K. Ritner – D.P. Silverman (eds.), *Religion and Philosophy in Ancient Egypt* (YES 3), New Haven 1989, pp. 135-159.

Aston, D.A., 'The Theban West Bank from the Twenty-fifth Dynasty to the Ptolemaic Period', in N. Strudwick – J.H. Taylor (eds.), *The Theban Necropolis. Past, Present and Future*, London: British Museum Press 2003, pp. 138-166.

Aston-Green, B., 'The Pottery', in M.J. Raven, *The Tomb of Pay and Raia at Saqqara*, London: Egypt Exploration Society 2005, pp. 94-128.

Aubert, J.-F. – Aubert, L., *Statuettes égyptiennes. Chaouabtis, ouchebtis*, Paris: Librairie d'Amérique et d'Orient 1974.

Aubert J.-F. – Aubert, L., *Bronzes et Or Egyptiens*, Paris: Cybèle 2001.

al-Ayedi, A., *Index of Egyptian Administrative, Religious and Military Titles of the New Kingdom*, Ismailiya: Obelisk Publications 2006.

Badawy, A., *A History of Egyptian Architecture I. From the Earliest Times to the End of the Old Kingdom*, Giza 1954.

Baines, J., 'Modelling Sources, Processes, and Locations of Early Mortuary Texts', in S. Bickel – B. Mathieu (eds.), *Textes des Pyramides. Textes des Sarcophages. D'un monde à l'autre. Actes de la table ronde internationale 'Textes des Pyramides versus Textes des Sarcophages', IFAO – 24-26 septembre 2001*, (BdE 139), Cairo: IFAO 2004, pp. 15-41.

Bareš, L., 'Saite-Persian Cemetery at Abusir (Situation Report for January–April 1995)', *GM* 151 (1996), pp. 7-17.

Bareš, L., *Abusir IV. The Shaft Tomb of Udjahorresnet at Abusir*, Prague: Universitas Carolina Pragensis 1999.

Bareš, L., 'The Destruction of the Monuments at the Necropolis of Abusir', in M. Bárta – J. Krejčí (eds.), *Abusir and Saqqara in the Year 2000*, (Supplementa Archivu Orientálního IX), Prague: Academy of Sciences of the Czech Republic – Oriental Institute 2000, pp. 1-16.

Bareš, L., 'Shabtis from the Late Period Tombs at Abusir (Preliminary Remarks)', in H. Győry (ed.), *'Le lotus qui sort de la terre'. Mélanges offerts à Edith Varga*, (Bulletin du Musée Hongrois des Beaux-Arts. Supplément 2001), Budapest 2001, pp. 23-28.

Bareš, L., 'Some remarks on Cult Installations in Late Period Shaft Tombs in Egypt', *BACE* 13 (2002), pp. 17-27.

Bareš, L., 'The Necropolis at Abusir in the First Millennium BC', in K. Daoud – S. Bedier – S. Adel Fattah (eds.), *Studies in Honour of Ali Radwan*, (Supplément aux Annales du Service des Antiquités de l'Egypte 34/1), Cairo: IFAO 2005, pp. 177-182.

Bareš, L., 'Some Notes on the Religious Texts and Scenes in the Tomb of Iufaa and Other Late Period Shaft Tombs at Abusir', in H. Győry (ed.), *Aegyptus et Pannonia III. Acta Symposii anno 2004*, Budapest: MEBT–ÓEB 2006, pp. 1-9.

Bareš, L., 'The Social Status of the Owners of the Large Late Period Shaft Tombs', in M. Bárta – F. Coppens – J. Krejčí (eds.), *Abusir and Saqqara in the Year 2005. Proceedings of the Conference Held in Prague (June 27– July 5, 2005)*, Prague: Czech Institute of Egyptology 2006, pp. 1-17.

Bareš, L., 'Late Period Shaft Tombs, Step Pyramid and the Dry Moat?', in K. Daoud – S. Abd el-Fattah (eds.), *The World of Ancient Egypt. Essays in honor of Ahmed Abd el–Qader el–Sawi*, (Supplément aux Annales du Service des Antiquités de l'Egypte 35), Cairo: IFAO 2006, pp. 31–33.

Bareš, L., 'The Late Period at the Abusir Necropolis', in *Abusir. Secrets of the Desert and the Pyramids* (exhibition catalogue), Prague: Czech Institute of Egyptology / National Museum – Náprstek Museum of Asian, African and American Cultures 2006, pp. 162-175.

Bareš, L., 'The Saite–Persian Cemetery at Abusir', in: J.-C. Goyon – C. Cardin (eds.), *Proceedings of the Ninth International Congress of Egyptologists. Grenoble, 6-12 septembre 2004* I, (OLA 150) Leuven: Peeters 2007, pp. 145-150.

Bareš, L., 'Lesser Burial Chambers in the Large Late Period Shaft Tombs and their Owners', in Z. Hawass – J. Richards (eds.), *The Archaeology and Art of Ancient Egypt. Essays in Honor of David B. O'Connor*, (CASAE 36), 2007, pp. 87-97.

Bareš, L., 'Personifications of the Day- and Night-Hours in the Tomb of Menekhibnekau at Abusir – A Preliminary Notice', in P. Maříková Vlčková – J. Mynářová – M. Tomášek (eds.), *My Things Changed Things. Social Development and Cultural Exchange in Prehistory, Antiquity, and Middle Ages*, Prague: Charles University in Prague 2009, pp. 16-24.

Bareš, L., 'A Case of Proofreading in Ancient Egypt', in I. Régen – F. Servajean (eds.), *Verba Manent. Recueil d'études dédiées à Dimitri Meeks*, (Cahiers 'Egypte Nilotique et Méditerranéenne' 2), Montpellier 2009, pp. 51-56.

Bareš, L. – Bárta, M. – Smolárikova, K. – Strouhal, E., 'Abusir – Spring 2002', *ZÄS* 130 (2003), pp. 147-159.

Bareš, L. – Dvořák, M. – Smoláriková, K. – Strouhal, E., 'The Shaft Tomb of Iufaa at Abusir in 2001', *ZÄS* 129 (2002), pp. 97-108.

Bareš, L. – Janák, J. – Landgráfová, R. – Smoláriková, K., 'The Shaft Tomb of Menekhibnekau at Abusir – Season of 2007', *ZÄS* 135 (2008), pp. 104-114.

Bareš, L. – Janák, J. – Landgráfová, R. – Smoláriková, K., 'The Shaft Tomb of Menekhibnekau at Abusir – season of 2008', *ZÄS* 137 (2010 – forthcoming).

Bareš, L. – Smoláriková, K., 'The Shaft Tomb of Iufaa at Abusir (Preliminary Report for 1995/1996)', *GM* 156 (1997), pp. 9-26.

Bareš, L. – Smoláriková, K., *The shaft tomb of Iufaa. vol. I: Archaeology*, (Abusir XVII), Prague: Czech Institute of Egyptology 2008.

Bareš, L. – Smoláriková, K. – Strouhal, E., 'The Saite Persian Cemetery at Abusir in 2003', *ZÄS* 132 (2005), pp. 95-106.

Bareš, L. – Strouhal, E., 'The Shaft Tomb of Iufaa – Season of 1997/98', *ZÄS* 127 (2000), pp. 5-14.

Barguet, P., *Les textes des sarcophages égyptiens du Moyen Empire. Introduction et traduction*, (LAPO 12), Paris: 1986.

Barsanti, A., 'II. Les tombeaux de Psammétique et de Setariban. I. Rapport sur la découverte', *ASAE* 1 (1900), pp. 161-166.

Barsanti, A., 'III. Le tombeau de Smendès', *ASAE* 1 (1900), pp. 189-190.

Barsanti, A., 'IV. Tombeau de Péténisis. I. Rapport sur la découverte', *ASAE* 1 (1900), pp. 230-234.

Barsanti, A., 'IV. Tombeau de Zannehibou. I. Rapport sur la découverte', *ASAE* 1 (1900), pp. 262-271.

Barsanti, A., 'VIII. Tombeau de Péténéith. I. Rapport sur la découverte', *ASAE* 2 (1901), pp. 97-104.

Barsanti, A., 'Rapports de M. Alexandre Barsanti sur les déblaiements opérés autour de la pyramide d'Ounas pendant les années 1899-1901', *ASAE* 2 (1901), pp. 244-257.

Barsanti, A., 'Sur la découverte du puits d'Ouazhorou à Sakkarah', *ASAE* 3 (1902), pp. 209-212.

Barsanti, A., 'XII. Le tombeau de Hikaoumsaf. Rapport sur la découverte', *ASAE* 5 (1904), pp. 69-78.

Bárta, M., 'The Title "Property Custodian of the King" during the Old Kingdom Egypt', *ZÄS* 126 (1999), pp. 79-90.

Bárta, M., 'The early Fourth and early Fifth Dynasty at Abusir South', in M. Bárta – J. Krejčí (eds.), *Abusir and Saqqara in the Year 2000*, (Supplementa Archivu Orientálního IX), Prague: Academy of Sciences of the Czech Republic – Oriental Institute 2000, pp. 331-346.

Bárta, M. – Brůna, V., *Satellite Atlas of the Pyramid Fields of Abusir, Saqqara and Dahshur*, Prague: Dryada 2006.

Barta, W., *Die altägyptische Opferliste von der Frühzeit bis zur griechisch-römischen Epoche*, (MÄS 3), Berlin: Verlag Bruno Hessling 1963.

Barta, W., 'Funktion und Lokalisierung der Zirkumpolarsterne in den Pyramidentexte', *ZÄS* 107 (1980), pp. 1-4.

Baud, M., *Famille royale et pouvoir sous l'Ancien Empire égyptien* I, (BdE 126/1), Cairo: IFAO 1999.

Bell, L.D., 'Ancient Egyptian Personhood (Anthropology/Psychology): The Nature of Humankind, Individuality and Self–identity', in H. Beinlich – J. Hallof – H. Hussy – C. von Pfeil (eds.), *5. Ägyptologische Tempeltagung. Würzburg, 23.–26. September 1999*, (ÄAT 33/3), Wiesbaden: Harrassowitz 2002, pp. 38-42.

Betro, M.C. – Silvano, F., 'Progetto visir. La simulazione nel restauro della tomba di Bekenrenef a Saqqara (L 24)', *EVO* 14-15 (1991–1992), pp. 5-8.

Bickel, S. – Tallet, P., 'La nécropole Saïte d'Héliopolis. Etude preliminaire', *BIFAO* 97 (1997), pp. 67-90.

Bidoli, D., *Die Sprüche der Fangnetze in den altägyptischen Sargtexten*, ADAIK 9 (1976), Glückstadt.

Björkman, G., 'A Funerary Statuette of Hekaemsaf, Chief of the Royal Ships in the Saitic Period', *From the Gustavianum Collections in Uppsala, 1974*, (BOREAS. Uppsala Studies in Ancient Mediterranean and Near Eastern Civilizations 6), Uppsala 1974, pp. 71-79.

Bolshakov, A., 'Ka', in D. Redford (ed.), *The Oxford Encyclopedia of Ancient Egypt* II, Oxford–New York: Oxford University Press 2001, pp. 215-217.

Bonnet, H., *Reallexikon der ägyptischen Religionsgeschichte*, Berlin: De Gruyter & Co. 1952.

Borchardt, L., *Statuen und Statuetten von Königen und Privatleuten* III *Catalogue Général des Antiquités Égyptiennes du Musée du Caire, Nos 654-950*, Berlin 1930.

Botti, G. – Romanelli, P., *Le sculture del Museo Gregoriano Egizio*, Vatican: Tipografia poliglotta Vaticano 1951.

Bourriau, J., 'Salbgefässe', in W. Helck – E. Otto (eds.), *Lexikon der Ägyptologie V*, Wiesbaden: Harrassowitz 1984, pp. 362-366.

Bourriau, J. – Aston, D., 'The Pottery', in G.T. Martin, *The Tomb Chapels of Paser and Ra'ia at Saqqara*, (Excavation Memoir 52), London: Egypt Exploration Society 1985.

Bresciani, E., *Le stele egiziane del Museo Civico Archeologico di Bologna*, Bologna: Grafis 1985.

Bresciani, E. – an-Nagar, S. – Pernigotti, S. – Silvano, F., *La Galleria di Padineit, visir di Nectanebo I*, (Saqqara 1), Pisa 1983.

Bresciani, E. – Pernigotti, S. – Giangeri Silvis, M.P., *La tomba di Ciennehebu, capo della flotta del Re*, (Biblioteca degli Studi Classici e Orintale 7) Pisa: Giardini 1977.

Briant, P., *Historie de l'Empire Perse, de Cyrus à Alexandre*, Paris: Fayard 1996.

Brunner, S., 'Der Bekannte des Königs', *SAK* 1 (1974), pp. 55-60.

Brunner-Traut, E., 'Chenti-irti', in W. Helck – E. Otto (eds.), *Lexikon der Ägyptologie I*, Wiesbaden: Harassowitz 1975, pp. 926-930.

Buongarzone, R., 'La funzionalita dei testi nel contesto architettonico della tomba di Bakenrenef', *EVO* 13 (1990), pp. 81-102.

Buongarzone, R., 'Su alcuni testi della tomba di Bakenrinef. A proposito di una redazione saitica', *EVO* 14-15 (1991–1992), pp. 31-42.

Buongarzone, R., 'Testi religiosi di epoca saitica e Testi delle piramidi', *EVO* 16 (1993), pp. 23-30.

Cauville, S., *La théologie d'Osiris à Edfou*, (BdE 91), Cairo: IFAO 1983.

Chrysikopoulos, V.I., 'The Statue of Padihor, General of the Army of Psammetichus I, at the National Archaeological Museum of Athens', in P. Kousoulis – K. Magliveras (eds.), *Moving Across Borders. Foreign Relations, Religion and Cultural Interactions in the Ancient Mediterranean*, (OLA 159), Leuven 2007, pp. 157-168.

Cook, R.M. – Dupont, P., *East Greek Pottery*, London: Routledge 1998.

Coppens, F., *The Wabet. Tradition and Innovation in Temples of the Ptolemaic and Roman Period*, Prague: Czech Institute of Egyptology 2007.

Coppens, F., 'Linen, Unguents and Pectorals. Instruments of Regeneration in Ptolemaic and Roman Temples', in M. Dolinska – H. Beinlich (eds.), *8th Egyptological Tempeltagung. Interconnections between Temples*, (Königtum, Staat und Gesellschaft Früher Hochkulturen 3/3), Wiesbaden (in press).

Coppens, F. – Vymazalová, H., 'Long Live the King! Notes on the Renewal of Divine Kingship in the Temple', in L. Bareš – F. Coppens – K. Smoláriková (eds.), *Social and Religious Development of Egypt in the First Millennium BCE*, Prague 2010 (in press).

Corteggiani, J.-P., 'Documents divers (I-VI)', *BIFAO* 73 (1973), pp. 143-153.

Coulon, L., 'Les uraei gardiens du fétiche abydénien. Un motif osirien et sa diffusion à l'époque saïte', in D. Devauchelle (ed.), *La XXVIe dynastie. Continuité ou rupture. Actes du colloque de l'Université de Lille-III. 26–27 novembre 2004*, in press.

Daressy, G., 'Inscriptions du tombeau de Psamtik à Saqqarah', *RT* 17 (1895), pp. 17-25.

Daressy, G., 'Tombe de Hor-Kheb à Saqqarah', *ASAE* 4 (1903), pp. 76-82.

Daressy, G., 'Samtauï-Tafnekht', *ASAE* 18 (1918), pp. 29-33.

Davis, W.M., 'The Ascension-Myth in the Pyramid Texts', *JNES* 36/3 (1977), pp. 161-179.

Dawson, W.R. – Uphill, E.P., *Who was who in Egyptology*, London: Egypt Exploration Society 1995.

De Meulenaere, H., 'Un titre memphite méconnu', in *Mélanges Mariette*, (BdE 32), Cairo: IFAO 1961, pp. 285-290.

De Meulenaere, H., 'La statue du général Djed–ptah–iouf–ankh (Caire JE 36949)', *BIFAO* 63 (1965), pp. 19-32.

De Meulenaere, H., 'Trois stèles inédites des Musées Royaux d'Art et d'Histoire', *CdE* 48 (1973), pp. 47-59.

De Meulenaere, H., 'Le clergé abydénien d'Osiris à la Basse Epoque', in P. Naster – H. De Meulenaere – J. Quaegebeur (eds.), *Miscellanea in honorem Joseph Vergote*, (OLP 6/7), Leuven: Departement Oriëntalistiek 1975–1976, pp. 133-151.

De Meulenaere, H., 'E Pluribus Una', *BIFAO* 87 (1987), pp. 135-140.

De Meulenaere, H. – De Strooper, I., 'Notes de prosopographie thébaine. Cinquième série', *CdE* 73 (1998), pp. 244-260.

Dodson, A. – Ikram, S., *The Tomb in Ancient Egypt. Royal and Private Sepulchers from the Early Dynastic Period to the Romans*, London: Thames & Hudson 2008.

Donatelli, L., *La raccolta egizia di Giuseppe Acerbi*, Mantova: Publi Paolini Editore 1983.

Drioton, E., 'Textes religieux des tombeaux saïtes', *ASAE* 52 (1954), pp. 105-128.

Drioton, E. – Lauer, J.-Ph., 'Les tombes jumeleés de Neferibrê-Sa-Neith et de Ouahibrê-Men', *ASAE* 51 (1951), pp. 469-489.

Dunsmore, A., 'Pottery from the Tomb of Meryneith', *JEOL* 40 (2006–2007), p. 18.

Edel, E., *Altägyptische Grammatik* I-II, (Analecta Orientalia 34/39), Roma: Pontificium Institutum Biblicum 1955–1964.

Eickstedt, E., *Die Forschung am Menschen. Teil 2. Physiologische und morphologische Anthropologie*, Stuttgart: Enke 1944.

Eigner, D., *Die monumentalen Grabbauten der Spätzeit in der thebanischen Nekropole*, (DÖAW 8), Wien 1984.

Eigner, D., 'Late Period Private Tombs', in K.A. Bard (ed.), *Encyclopedia of the Archaeology of Ancient Egypt*, London – New York: Routledge 1999, pp. 432-438.

Englund, G., *Akh – une notion religieuse dans l'Egypte pharaonique*, (BOREAS. Uppsala Studies in Ancient Mediterranean and Near Eastern Civilizations 11), Uppsala 1974.

Faulkner, R.O., *The Ancient Egyptian Pyramid Texts*, Oxford: Oxford University Press 1969.

Faulkner, R.O., *The Ancient Egyptian Coffin Texts* I-III, Warminster: 1973–1978.

Feucht, E., *Das Kind im alten Ägypten. Die Stellung des Kindes in Familie und Gesellschaft nach altägyptischen Texten und Darstellungen*, Frankfurt – New York: Campus Verlag 1995.

Firth, C.M., 'Excavations of the Service des Antiquités at Saqqara (October 1927 – April 1928)', *ASAE* 28 (1928), pp. 81-88.

Firth, C.M., 'Excavations of the Department of Antiquities at Saqqarah (October 1928 to March 1929)', *ASAE* 29 (1929), pp. 64-70.

Firth, C.M. – Quibell, J.E., *The Step Pyramid* I-II (with plans by J.-Ph. Lauer), Cairo: IFAO 1935.

Fischer, H.G., *Egyptian Titles of the Middle Kingdom: A Supplement to Wm. Ward's Index*, New York: Metropolitan Museum of Art 1985.

French, P., 'An Embalmer's Cache of the Late Dynastic Period', in U. Hartung – P. Ballet – F. Béguin – J. Bourriau – P. French – T. Herbich – P. Kapp – G. Lecuyot – A. Schmitt, 'Tell el-Fara'in-Buto. 8. Vorbericht', *MDAIK* 59 (2003), pp. 221-224.

French, P., 'Distinctive Pottery from the Second Half of the 6th Century B.C.', *CCE* 5 (2004), pp. 91-97.

French, P., 'The Pottery', in L. Giddy, *The Anubieion at Saqqara II: Cemeteries*, London: Egypt Exploration Society 1992, pp. 79-85.

French, P. – Ghaly, H., 'Pottery of the Late Period at Saqqara', *CCE* 2 (1987), pp. 93-124.

Frick, F.S., 'Pottery at Taanach', in S. Kreuzer (ed.), *Taanach/Tell Ta'annek. 100 Jahre Forschungen zur Archäologie, zur Geschichte, zu den Fundobjekten und zu den Keilschrifttexten*, (Wiener Alttestamentliche Studien 5), Frankfurt 2006, p. 35-47.

Galan, J.M. – el-Bialy, M., 'An apprentice's board from Dra Abu el-Naga', *EA* 25 (2004), pp. 38-40.

Gauthier, H., 'A travers la Basse Egypte. VII: Tombeau d'un certain Rames à Materia', *ASAE* 21, pp. 197-203.

Gauthier, H., 'Tombe d'époque Saïte à Héliopolis', *ASAE* 27 (1927), pp. 1-18.

Gestermann, L., 'Zu den spätzeitlichen Bezeugungen der Sargtexte', *SAK* 19 (1992), pp. 117-132.

Gestermann, L., '"Neue" Texte in spätzeitlichen Grabanlage von Saqqara und Heliopolis', in M. Minas – J. Zeidler (eds.), *Aspekte spätägyptische Kultur. Festschrift für Erich Winter zum 65. Geburtstag*, (Aegyptiaca Treverensia 7), Mainz: Verlag Philipp von Zabern 1994, pp. 89-95.

Gestermann, L., *Die Überlieferung ausgewählter Texte altägyptischer Totenliteratur ('Sargtexte') in spätzeitlichen Grabanlagen, Teil 1: Text, Teil 2: Textanhang*, (ÄA 68), Wiesbaden: Harrassowitz 2005.

Gestermann, L., 'Das spätzeitliche Schachtgrab als memphitischer Grabtyp', in G. Moers – H. Behlmer – K. Demuss – K. Widmaier (eds.), *jn.t ḏr.w. Festschrift für Friedrich Junge*, Göttingen: Seminar für Ägyptologie und Koptologie 2006, pp. 195-206.

Giles, E. – Elliot, O., 'Sex Determination by Discriminant Function Analysis of Crania', *AJPA* 21 (1963), pp. 53-68.

Gilula, M., 'An Adjective Predicative Expression of Possession in Middle Egyptian', *RdE* 20 (1968), pp. 55-61.

Goedicke, H., '*Rs m ḥtp*', *SAK* 34 (2006), pp. 187-204.

Gorre, G., '*Rḫ-nswt*: titre aulique ou titre sacerdotal "spécifique"?', *ZÄS* 136 (2009), pp. 8-18.

Goyon, J.-C., 'La statuette funéraire I.E. 84 de Lyon et le titre saïte , *BIFAO* 67 (1967), pp. 159-171.

Graefe, E., 'Das Stundenritual in thebanischen Gräbern der Spätzeit (Über den Stand der Arbeit an der Edition)', in J. Assmann – E. Dziobek – H. Guksch – F. Kampp (eds.), *Thebanische Beamtennekropolen. Neue Perspektiven der archäologischen Forschung. Internationales Symposium Heidelberg 9.-13.6.1993*, (SAGA 12), Heidelberg 1995, pp. 85-93.

Grimal, N., *Histoire de l'Egypte ancienne*, Paris: Fayard 1988.

Grimm, A., 'Ein Zitat aus den Pyramidentexten in einem ptolemäischen Ritualtext des Horus-Tempels von Edfu. Edfu III, 130, 14-15 = Pyr. 376b (Spr. 269). Zur Tradition altägyptischer Texte. Voruntersuchungen zu einer Theorie der Gattungen', *GM* 31 (1979), pp. 35-45.

Guermeur, I., 'Glanures (3-4)', *BIFAO* 106 (2006), pp. 105-126.

Guilhou, N. – Mathieu, B., 'Cent dix ans d'étude des Textes des Pyramides (1882-1996)', in C. Berger – B. Mathieu (eds.), *Etudes sur l'Ancien Empire et la nécropole de Saqqâra dédiées à Jean-Philippe Lauer*, (Orientalia Monspeliensia 9), Montpellier 1997, pp. 233-244.

Hannig, R., *Die Sprache der Pharaonen. Grosses Handwörterbuch Ägyptisch-Deutsch (2800-950 v. Chr.)*, (Kulturgeschichte der Antiken Welt 64), Mainz: Philipp von Zabern 2006 (4. überarbeitete auflage).

Harpur, Y., *Decoration in Egyptian Tombs of the Old Kingdom: Studies in Orientation and Scene Content*, London – New York: KPI 1987.

Hawass, Z., 'The Discovery of the Osiris Shaft at Giza', in Z. Hawass – J. Richards (eds.), *The Archaeology and Art of Ancient Egypt. Essays in Honor of David B. O'Connor*, (CASAE 36), 2007, pp. 379-397.

Hays, H.M., 'Transformation of Context: The Field of Rushes in Old and Middle Kingdom Mortuary Literature', in S. Bickel – B. Mathieu (eds.), *Textes des Pyramides. Textes des Sarcophages. D'un monde à l'autre*, (BdE 139), Cairo: IFAO 2004, pp. 175-200.

Heerma van Voss, M.S.H.G., 'An Egyptian Magical Brick', *JEOL* 18 (1964), pp. 314-317.

Heerma van Voss, M.S.H.G., 'Ziegel (magische)', in W. Helck – E. Otto (eds.), *Lexikon der Ägyptologie VI*, Wiesbaden: Harrassowitz 1986, p. 1402.

Helck, W., *Zur Verwaltung des Mittleren und Neuen Reiches*, Leiden: Brill 1958.

Holladay, J.S., *Cities of the Delta III. Tell el-Maskhuta*, (ARCE Reports, 6), Malibu: Undena 1982.

Holm-Rasmussen, T., 'Collaboration in Early Achaemenid Egypt. A New Approach', in E. Christiansen – A. Damsgaard-Madsen – E. Hallager (eds.), *Studies in Ancient History and Numismatics, presented to Rudi Thomsen*, Aarhus: Aarhus University Press 1988, pp. 29-38.

Hornung, E., *The Ancient Egyptian Book of the Afterlife*, Ithaca – London: Cornell University Press 1999.

Hornung, E., *Das Totenbuch der Ägypter*, Düsseldorf: Artemis & Winkler 2000.

Hussein, R.B., *The Saite Pyramid Text Copies in the Memphite and Heliopolitan Shaft-Tombs: A Study of their Selection and Layout*, Brown University 2009 (unpublished PhD thesis).

Ikram, S. – Dodson, A., *The Mummy in Ancient Egypt. Equipping the Dead for Eternity*, Cairo: American University in Cairo Press 1998.

Janák, J., *Staroegyptská Kniha mrtvých. Kapitola 105*, (Pontes Pragenses 29), Prague: Centrum pro náboženský a kulturní dialog při Husitské teologické fakultě Univerzity Karlovy v Praze 2003 [in Czech, The Ancient Egyptian Book of the Dead. Chapter 105].

Janák, J., 'Journey to the Resurrection. Chapter 105 of the Book of the Dead in the New Kingdom', *SAK* 31, (2003), pp. 13-210.

Janák, J., 'Migratory Spirits. Remarks on the Akh Sign', in M. Cannata (ed.), *Current Research in Egyptology 2006*, Oxford: Oxbow Books 2007, pp. 116-119.

Janák, J., *Staroegyptské náboženství I. Bohové na zemi a v nebesích*, (Oikúmené 151), Prague: OIKOYMENH 2009 [in Czech, Ancient Egyptian Religion I. Gods on Earth and in the Heavens].

Janák, J – Landgráfová, R., 'Wooden fragments with some chapters of the Book of the Dead belonging to Neferibreseneb Nekau', in B. Backes – I. Munro – S. Stöhr (eds.), *Totenbuch-Forschungen: Gesammelte Beiträge des 2. Internationalen Totenbuch-Symposiums, Bonn 25.-29. September 2005*, [SAT 11], Wiesbaden: Harrassowitz 2006, pp. 135-144.

Janák, J – Landgráfová, R., 'Wooden fragments with some chapters of the Book of the Dead belonging to Neferibreseneb Nekau', in M. Bárta – F. Coppens – J. Krejčí (eds.), *Abusir and Saqqara in the Year 2005. Proceedings of the Conference Held in Prague (June 27–July 5, 2005)*, Prague: Czech Institute of Egyptology 2006, pp. 28-33.

Janák, J – Landgráfová, R., 'The Book of the Dead belonging to Neferibre-seneb Nekau inscribed on Wooden Tablets', in L. Bareš – K. Smoláriková, *The shaft tomb of Iufaa. vol. I: Archaeology*, (Abusir XVII), Prague: Czech Institute of Egyptology 2008, pp. 148-155.

Jansen-Winkeln, K., ''Horizont' und 'Verklärheit': Zur Bedeutung der Wurzel *3ḫ*', *SAK* 23 (1996), pp. 201-215.

Jelínková, E., 'Recherches sur le titre *ḫrp ḥwwt Nt* 'Administrateur des Domaines de la Couronne Rouge'', *ASAE* 50 (1950), pp. 321-362.

Jelínková, E., 'Une titre saïte emprunté à l'Ancien Empire', *ASAE* 55 (1958), pp. 79-125.

Jéquier, G., 'Les pyramides non funéraires', *CRAIBL* 1927, pp. 188-193.

Jones, D., *An Index of Ancient Egyptian Titles, Epithets and Phrases of the Old Kingdom* I-III, (BAR International Series 866), Oxford: Hadrian Books Ltd. 2006.

Kahl, J., 'Religiöse Sprachensensibilität in den Pyramidentexten und Sargtexten am Beispiel des Namens des Gottes Seth' in S. Bickel – B. Mathieu (eds.), *Textes des Pyramides. Textes des Sarcophages. D'un monde à l'autre*, (BdE 139), Cairo: IFAO 2004, pp. 219-246.

Kákosy, L., 'Magical Bricks from TT 32', in J.H. Kamstra – H. Milde – K. Wagtendonk (eds.), *Funerary Symbols and Religion: Essays dedicated to M.S.H.G. Heerma van Voss on the Occasion of his Retirement from the Chair in History of Ancient Religions at the University of Amsterdam*, Kampten: Kok 1988, pp. 60-72.

Kaplony, P., 'Ka', in W. Helck – E. Otto (eds.), *Lexikon der Ägyptologie III*, Wiesbaden: Harrassowitz 1980, pp. 275-282.

Kees, H., *Horus und Seth als Götterpaar* II, (MVAG 29/1), Leipzig: Hinrichs'sche Buchhandlung 1924.

Kees. H., 'Zur Familie des 3. Amonspropheten Amenophis', *ZÄS* 84 (1959), pp. 54-67.

Kemp, B., 'Soil (including mud-brick architecture)', in P.T. Nicholson – I. Shaw (eds.), *Ancient Egyptian Materials and Technology*, Cambridge: Cambridge University Press 2000, pp. 78-103.

el-Khouli, A., 'Excavations at the Pyramid of Userkaf, 1976: Preliminary Report', *JEA* 64 (1978), pp. 35-43.

el-Khouli, A., 'Excavations at the Pyramid of Userkaf, 1979: Preliminary Report', *JEA* 66 (1980), pp. 46-47.

el-Khouli, A., 'Excavations at the Pyramid of Userkaf', *JSSEA* 15 (1985), pp. 86-93.

Kienitz, F.K., *Die politische Geschichte Ägyptens vom 7. bis zum 4. Jahrhundert vor der Zeitwende*, Berlin: Akademie Verlag 1953.

Krejčí, J. – Verner, M. – Callender, V.G., *Abusir XII. Minor Tombs in the Royal Necropolis I (The Mastabas of Nebtyemneferes and Nakhtsare, Pyramid Complex Lepsius no. 24 and Tomb complex Lepsius no. 25)*, Prague: Czech Institute of Egyptology 2008.

Labrousse, A. – Lauer, J.-Ph., *Les complexes funéraires d'Ouserkaf et de Néferhétepès I. Texte*, (BdE 130/1), Cairo: IFAO 2000.

Labrousse A. – Lauer, J.-Ph. – Leclant, J., *Mission archéologique de Saqqarah II. Le temple haut du complexe funéraire du roi Ounas*, (BdE 73), Cairo: IFAO 1977.

Lacau, P., 'Textes religieux écrits sur les sarcophages', in J.E. Quibell, *Excavations at Saqqara (1906–1907)*, Cairo: IFAO 1908, pp. 21-61.

Lapp, G., *Die Opferformel des Alten Reiches unter berücksichtigung einiger späterer Formen*, (SDAIK 21), Mainz: Verlag Philipp von Zabern 1986.

Lauer, J.-Ph., *La pyramide à degrés. I-II L'Architecture*, Cairo: IFAO 1936.

Lauer, J.-Ph., 'La structure de la tombe de Hor à Saqqarah (XXVIe Dynastie)', *ASAE* 52 (1954), pp. 133-136.

Lauer, J.-Ph., *Les pyramides de Sakkarah*, (BiGen 3), Cairo: IFAO 1972.

Lauer, J-Ph. – Iskander, Z., 'Donnés nouvelles sur la momification dans l'Egypte ancienne', *ASAE* 53 (1956), pp. 167-195.

Leahy, A., 'Two Donation Steale of Necho II', *RdE* 34 (1982–1983), pp. 72-91.

Lepsius, K.R., *Denkmaeler aus Aegypten und Aethiopien* I–XII, Berlin: Ressersche Buchhandlung 1849–1858.

Lepsius, K.R., *Denkmaeler aus Aegypten und Aethiopien. Text* I–V, Leipzig: Nicolaische Buchhandlung 1897–1913.

Lloyd, A.B., 'The Late Period (664-332 BC)', in I. Shaw (ed.), *The Oxford History of Ancient Egypt*, Oxford: Oxford University Press 2000, pp. 369-394.

Loukianoff, G., 'Les statues et les objets funéraires de Pedamenopet', *ASAE* 37 (1937), pp. 219-232.

Lüddeckens, E. – Brusch, W. – Vittmann, G. – Zauzich, K.-Th., *Demotisches Namenbuch. Band I, Lieferung 5. p3-ty-wp-w3.wt – pa-nfr*, Wiesbaden: Reifert 1985.

Mariette, A., *Notice des principaux monuments exposés dans les galeries provisoires du Musée d'antiquités égyptiennes de S.A. le khédive à Boulaq*, Paris 1872.

Mariette, A. – Maspero, G., *Monuments divers recueillis en Egypte et en Nubie*, Paris 1872–1889.

Martin, R. – Saller, K., *Lehrbuch der Anthropologie in systematischer Darstellung* II, 3. Auflage, Stuttgart: G. Fischer 1959.

Maspero, G., 'II. Les tombeaux de Psammétique et de Setariban. II. Les inscriptions de la chambre de Psammétique', *ASAE* 1 (1900), pp. 166-184.

Maspero, G., 'II. Les tombeaux de Psammétique et de Setariban. III. La date précise du tombeau de Psammétique', *ASAE* 1 (1900), pp. 185-188.

Maspero, G., 'IV. Tombeau de Péténisis. II. Les inscriptions du tombeau de Péténisis', *ASAE* 1 (1900), pp. 234-261.

Maspero, G., 'IV. Tombeau de Zannehibou. II. Les inscriptions du tombeau de Zannehibou', *ASAE* 1 (1900), pp. 271-282.

Maspero, G., 'VIII. Tombeau de Péténéith. II. Les inscriptions du tombeau de Péténéith', *ASAE* 2 (1901), pp. 104-111.

Maspero, G., 'XIII. Les inscriptions du tombeau de Hikaoumsaf', *ASAE* 5 (1904), pp. 78-83.

Meeks, D., 'Les donations aux temples dans l'Égypte du Ier millénaire avant J.-C.', in E. Lipinski (ed.), *State and Temple Economy in the Ancient Near East* II, (OLA 6), Leuven: Peeters 1979.

Mercer, S.A., *The Pyramid Texts in Translation and Commentary* I–IV, New York – London – Toronto: Longmans 1952.

Mond, R. – Myers, O.H., *The Bucheum II. The Inscriptions*, London: The Egypt Exploration Society 1934.

Monnet, J., 'Les briques magiques du Musée du Louvre', *RdE* 8 (1951), pp. 151-162.

Munro, P., *Die spätägyptischen Totenstelen*, (AF 25), Glückstad 1973.

Myśliwiec, K., *Keramik und Kleinfunde aus der Grabung im Tempel Sethos' I in Gurna*, (AV 57), Mainz: Philipp von Zabern 1987.

Myśliwiec, K. – Herbich, T. (with contribution by A. Niwinski), 'Polish Research at Saqqara in 1987', *EtTrav* 17 (1995), pp. 177-203.

el-Naggar, S., *Les voutes dans l'architecture de l'Egypte ancienne*, (BdE 128), Cairo: IFAO 1999.

Neureiter, S., 'Eine neue Interpretation des Archaismus', *SAK* 21 (1994), pp. 219-254.

Nicholson, P.T., 'Faience Technology', in W. Wendrich (ed.), *UCLA Encyclopedia of Egyptology*, Los Angeles 2009 [= http://escholarship.org/uc/item/9cs9x41z].

Nicholson, P.T. – Peltenburg, E., 'Egyptian Faience', in P.T. Nicholson – I. Shaw (eds.), *Ancient Egyptian Materials and Technology*, Cambridge: Cambridge University Press 2000, pp. 177-194.

Oren, E.D., 'Migdol: A New Fortress on the Edge of the Eastern Delta', *BASOR* 256 (1984), pp. 7-44.

Otto, E., 'Sprüche auf altägyptischen Särgen', *ZDMG 102* (1952), pp. 187-200.

Otto, E., *Das ägyptische Mundöffnungsritual* I-II. (ÄA 3), Wiesbaden 1960.

Otto, E., 'Ach', in W. Helck – E. Otto (eds.), *Lexikon der Ägyptologie I*, Wiesbaden: Harassowitz 1975, pp. 49-52.

Otto, E., 'Anedjti', in W. Helck – E. Otto (eds.), *Lexikon der Ägyptologie I*, Wiesbaden: Harrassowitz 1975, pp. 269-270.

Patanè, M., *Les variantes des textes de pyramides à la Basse Epoque*, Genève 1992.

Pernigotti, S., 'Saitica I', *EVO* 7 (1984), pp. 23-40.

Pernigotti, S., 'Saitica II', *EVO* 8 (1985), pp. 7-18.

Perring, J.S., *The Pyramids to the Southward of Gizeh and at Abou Roash; also Campbell's tomb and a section of the rock of Gizeh from actual survey and admeasurements*, London 1842.

Pischikova, E.V., 'Representations of Ritual and Symbolic Objects in Late XXVth Dynasty and Saite Private Tombs', *JARCE* 31 (1994), pp. 63-77.

Pörtner, B., *Aegyptische Grabsteine und Denksteine aus Athen und Konstantinopel*, Strasbourg: Schlesier & Schweikhardt 1908.

Posener, G., *La première domination Perse en Égypte. Recueil d'inscriptions hiéroglyphiques*, Cairo: IFAO 1936.

Pressl, D.A., *Beamte und Soldaten, Die Verwaltung in der 26. Dynastie in Ägypten (664-525 v. Chr.)*, (Europäische Hochschulschriften III. Geschichte und ihre Hilfswissenschaften. Serie III, vol. 779), Frankurt: Peter Lang 1998.

Quibell, J.E. *Excavations at Saqqara, 1908–09, 1909–10. The Monastery of Apa Jeremias*, Cairo: IFAO 1912.

Quirke, S., *Titles and Bureaux of Egypt 1850–1700 BC*, London: Golden House Publications 2004.

Ranke, H., 'Statue eines hohen Beamten under Psammetich I', *ZÄS* 44 (1907), pp. 42-54.

Ranke, H., *Die ägyptischen Personennamen I. Verzeichnis der Namen*, Glückstad: Augustin 1935.

Raven, M.J., 'Egyptian Concepts on the Orientation of the Human Body', *JEA* 91 (2005), pp. 31-53.

Ray, J.D., 'Saqqara, Late Period and Graeco-Roman Tombs', in K.A. Bard (ed.), *Encyclopedia of the Archaeology of Ancient Egypt*, London-New York: Routledge 1999, pp. 691-694.

Reader, C., 'The Geology of Abusir', in M. Bárta, *Abusir XIII. Abusir South 2. Tomb Complex of the Vizier Qar, his sons Qar Junior and Senedjemib, and Iykai*, Prague: Czech Institute of Egyptology – Dryada 2009, pp. 9-16.

Régen, I., *Les quatres amuletes protectrices ou 'briques magiques'. Etude d'un ritual funéraire égyptien (chap. 151 A LdM sections g-h)*, Montpellier : Université Paul Valéry 1999 (unpublished PhD thesis).

Ricke, H., *Bemerkungen zur ägyptischen Baukunst des Alten Reiches* I, (Beiträge Bf 4), Zürich: Schweizerisches Institut für ägyptische Bauforschung und Altertumskunde 1944.

Ricke, H. – Schott, S., *Bemerkungen zur ägyptischen Baukunst des Alten Reiches* II, (Beiträge Bf 5), Cairo: Schweizerisches Institut für ägyptische Bauforschung und Altertumskunde 1950.

Rostem, O.M., 'Note on the Method of Lowering the Lid of the Sarcophagus in a Saite Tomb at Saqqara', *ASAE* 43 (1943), pp. 351-356.

Roth, A.M. – Roehrig, C.H., 'Magical Bricks and the Bricks of Birth', *JEA* 88 (2002), pp. 121-139.

Rummel, U., 'Weihrauch, Salböl und Leinen. Balsamierungsmaterialien als Medium der Erneuerung im Sedfest', *SAK* 34 (2006), pp. 381–407.

Ryan, D.P. – Hansen, D.H., *A Study of Ancient Egyptian Cordage in the British Museum*, (British Museum Occasional Paper 62), London: British Museum Press 1987.

Saad, Z.Y., 'Preliminary Report on the Royal Excavations at Saqqarah 1939–1940', *ASAE* 40 (1941), pp. 675-693.

Saad, Z.Y., 'Preliminary Report on the Royal Excavations at Saqqarah 1941–1942', *ASAE* 41 (1942), pp. 381-393.

Saad, Z.Y., *Royal Excavations at Saqqara and Helwan (1941-1945)*, (CASAE 3), Cairo 1947.

el-Sadeek, W., *Twenty-Sixth Dynasty Necropolis at Gizeh*, (Veröffentlichungen der Institute für Afrikanistik und Ägyptologie der Universität Wien 29, Beiträge zur Ägyptologie 5), Wien 1984.

Sampsell, B.M., *A Traveller's Guide to the Geology of Egypt*, Cairo 2003, pp. 96-101.

el-Sayed, R., *Documents relatifs à Sais et ses divinités*, (BdE 69), Cairo: IFAO 1975.

el–Sayed, R., 'À propos du titre *ḫrp ḥwwt*', *RdE* 28 (1976), pp. 97-110.

el-Sawi, A. – Gomaa, F., *Das Grab des Panehsi, Gottesvaters von Heliopolis in Matariya*, (ÄAT 23), Wiesbaden: Harrassowitz 1993.

Schenkel, W., 'Zur Frage der Vorlagen spätzeitlicher "Kopien"', in J. Assmann – E. Feucht – R. Grieshammer (eds.), *Fragen an die altägyptische Literatur. Studien zum Gedenken an Eberhard Otto*, Wiesbaden: Reichert 1977, pp. 417-441.

Schlögl, H.A. – Meves-Schlögl, C., *Ushebti. Arbeiter im ägyptischen Totenreich*, Wiesbaden: Harrassowitz 1993.

Schneider, H.D., *Shabtis* I-III. *An Introduction to the History of the Ancient Egyptian Funerary Statuettes with a Catalogue of the Collection of Shabtis in the National Museum of Antiquities at Leiden*, (Collections of the National Museum of Antiquities at Leiden 2), Leiden: Rijksmuseum van Oudheden 1977.

Schweitzer, U., *Das Wesen des Ka im Diesseits und Jenseits der alten Ägypter*, (ÄF 19), Glückstadt 1956.

Smith, H.S. 'Saqqara. Late Period', in W. Helck – E. Otto (eds.), *Lexikon der Ägyptologie V*, Wiesbaden: Harrassowitz 1984, pp. 412-428.

Smoláriková, K., 'The Pottery', in L. Bareš, *The shaft tomb of Udjahorresnet at Abusir* (Abusir IV), Prague: Universitas Carolina Pragensis 1999, pp. 90-98.

Smoláriková, K., *Abusir VII. Greek Imports in Egypt. Graeco-Egyptian Relations During the First Millennium BC*, Prague 2002.

Smoláriková, K., 'Some Remarks on Embalmers' Caches from the Saite-Persian Cemetery at Abusir', in H. Györy (ed.), *Aegyptus et Pannonia III. Acta Symposii anno 2004*, Budapest: MEBT–ÓEB 2006, pp. 261-268.

Smoláriková, K., 'The Step Pyramid – A Constant Inspiration to the Saite Egyptians', in M. Bárta – F. Coppens – J. Krejčí (eds.), *Abusir and Saqqara in the Year 2005. Proceedings of the Conference Held in Prague (June 27– July 5, 2005)*, Prague: Czech Institute of Egyptology 2006, pp. 42-49.

Smoláriková, K., *Saite forts in Egypt. Political-military History of the Saite Dynasty*, Prague: Czech Institute of Egyptology 2008.

Smoláriková, K., 'The Embalmer's Cache as an Heir of the South Tomb', in P. Maříková Vlčková – J. Mynářová – M. Tomášek (eds.), *My Things Changed Things. Social Development and Cultural Exchange in Prehistory, Antiquity, and Middle Ages*, Prague: Charles University in Prague 2009, pp. 58-63.

Soukiassian, G., 'Textes de pyramides et formules apparantés. Remarques à propos des tombes saïtes', *L'Egyptologie en 1979: Axes prioritaires des recherches II*, (Colloques internationaux du CNRS 595), Paris: Editions du Centre national de la recherche scientifique 1982, pp. 55-61.

Spencer, A.J., *Brick Architecture in Ancient Egypt*, Warminster: Aris & Phillips Ltd 1979.

Spencer, A.J., *Excavations at Tell el-Balamun 1991–1994*, London: British Museum Press 1996.

Stadelmann, R., 'Pyramiden AR', in W. Helck – E. Otto (eds.), *Lexikon der Ägyptologie IV*, Wiesbaden: Harrassowitz 1982, pp. 1205-1263.

Stadelmann, R., *Die ägyptischen Pyramiden. Vom Ziegelbau zum Weltwunder*, Mainz: Philipp von Zabern 1991.

Stammers, M., *The Elite Late Period Egyptian Tombs of Memphis*, (BAR International Series 1903), Oxford: Hadrian Books Ltd. 2009.

Strouhal, E., 'The Relation of Iufaa to Persons found beside his Shaft-tomb at Abusir', in Coppens, F. (ed.), *Abusir and Saqqara in the Year 2001. Proceedings of the Symposium (Prague, September 25th – 27th 2001), Archiv Orientální* 70.3 (2002), pp. 403-414.

Strouhal, E., 'Relation of Iufaa to Persons found beside his Shaft-tomb at Abusir', *Anthropologie* 40 (2002), pp. 37-50.

Strouhal, E. – Bareš, L. *Secondary Cemetery in the Mastaba of Ptahshepses at Abusir,* Prague: Czechoslovak Institute of Egyptology 1993.

Strouhal, E. – Němečková, A., 'Paleopathological Find of a Sacral Neurilemmoma from Ancient Egypt', *AJPA* 125 (2004), pp. 320-328.

Strouhal, E. – Němečková, A. – Kouba, M., 'Palaeopathology of Iufaa and Other Persons found beside his Shaft Tomb at Abusir (Egypt)', *International Journal of Osteoarchaeology* 13 (2003), pp. 331-338.

Swelim, N., 'The Dry Moat of the Netjerykhet Complex', in J. Baines – T.G.H. James – A. Leahy – A.F. Shore (eds.), *Pyramid Studies and Other Essays Presented to I.E.S. Edwards*, (Occasional Publications 7), London: Egypt Exploration Society 1988, pp. 12-22.

Tait, W.J., 'Exuberance and Accessibility: Notes on Written Demotic and the Egyptian Scribal Tradition', in: T. Gagos – R.S. Bagnall (eds.), *Essays and Texts in Honor of J. David Thomas*, (American Studies in Papyrology 42), London 2001, pp. 31-39.

Tawfik, S., 'Die Alabasterpaletten für die sieben Salböle im Alten Reich', *GM* 30 (1978), pp. 77-87.

te Velde, H., *Seth, God of Confusion. A Study of his Role in Egyptian Mythology and Religion*, (PdÄ 6), Leiden: Brill 1967.

te Velde, H., 'Seth', in W. Helck – E. Otto (eds.), *Lexikon der Ägyptologie V*, Wiesbaden: Harassowitz 1984, pp. 908-911.

Teeter, E., 'Techniques and Terminology of Rope-Making in Ancient Egypt', *JEA* 73 (1987), pp. 71-77.

Teeter, E., *Ancient Egypt. Treasures from the Collection of the Oriental Institute, University of Chicago*, (OIMP 23), Chicago: The Oriental Institute 2003.

Thomas, E., 'The Four Niches and the Amuletic Figures in Theban Royal Tombs', *JARCE* 3 (1964), pp. 71-78.

Trotter, M. – Gleser, G.C., 'Estimation of Stature from Long Bones of American Whites and Negroes', *AJPA* 10 (1952), pp. 463-514.

Vachala, B., 'Neue Salbölpaletten aus Abusir', *ZÄS* 108 (1981), pp. 61-67.

Vachala, B., 'Neue Salbölpaletten aus Abusir – Addendum', *ZÄS* 109 (1982), p. 171.

Veldmeijer, A.J., 'Cordage Production', in W. Wendrich (ed.), *UCLA Encyclopedia of Egyptology*, Los Angeles 2009 [= http://escholarship.org/uc/item/1w90v76c].

Verner, M., 'Excavations at Abusir, Season 1980/1981 – Preliminary Report', *ZÄS* 109 (1982), pp. 157-166.

Verner, M., 'Archaeological Survey at Abusir, Season 1990/1991 – Preliminary Report II: Archaeological Survey of Abusir', *ZÄS* 119 (1992), pp. 116-124.

Verner, M., *The Pyramids. Their Archaeology and History*, London: Atlantic Books 2001.

Verner, M., *Abusir. Realm of Osiris*, Cairo-New York: The American University in Cairo Press 2002.

Verner, M. – Benešovská, H., *Unearthing Ancient Egypt. Fifty Years of the Czech Archaeological Exploration in Egypt*, Prague: Czech Institute of Egyptology 2008.

Verner, M. – Callender, V.G., *Djedkare's Family Cemetery (Abusir VI)*, Prague: Czech Institute of Egyptology 2002.

Vittmann, G., 'Zwei Königinnen der Spätzeit namens Chedebnitjebone', *CdE* 49 (1974), pp. 43-51.

Vittmann, G.,'Die Familie der saitischen Könige', *Orientalia* 44 (1975), pp. 375-387.

Vyse, H., *Operations Carried on at the Pyramids of Gizeh in 1837* I-II, London 1840.

Ward, W.A. *Index of Egyptian Administrative and Religious Titles of the Middle Kingdom, with a glossary of words and phrases used*, Beirut: American University of Beirut 1982.

Weill, R., *Le Champ des Roseaux et le Champ des Offrandes*, Paris: Geuthner 1936.

Wendrich, W., 'Preliminary Report on the Amarna Basketry and Cordage', in B.J. Kemp (ed.), *Amarna Report V*, (Occasional Publications 6), London 1989: Egypt Exploration Society, pp. 169-201.

Willems, H., *The Coffin of Heqata (Cairo JdE 36418). A Case Study of Egyptian Funerary Culture of the Early Middle Kingdom*, (OLA 70), Leuven: Peeters 1996.

Wilson, P. – Gilbert, P., 'Sais and its Trading Relations with the Eastern Mediterranean', in P. Kousoulis – K. Magliveras (eds.), *Moving Across Borders. Foreign Relations, Religion and Cultural Interactions in the Ancient Mediterranean*, (OLA 159), Leuven – Paris – Dudley, MA 2007, pp. 251-265.

Zivie-Coche, C.-M., *Giza au premier millénaire autour du temple d'Isis dame des pyramides*, Boston: Museum of Fine Arts 1991.

Preface

Ladislav Bareš

The present volume offers the results of excavations in two shaft tombs of small dimensions which have been unearthed in the Late Period cemetery at Abusir and represent the first two of some five to ten such structures that are potentially located on the site as the archaeological survey and geophysical measurements suggest. As it happens, both tombs (as different as they are) represent most interesting and unique structures of their kind. The tomb of Padihor, which has been unearthed in 2001 and is situated just to the east from the large and very complex tomb of Iufaa, is without doubt the smallest such structure known from Egypt so far. Despite its small size it contains all the appropriate features of a Saite-Persian shaft tomb, namely a burial chamber situated at the bottom of a relatively wide and deep shaft and a much smaller shaft which is connected at its bottom with the burial chamber by means of a narrow corridor. Interestingly enough, the tomb of Padihor has been completely finished despite its small dimensions (or, perhaps, precisely because it was so small?), unlike the much larger structures of Udjahorresnet and Iufaa and the anonymous tomb R3, which is also published in this volume.

The tomb dubbed R3, whose owner is unknown at present and will perhaps always remain so, is quite unique in its outer shape and in the arrangement of its superstructure, perhaps due to the fact that this part of the tomb had to be completed in haste after the premature death of its owner or, possibly, because it represents the last such structure built in this part of the cemetery. In any case, it clearly corroborates the idea (once presented by J.-Ph. Lauer) that the builders of the Saite-Persian shaft tombs drew their inspiration directly from the oldest pyramid in Egypt (and the oldest surviving monument completely built of stone), the step pyramid of Djoser at Saqqara and its enclosure.

Both tombs clearly differ in one important respect, however. While the tomb of Padihor seems to have been built for one person only (thus resembling the tombs of Udjahorresnet and Menekhibnekau), structure R3 might have been intended for the burials of not only its owner (for whom the sarcophagus placed directly at the bottom of the main shaft might have been meant) but of at least two more persons (most probably other members of his family if a parallel with the tomb of Iufaa may be drawn), for whom two large niches have been dug at about the mid-depth of the main shaft.

In many respects, the tomb of Padihor and the anonymous structure R3 represent interesting and important counterparts to the much larger burial enclosures of Udjahorresnet, Iufaa and Menekhibnekau which are situated nearby. They contribute greatly to our knowledge of the development of the funeral architecture, burial habits and religious thought of their time. The owners of these smaller tombs will perhaps never become known to us from other (especially written) sources as Udjahorresnet and Menekhibnekau have, but their tombs help improve our understanding of historical developments during the troubled era of the transition between the Twenty-Sixth and Twenty-Seventh Dynasties.

Chapter 1
The Tomb of Padihor

Filip Coppens

1.1. Architecture of the tomb complex

1.1.1. The location

The Saite-Persian cemetery of Abusir is located in the south-west of the Abusir plateau, about 200 m to the south-west of the Fifth Dynasty pyramid complexes of pharaohs Sahura, Neferirkara, Raneferef and Niussera, on top of a low hill sloping down towards the south-east and the former Lake of Abusir.[1] The small tomb of Padihor (also designated R1)[2] was excavated on this site during the spring season of 2001 (Fig. 1 and Pl. 1).[3] It is located immediately to the east of a series of larger burial complexes, five or perhaps six in number, that appear to have been loosely arranged in the shape of the letter V (or perhaps L),[4] with its focal point – the monumental shaft tomb of Udjahorresnet – located furthermost to the west at the highest point of the hill.[5] Three of these large tombs have already been excavated, namely the burial complexes

[1] For a general introduction to the Saite-Persian shaft tomb cemetery at Abusir, consult for instance M. Verner, *Abusir. Realm of Osiris*, Cairo-New York 2002, pp. 177-205; L. Bareš, 'The Late Period at the Abusir Necropolis', in *Abusir. Secrets of the Desert and the Pyramids* (exhibition catalogue), Prague 2006, pp. 162-175, and M. Verner – H. Benešovská, *Unearthing Ancient Egypt. Fifty Years of the Czech Archaeological Exploration in Egypt*, Prague 2008, pp. 47-51, 181-203, and 247-249.

[2] The preliminary excavation report of the tomb of Padihor was published in L. Bareš – M. Dvořák – K. Smoláriková – E. Strouhal, 'The shaft tomb of Iufaa at Abusir in 2001', *ZÄS* 129 (2002), pp. 105-106. Information on the tomb can also be found in Bareš, in *Abusir. Secrets of the Desert and the Pyramids*, pp. 173-175, and M. Stammers, *The Elite Late Period Egyptian Tombs of Memphis*, (BAR International Series 1903), Oxford 2009, esp. pp. 114, 135 and 158. Specific aspects of the tomb have been discussed in a variety of articles. Consult for instance: L. Bareš, 'Shabtis from the Late Period Tombs at Abusir (Preliminary Remarks)', in H. Győry (ed.), *'Le lotus qui sort de la terre'. Mélanges offerts à Edith Varga*, (Bulletin du Musée Hongrois des Beaux-Arts. Supplément 2001), Budapest 2001, p. 27; L. Bareš, 'Some Notes on the Religious Texts and Scenes in the Tomb of Iufaa and Other Late Period Shaft Tombs at Abusir', in H. Győry (ed.), *Aegyptus et Pannonia III. Acta Symposii anno 2004*, Budapest 2006, pp. 5-6; L. Bareš, 'The Saite–Persian Cemetery at Abusir', in: J.-C. Goyon – C. Cardin (eds.), *Proceedings of the Ninth International Congress of Egyptologists. Grenoble, 6-12 Septembre 2004* I, (OLA 150) Leuven 2007, p. 148, and L. Bareš, 'A Case of Proofreading in Ancient Egypt', in I. Régen – F. Servajean (eds.), *Verba Manent. Recueil d'études dédiées à Dimitri Meeks*, (Cahiers 'Egypte Nilotique et Méditerranéenne' 2), Montpellier 2009, pp. 51-56.

[3] The excavation of the tomb and its documentation was carried out by Květa Smoláriková and Petra Maříková Vlčková. The author wishes to thank both for providing him with the documentary material and information. A final check of the inscriptions on the walls of the tomb was carried out by the author during the fall season of 2008.

[4] This is most evident on the plan published in M. Bárta, 'The early Fourth and early Fifth Dynasty at Abusir South', in M. Bárta – J. Krejčí (eds.), *Abusir and Saqqara in the Year 2000*, Prague 2000 (Supplementa Archivu Orientálního, IX), p. 345.

[5] Stammers, *Elite Late Period Egyptian Tombs*, pp. 21, 24 and 28 suggested that if one would extend further south-westwards the geodetic line that passes through the northwest corners of the pyramids of Raneferef, Neferirkare and Sahura at Abusir, one would end up in the centre of the tomb of Udjahorresnet. The geodetic line is possibly directed at the obelisk in Heliopolis according to M. Verner, *The Pyramids. Their Archaeology and History*, London 2001, pp. 302-303. The association with the sun temple in Heliopolis might, according to Stammers, have been one of the main reasons why Udjahorresnet positioned his tomb specifically in this location in Abusir, but the relation between the Abusir pyramids and Heliopolis still needs to be explored in more detail. Bareš, in *Abusir. Secrets of the Desert and the Pyramids*, p. 165, and Stammers, *Elite Late Period Egyptian Tombs*, pp. 21-22 and 24-25 provide a general overview of the various theories, technical and religious, proposed for the foundation of the Saite-Persian shaft tomb cemetery in this particular location in Abusir.

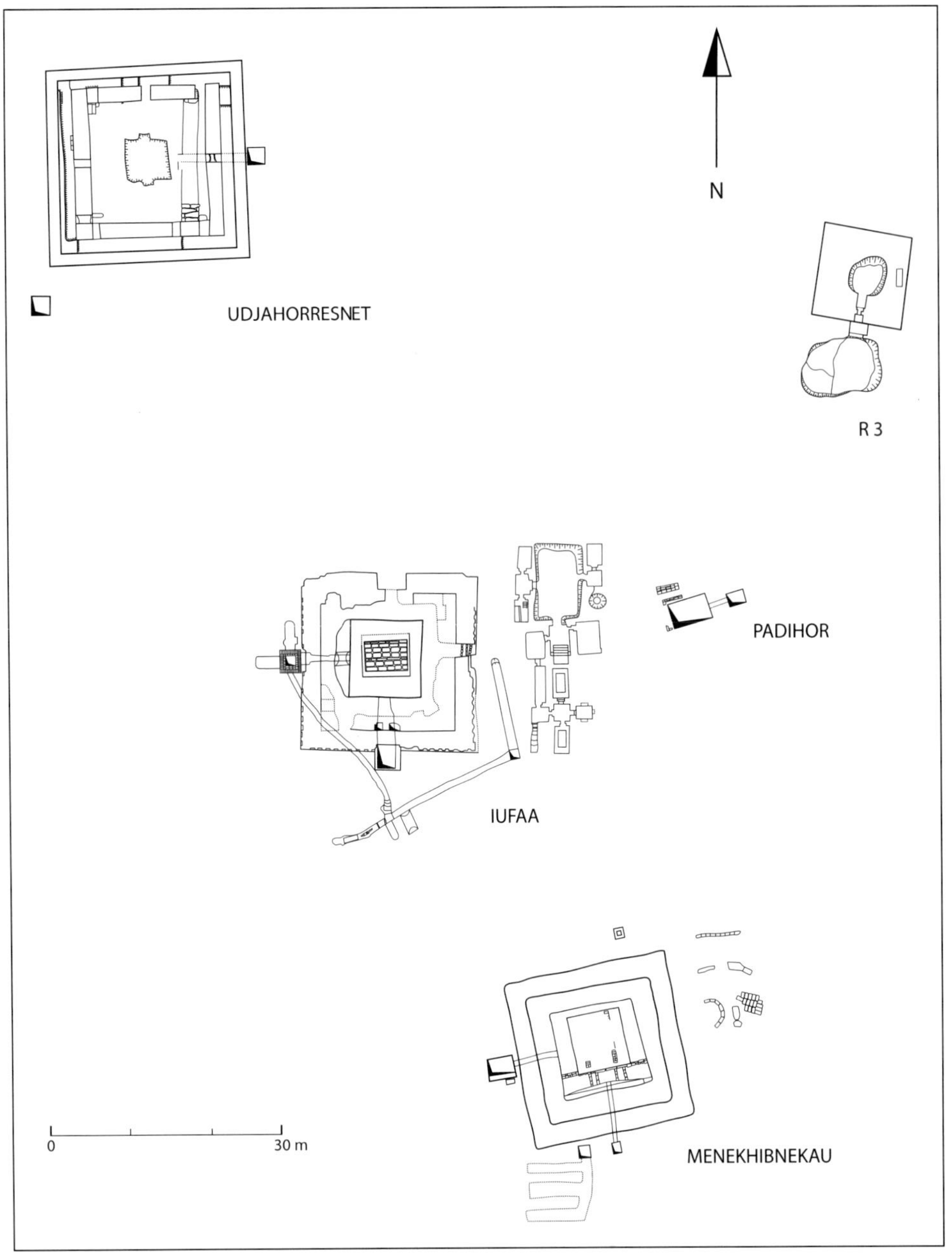

Fig. 1
The Saite-Persian cemetery at Abusir

of Udjahorresnet,[6] Iufaa (also designated R)[7] and Menekhibnekau (Fig. 1).[8] The tomb of Padihor is located between these large sized tombs and a group of several for the most part not yet cleared middle-sized and smaller tombs, including the anonymous tomb R3,[9] which appear to form a second row of funerary complexes from the north-west to the south-east. Padihor's tomb is located 26.50 m to the east of the enclosure wall of the tomb of Iufaa and adjoins the east side of the cult installation situated in front of the east facade of Iufaa's central shaft.[10] (Pl. 2a)

1.1.2. The superstructure

Padihor's burial complex was located under a large mound consisting mainly of sand mixed with pebbles, crushed *tafla* (soft and only partially petrified marl clay resulting from tertiary marine deposits of the Tethys sea)[11] and crushed mud bricks, which sloped from Iufaa's tomb towards the east (Fig. 1). The dump was probably created by the robbers who entered Iufaa's tomb and emptied its main shaft.[12] At the surface only very little remains of the superstructure of the east-west orientated tomb – with the exception of the openings of the main shaft, at whose bottom the burial chamber was located, and the subsidiary shaft leading to the substructure of the monument

(Fig. 2). The burial complex appears to have been originally surrounded by a mud brick enclosure wall of whose outer face only a very small part remains, located 2.10 to 2.20 m to the north of the north edge of the opening of the main shaft and running from east to west (Fig. 3, a and c). The remaining part of the wall measures 2.55 by 0.63-0.69 m. At its highest remaining level, at the east edge of the structure, it still consists of two courses of mud bricks (ca. 38×19-20×10 cm)[13] and the bottom part of a third course. The mud used for the construction of the bricks was tempered with a large addition of chopped straw.[14] The mud bricks were without exception placed horizontally in alternating layers of headers and stretchers[15] and a small layer of clean sand was used as a binding agent between the courses of mud brick.[16] The remaining parts of the wall currently reach no higher than 45 cm. The bottom of the wall was located on top of a compact layer (10-12 cm) containing small fragments of crushed *tafla*, limestone chips, pebbles and a small amount of sand. Underneath still featured a compact hard layer of sand of varied height (between 3 and 10 cm) that was placed on top of

---

[6] L. Bareš, *Abusir IV. The Shaft Tomb of Udjahorresnet at Abusir*, Prague 1999, with references to older publications. More recently, Stammers, *Elite Late Period Egyptian Tombs*, pp. 27-28, 111-112, 133 and 156.

[7] The final archaeological report of the excavation of the tomb of Iufaa can be consulted in L. Bareš – K. Smoláriková, *Abusir XVII. The shaft tomb of Iufaa. vol. I: Archaeology*, Prague 2008, with references to previous publications. The publication dealing with the scenes and inscriptions found on the walls of the tomb, sarcophagus and coffin is in preparation. See also L. Gestermann, *Die Überlieferung ausgewählter Texte altägyptischer Totenliteratur ("Sargtexte") in spätzeitlichen Grabanlagen, Teil 1: Text*, (ÄA 68), Wiesbaden 2005, pp. 101-105 and Stammers, *Elite Late Period Egyptian Tombs*, pp. 112-114, 133-135 and 156-157. A separate volume will be dedicated to the unique Book of the Dead, written on wooden tablets, of the priest Neferibre-seneb Nekau, who was buried in a small chamber cut into the west shaft of the tomb of Iufaa. On this Book of the Dead, see already J. Janák – R. Landgráfová, 'The Book of the Dead belonging to Neferibre-seneb Nekau inscribed on Wooden Tablets', in Bareš – Smolárikova, *Abusir XVII*, pp. 148-155; J. Janák – R. Landgráfová, 'Wooden fragments with some chapters of the Book of the Dead belonging to Neferibreseneb Nekau', in B. Backes – I. Munro – S. Stöhr (eds.), *Totenbuch-Forschungen: Gesammelte Beiträge des 2. Internationalen Totenbuch-Symposiums, Bonn 25.-29. September 2005*, (SAT 11), Wiesbaden 2006, pp. 135-144, and J. Janák – R. Landgráfová, 'Wooden fragments with some chapters of the Book of the Dead belonging to Neferibreseneb Nekau', in M. Bárta – F. Coppens – J. Krejčí (eds.), *Abusir and Saqqara in the Year 2005. Proceedings of the Conference Held in Prague (June 27– July 5, 2005)*, Prague 2006, pp. 28-33.

[8] Preliminary reports on the excavation of the tomb of Menekhibnekau can be found in L. Bareš – M. Bárta – K. Smoláriková – E. Strouhal, 'Abusir – Spring 2002', *ZÄS* 130 (2003), pp. 151-153; L. Bareš – K. Smoláriková – E. Strouhal, 'The Saite Persian Cemetery at Abusir in 2003', *ZÄS* 132 (2005), pp. 96-98; L. Bareš – J. Janák – R. Landgráfová – K. Smoláriková, 'The Shaft Tomb of Menekhibnekau at Abusir – Season of 2007', *ZÄS* 135 (2008), pp. 104-114, and L. Bareš – J. Janák – R. Landgráfová – K. Smoláriková, 'The shaft tomb of Menekhibnekau at Abusir – season of 2008', *ZÄS* 136 (2010 – forthcoming). See also Stammers, *Elite Late Period Egyptian Tombs*, pp. 114, 135 and 158.

[9] See the chapter by K. Smoláriková further in this volume.

[10] On this cult installation, consult Bareš – Smoláriková, *Abusir XVII*, pp. 73-80, and L. Bareš, 'Some Remarks on Cult Installations in Late Period Shaft Tombs in Egypt', *BACE* 13 (2002).

[11] In general: B.M. Sampsell, *A Traveller's Guide to the Geology of Egypt*, Cairo 2003, pp. 1-24 and 96-101. On the geology of Abusir, consult especially C. Reader, 'The Geology of Abusir', in M. Bárta, *Abusir XIII. Abusir South 2. Tomb Complex of the Vizier Qar, his sons Qar Junior and Senedjemib and Iykai*, Prague 2009, pp. 9-16.

[12] Bareš – Smoláriková, *Abusir XVII*, pp. 31-32.

[13] The size of the bricks corresponds to the 'smaller' type of bricks used in the nearby tomb of Iufaa according to Bareš – Smoláriková, *Abusir XVII*, p. 37 (n. 28). According to A.J. Spencer, *Brick Architecture in Ancient Egypt*, Warminster 1979, pp. 52-53; 147-148 and pls. 41-44, these dimensions are quite common in Late Period Egypt. In general on mud-brick architecture, consult B. Kemp, 'Soil (including mud-brick architecture)', in P.T. Nicholson – I. Shaw (eds.), *Ancient Egyptian Materials and Technology*, Cambridge 2000, pp. 78-103.

[14] Spencer, *Brick Architecture*, p. 3. The mud bricks from the nearby tomb of Iufaa were also tempered with (a large amount of) chopped straw – Bareš – Smoláriková, *Abusir XVII*, pp. 31 (n. 9); 35; 37 (n. 28); 38 (n. 33); 41; 48 (n. 85); 49 (n. 91); 50 (n. 98) and further.

[15] Bond A_1 according to Spencer, *Brick Architecture*, pl. 1.

[16] Spencer, *Brick Architecture*, p. 133.

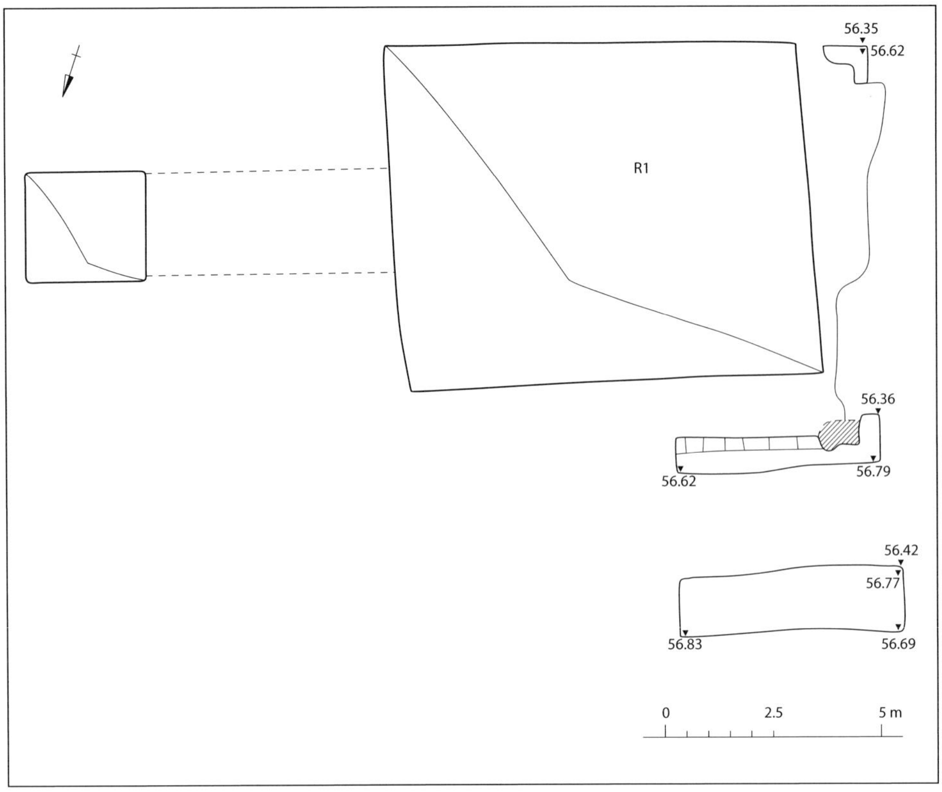

Fig. 2
The superstructure of the burial complex of Padihor

the *tafla* bedrock to even out the surface for the mud brick wall.[17] No foundation deposits have been found in the course of the excavation.[18]

Other remains of the mud brick wall could still be observed on the surface near the main shaft of the burial complex (Fig. 2). The best preserved part of the wall, measuring 2.35× 0.45 m and running from east to west, is located 65 to 70 cm to the north of the opening of the main shaft (Fig. 3b). It consists of three courses of mud bricks (ca. 38×19-20×10 cm)[19] and the bottom part of a fourth row. The mud bricks were without exception placed horizontally.[20] At present the remains of the wall reach a maximum height of 43 cm (Fig. 3, d and e). A second, smaller part (ca. 0.45×0.50 m) of most likely the same structure is still preserved at the south-west corner of the shaft. Only the top part of the lowest course of mud bricks, the second course and the bottom part of the third row remain. The maximum height of this part of the wall is 28 cm. In both remaining parts of the wall a small layer of clean sand was used as a binding material between the rows of mud bricks and both walls were placed directly on top of the *tafla* bedrock. The two remaining parts of this wall might, in combination with the aforementioned wall further to north of the opening of the main shaft (Fig. 2 and 3, a and c), represent the inner and outer casing of a single wall whose interior would have been filled with limestone chips, crushed *tafla* and mud.[21] The wall did

[17] The compact layer of sand is vaguely reminiscent of the sand-bed foundation, a typical component of many buildings from Saite times. See for instance A.J. Spencer, *Excavations at Tell el-Balamun 1991-1994*, London 1996, pp. 37-38 and 46, and D. Arnold, *Building in Egypt. Pharaonic Stone Masonry*, New York-Oxford 1991, pp. 113-114. In general on the building techniques of the Saite Period, consult D. Arnold, *Temples of the Last Pharaohs*, New York-Oxford 1999, pp. 66-70.

[18] In the Saite-Persian cemetery at Abusir foundation deposits have, until now, only been discovered during the clearance of the superstructure of Udjahorresnet's tomb – Bareš, *Abusir IV*, pp. 65-66. On the topic, see also Bareš – Smoláriková, *Abusir XVII*, p. 39 (n. 38).

[19] The mud used for the construction of the bricks was tempered with a large amount of chopped straw – see footnote 14.

[20] There remains too little of this wall to define with absolute certainty the type of bonding used – the bricks seem to have been roughly arranged without any proper bond.

[21] See already Bareš – Smoláriková, *Abusir XVII*, p. 32 (n. 14). The foundations of both walls differ: the outer wall is built on top of two man-made layers (crushed *tafla* with pebbles, limestone chips and sand, and a compact layer of sand, respectively) above the *tafla* bedrock, while the wall closer to the main shaft was constructed directly onto the *tafla* bedrock.

Fig. 3
Remains of the mud brick walls surrounding the burial complex of Padihor

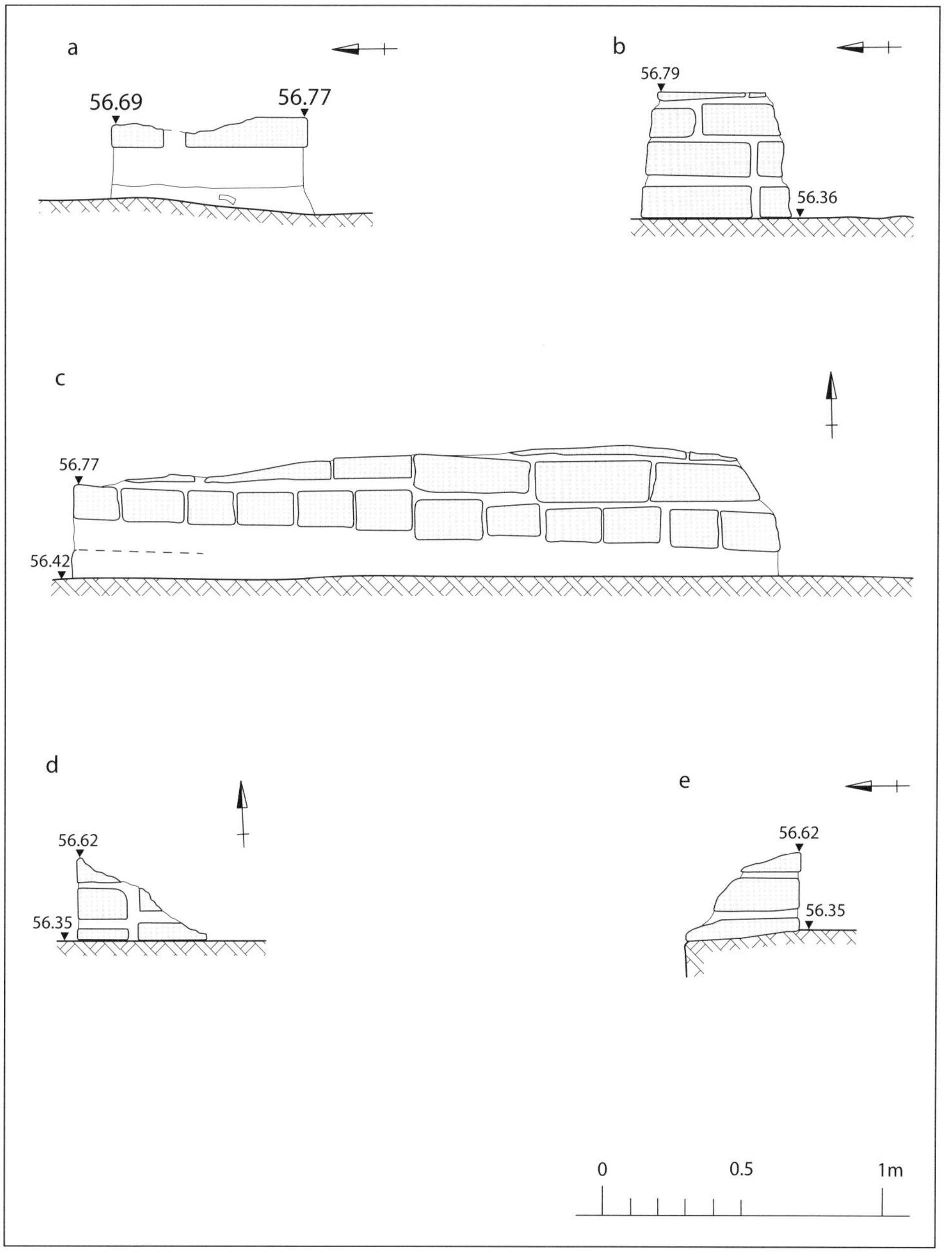

not show any evidence of plastering and it is most probable that the part of the masonry preserved to this day was originally located below ground.[22]

Another mound consisting of very dark sand with an addition of soil and small chips of white limestone reached up to the top of both walls and covered the opening of the main shaft. A similar dump was found also immediately to the south of the shaft. Fragments of shabtis, inscribed with Padihor's name, have been found during the clearance of the area about two m north of the north-west corner of the shaft, in a layer of dark sand above the bedrock.[23] The shabtis might have been lost when the tomb was being cleared by robbers.[24]

---

[22] A similar situation was attested in the nearby anonymous tomb R3 (see Chapter 2.1). On the east facade of Iufaa's enclosure wall the Nile mud plaster ends about 50 cm above the lowest course of masonry, indicating the original ground level. It could not be established either whether the enclosure wall of Padihor's burial complex had a panelled facade like the nearby tomb of Iufaa – Bareš – Smoláriková, *Abusir XVII*, pp. 34-43.

[23] Excavation nos. 99/R/01 and 131/R/01a (bottom fragment). The shabtis and other remains of the burial equipment revealed during the excavation of the tomb will be discussed in Chapter 1.4.

[24] The excavation of the burial complex did not provide any evidence that would enable us to date the tomb robbery with any degree of certainty.

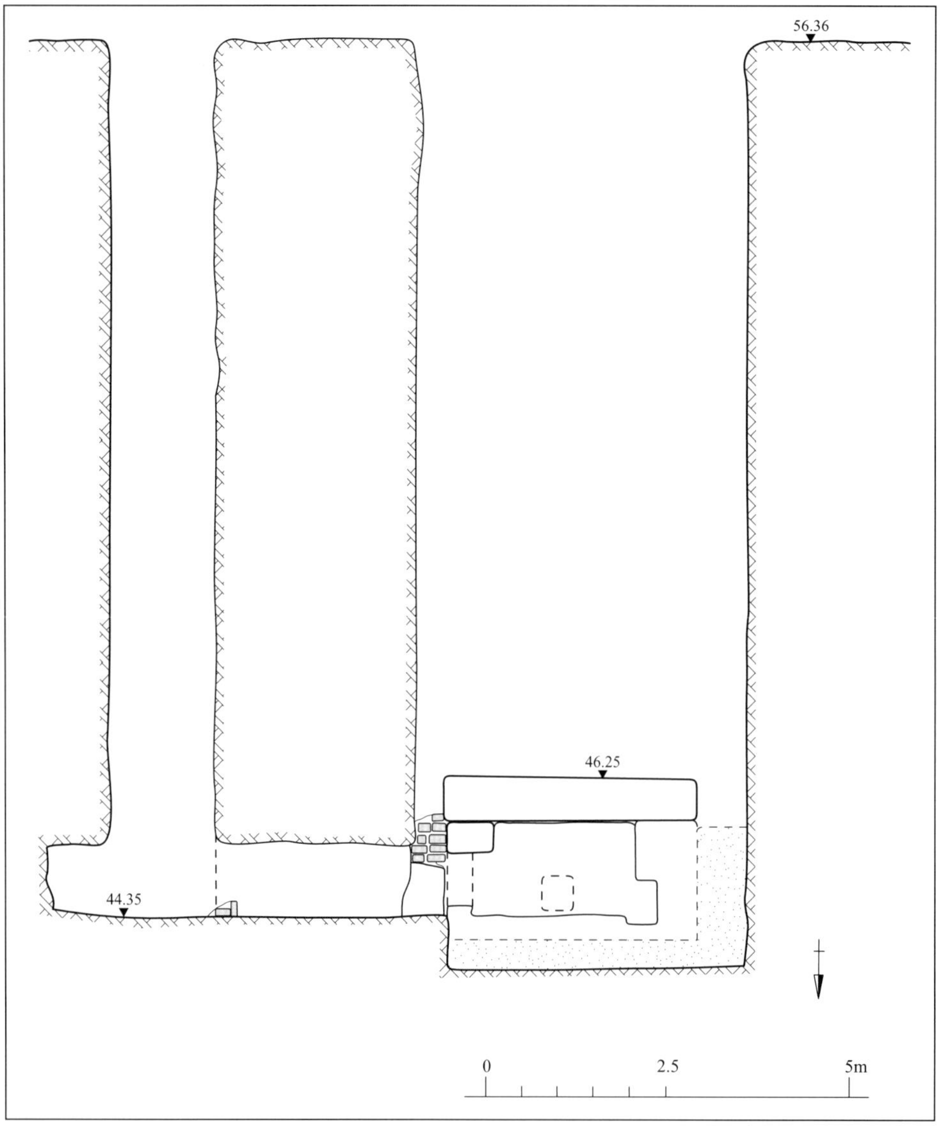

Fig. 4
The east-west section of Padihor's burial complex

The few remains of the walls and other elements do not allow for any reconstruction of the outlook of the superstructure of this funerary monument[25] – with the minor exception that the entire complex appears to have been surrounded by a mud brick wall of unknown dimensions.

1.1.3. The substructure

The main shaft of the tomb, at whose bottom the burial chamber is located, measures 4.80×3.20 m and was dug to a depth of 12 m into the *tafla* bedrock (Figs. 4 and 5).[26] The shaft is orientated north-east to south-west. All sides of the shaft were uneven, roughly worked and much weathered. The walls of the shaft did not show any traces of lining or plastering. The filling of the shaft consisted of clean yellow windblown sand inter-

[25] For the most recent overviews of the many suggested outlooks (e.g. mastaba, chapel, pyramidion, primeval hill) of the typical structure(s) that featured above ground, see Bareš, *Abusir IV*, pp. 48-49; Gestermann, *Sargtexte in spätzeitlichen Grabanlagen*, pp. 357-358; L. Gestermann, 'Das spätzeitliche Schachtgrab als memphitischer Grabtyp', in G. Moers – H. Behlmer – K. Demuss – K. Widmaier (eds.), *jn.t ḏr.w. Festschrift für Friedrich Junge*, Göttingen 2006, p. 199, and Stammers, *Elite Late Period Egyptian Tombs*, pp. 30-31.

[26] For a general introduction to the various stages in the construction of a typical shaft tomb, consult Bareš, *Abusir IV*, pp. 21-26. See also O.R. Rostem, 'Note on the Method of Lowering the Lid of the Sarcophagus in a Saite Tomb at Saqqara', *ASAE* 43, pp. 351-356, and Arnold, *Building in Egypt*, pp. 74-78; 104-105 (n. 77), and fig. 3.28.

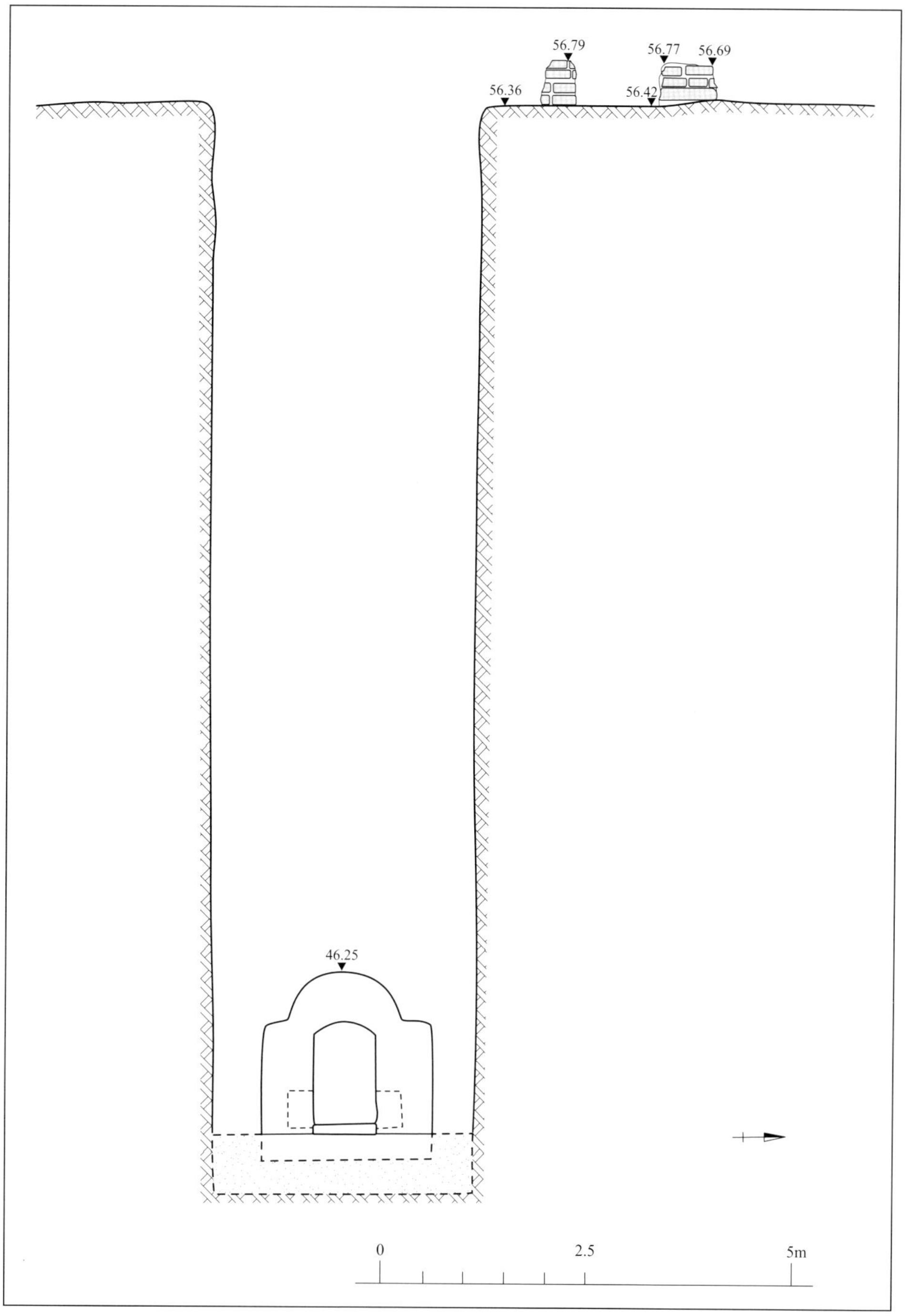

Fig. 5
The north-south section
of Padihor's burial complex

spersed with darker and firmer micro layers consisting mainly of organic remains (parts of insects, remains of leaves, etc.) and particles of eroded *tafla* and running down from south to north. The clear presence of wind erosion in most of the filling suggests that the shaft must have remained open for a considerable period of time, most likely after the tomb robbers had cleared the burial chamber. As a consequence the walls of the shaft are for the most part badly eroded. The south half of the west wall is in the worst state and a deep crevice runs down this wall from south to north.[27] A series of small irregular man-made openings occur in the west and south walls (the south-west

[27] The heavier damage suffered by the south half of the west wall of the shaft might be related to the prevailing direction of the wind in this area – from the north. The general position of the micro layers in the filling of the shaft (running down from south to north) is also in accordance with a prevailing north wind: sand and other particles are deposited against the south/south-west wall of the shaft and roll down towards the north. A similar situation was observed in the central shaft of the burial complex of Udjahorresnet according to Bareš, *Abusir IV*, p. 50.

corner of the shaft) until a depth of 8 m. These openings were most likely used as a means for the workers to exit the main shaft during its construction.[28]

The subsidiary shaft of the tomb lies 2.84 m to the east of the main shaft (Figs. 2 and 4). It is orientated east to west and measures 1.50×1.20 m and is 12 m deep. The walls of the shaft did not show any traces of lining or plastering. The clearance of the west half of the sand filling of the shaft uncovered numerous fragments of completely rotten wood with small remains of black paint (most likely the remains of the wooden coffin), fragments of blackened resin from the burial and some human remains, including a skull.[29] At the bottom of the subsidiary shaft a large irregular niche was dug into its east wall (max. dimensions 0.85×0.80×1.00 m, Fig. 4). The unfinished area is perhaps the initial stage in the building of a room similar to those located at the bottom of the subsidiary shaft in the almost contemporary tombs of Hor and Neferibra-sa-Neith in Saqqara,[30] or it might have been intended to once house the burial of the members of Padihor's family.[31]

At the opposite west wall of Padihor's shaft a few remains of mud bricks on the floor still indicate the mud brick wall that originally blocked the entrance into an east-west running corridor. This 2.80 m long and on average 0.95 m wide and 1 m high horizontal corridor was dug in the *tafla* bedrock and connected the bottom of the subsidiary shaft with the vaulted burial chamber located at the bottom of the main shaft (Figs. 2 and 4).

The burial chamber was not positioned directly at the edge of the west wall of the shaft where the corridor from the entrance shaft arrives. There is a small open space between the chamber and shaft walls which measures between 46 and 52 cm. The massive mud brick walls on both sides of the east wall of the tomb connected the chamber with the east wall of the main shaft (Pl. 2b, Fig. 4). A brick vault originally covered the open space between the corridor and the burial chamber.[32] This roof might have been

---

[28] D. Arnold, *The Encyclopaedia of Ancient Egyptian Architecture*, London – New York 2003, p. 221. In the west wall of a recess in the west side of the main shaft of Iufaa's burial complex a number of shallow holes were dug in two crossed lines to allow the workmen to climb down into the deep shaft – Bareš – Smoláriková, *Abusir XVII*, p. 47. The east wall of the subsidiary shaft in the corridor of Udjahorresnet's tomb contains similar small openings – Bareš, *Abusir IV*, p. 62. In the burial shaft of Udjahorresnet's tomb much larger recesses (1.4 m wide, 1 m deep) in the north and south walls of the shaft were used for removing the sand and lowering the sarcophagus – Bareš, *Abusir IV*, p. 49. The main shaft of the tomb of Hor-khebit has similar recesses – G. Daressy, 'Tombe de Hor-Kheb à Saqqarah', *ASAE* 4 (1903), p. 76.

[29] For more detailed information on the human remains see Chapter 1.3.3.

[30] E. Drioton – J.-Ph. Lauer, 'Les tombes jumeleés de Neferibrê-Sa-Neith et de Ouahibrê-Men', *ASAE* 51 (1951), pp. 477-478, and pl. I (M) (measuring 6.40×4.80 m), and J.-Ph. Lauer, 'La structure de la tombe de Hor à Saqqarah (XXVIe Dynastie)', *ASAE* 52 (1954), p. 136 and pl. I (M). The function of this room is still unclear. Lauer has suggested that it might have housed, during the construction of the tomb, the material necessary for its closure, or it might have functioned as a storage room. See also D. Eigner, 'Late Period Private Tombs', in K.A. Bard (ed.), *Encyclopedia of the Archaeology of Ancient Egypt*, London-New York 1999, p. 437, fig. 56 (no. 6).

[31] In general on the burial of family members in supplementary burial chambers next to the main one, see L. Bareš, 'Lesser Burial Chambers in the Large Late Period Shaft Tombs and their Owners', in Z. Hawass – J. Richards (eds.), *The Archaeology and Art of Ancient Egypt. Essays in Honor of David B. O'Connor*, (CASAE 36), 2007. For parallels, see for instance the shaft tombs of Hekaemsaf and Padineith or the burial of Setirben in the burial complex of Psamtek: A. Barsanti, 'II. Les tombeaux de Psammétique et de Setariban. I. Rapport sur la découverte', *ASAE* 1 (1900), pp. 161-162 and figs. 1-2; A. Barsanti, 'VIII. Tombeau de Péténéith. I. Rapport sur la découverte', *ASAE* 2 (1901), pp. 97-98 and figs. 1-4, and A. Barsanti, 'XII. Le tombeau de Hikaoumsaf. Rapport sur la découverte', *ASAE* 5 (1904), p. 70 and fig. 1. On the burials of family members in and around Iufaa's tomb, consult Bareš – Smoláriková, *Abusir XVII*, pp. 97-162.

[32] A vaulted brick passageway between the corridor and the burial chamber occurs for instance also in the shaft tombs of Hor, Neferibra-sa-Neith and Menekhibnekau: Z.Y. Saad, 'Preliminary Report on the Royal Excavations at Saqqarah 1941–1942', *ASAE* 41 (1942), p. 391 and pl. XXVIIb; Drioton – Lauer, *ASAE* 51 (1951), p. 472; Lauer, *ASAE* 52 (1954), p. 136 and plate I, and Bareš – Janák – Landgráfová – Smoláriková, *ZÄS* 135 (2008), p. 105. In the tomb of Udjahorresnet, a mud brick vault featured in the middle of the corridor connecting the secondary shaft with the burial chamber – Bareš, *Abusir IV*, p. 62 and fig. 6. On (brick) vaults in general, consult A.J. Spencer, *Brick Architecture*, pp. 123-126, and S. el-Naggar, *Les voutes dans l'architecture de l'Egypte ancienne*, (BdE 128), Cairo 1999.

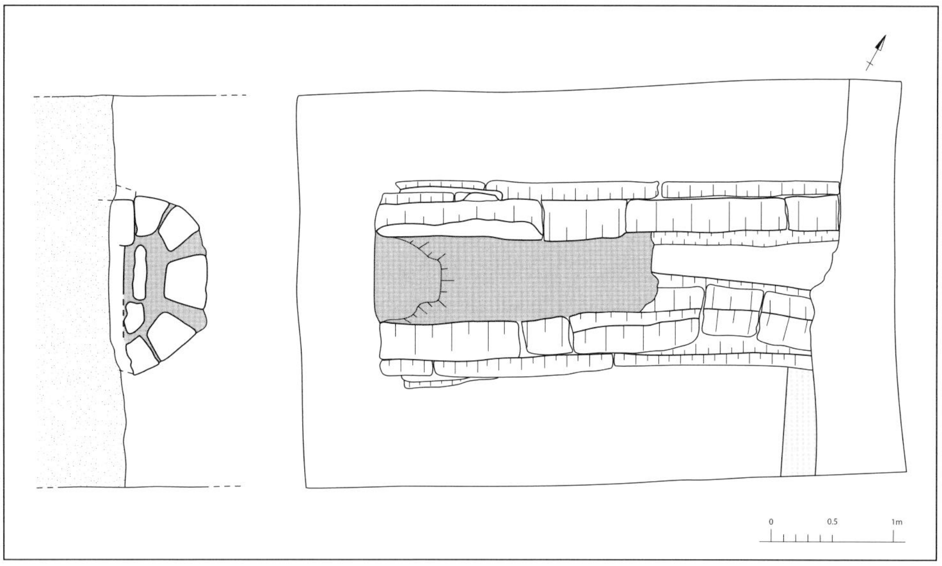

Fig. 6
The roof of Padihor's burial chamber

pierced immediately after the burial as a protective measure[33] or it could have been destroyed later on by the activities of the tomb robbers. In the small area between the burial chamber and the wall of the main shaft more remains of completely rotten wood from a coffin, resin and bones were found. Fragments of several shabtis[34] and bones from a scattered burial[35] were also found in the heap of sand that sloped down from the entrance into the burial chamber.

The burial chamber was located more or less in the centre of the bottom of the main shaft, which is slightly larger than the top, measuring 4.85/4.90×3.14/3.18 m (Figs. 4, 5 and 6). The outer walls of the chamber are located between 46 and 52 cm from the east wall, 64 to 68 cm from the west wall, 78 to 92 cm from the south wall and 76 to 82 cm from the north wall of the shaft. The highest point of the roof is located 10.10 m below the surface of the desert. The general shape of the chamber, measuring 3.75×1.60×1.90 m at its largest (on the outside), imitates the typical form of a giant sarcophagus with a vaulted ceiling. It was constructed from limestone ashlars, greyish to yellowish in colour. The outer face of the blocks were left rough. The origin of the material is for the time being still unknown, but it seems to represent the better-quality variety of local limestone.[36] The chamber was orientated from east to west, with an entrance in its east wall (Pl. 3a). Despite the fact that no remains of Padihor's mummy or

[33] The absence of openings or channels in the ceiling of the tomb (which would allow the sand filling of the main shaft to descend in order to cover and protect the burial chamber and its contents – on this technique see for instance Arnold, *Building in Egypt*, pp. 229-230) suggests that the small vaulted passage between the wall of the shaft and the burial chamber might have been destroyed immediately after the burial took place to protect the deceased – see Bareš, *Abusir IV*, pp. 25-26. For examples of the use of channels in the ceiling of the tomb, consult Barsanti, *ASAE* 1 (1900), p. 165 (tomb of Psamtek); A. Barsanti, 'IV. Tombeau de Péténisis. I. Rapport sur la découverte', *ASAE* 1 (1900), p. 233 (Padinese); Barsanti, *ASAE* 5 (1904), p. 71 (Hekaemsaf); Saad, *ASAE* 41 (1942), pp. 383-384, and 388-389 (Amuntefnakht); Drioton – Lauer, *ASAE* 51 (1951), pp. 472-473 (Neferibra-sa-Neith); Bareš, *Abusir IV*, p. 50 and figs. 32 and 33 (Udjahorresnet), and Bareš – Janák – Landgráfová – Smoláriková, *ZÄS* 135 (2008), p. 105 (Menekhibnekau). See also Gestermann, *Sargtexte in spätzeitlichen Grabanlagen* I, pp. 356-357.

[34] Excavation no. 131/R/01a-o.

[35] Excavation no. 132/R/01.

[36] It could not be established whether the blocks derived from older constructions in its vicinity, such as the pyramid complexes of the kings of the Fifth Dynasty. On the possible destruction and reuse of older monuments in Abusir at the time of the Late Period in general, consult L. Bareš, 'The Destruction of the Monuments at the Necropolis of Abusir', in M. Bárta – J. Krejčí (eds.), *Abusir and Saqqara in the Year 2000*, (Supplementa Archivu Orientálního IX), Prague 2000, pp. 1-16, and L. Bareš, 'The Necropolis at Abusir in the First Millennium BC', in K. Daoud – S. Bedier – S. Adel Fattah (eds.), *Studies in Honour of Ali Radwan*, (Supplements aux ASAE 34/1), Cairo 2005, pp. 177-182.

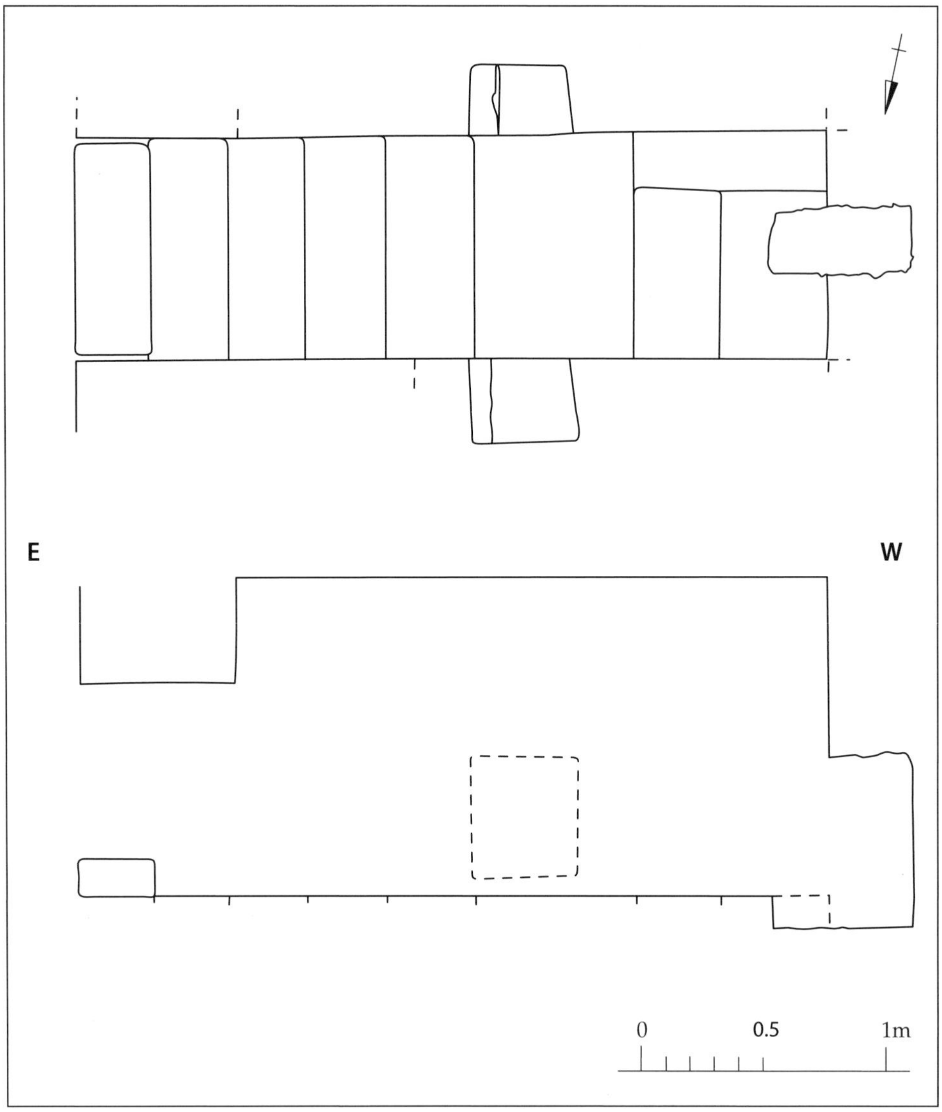

Fig. 7
The floor plan and section of Padihor's burial chamber

coffin were recovered in situ from his burial chamber, it is most probable that his head was positioned towards the west and the rear wall of the chamber. In the Saite-Persian cemetery at Abusir, the orientation of the head of the deceased was similar in the burial chambers of Udjahorresnet and the anonymous tomb R3, while in the tombs of Iufaa and Menekhibnekau the head of the deceased was orientated towards the east and north, respectively.[37]

The entrance to the burial chamber was originally closed with limestone blocks – one of these blocks still lies in the sand in front of the entrance. The entrance itself con-

[37] The large variety in the orientation of the heads of the deceased in the Saite-Persian cemetery at Abusir contradicts an earlier suggestion by Lauer, *ASAE* 52 (1954), p. 134, based on various Saqqara shaft tombs, that tombs orientated in an east-west direction were slightly older than tombs with a north-south orientation. The tombs in the Abusir cemetery appear however to have been built almost simultaneously according to Bareš, in *Abusir. Secrets of the Desert and the Pyramids*, p. 175. The decision to orientate the tomb north-south (perhaps following the orientation in Old Kingdom pyramids) or east-west (according to the prevailing Osirian beliefs) could have represented a personal choice of the deceased or it could have been chosen for reasons of expediency. In Saqqara and Giza, the shaft tombs of Amenutefnakht, Udjahor, Hekaemsaf, Hor, Neferibra-sa-Neith/Wahibremen and Pakap are also orientated east-west, while the tombs of Tjannehebu, Padineith, Padinese and Psamtek are orientated north-south. On this topic see also Stammers, *Elite Late Period Egyptian Tombs*, pp. 13-14; 30-31, and 91. On the orientation of the body of the deceased, consult A.M. Roth – C.H. Roehrig, 'Magical Bricks and the Bricks of Birth', *JEA* 88 (2002), p. 123 (n. 16); M.J. Raven, 'Egyptian Concepts on the Orientation of the Human Body', *JEA* 91 (2005), pp. 31-53, and Stammers, *Elite Late Period Egyptian Tombs*, p. 31.

sists of a small rectangular opening, about 69 cm high and 85 cm wide, demarcated at the top by the entrance lintel and at the bottom by the threshold. The lintel above the entrance is 85 cm wide, 65 cm deep and has a maximum height of 44 cm. The inner west face of the lintel, which features an inscription, was only roughly worked and not smoothed. The east half of the lintel (32 cm) hangs over the threshold (85 cm long, 32 cm wide and 15 cm high). The west part of the lintel (33 cm) sticks out into the tomb and over the floor (84 cm above the floor level).

The interior of the burial chamber measures 2.770×0.875×1.280 m. The floor, like all other parts of the tomb, was constructed out of eight regularly placed rectangular limestone slabs, greyish to yellowish in colour (Fig. 7). The thickness of the floor could not be established with precision[38] nor could it be ascertained whether it was constructed on a layer of sand[39] since for safety reasons the foundation of the burial chamber and the bottom of the main shaft could not be cleared.

The roof of the tomb is a true vault constructed as a single ring of blocks made of wedge-shaped keystones or *voussoirs* (Fig. 6 and Pl. 3a).[40] The ceiling reaches a maximum thickness of 60 cm. Inside the chamber, the ceiling is on average 125 cm high, the highest point reaching 128 cm, and it spans an area of about 85 cm.

The surface of the five rows of limestone ashlars, greyish to yellowish in colour and forming the north, south and west walls of the tomb, was smoothed (Pl. 3b). The four walls of the burial chamber and its ceiling were inscribed with hieroglyphic texts, mostly passages from the Pyramid Texts and the Coffin Texts (Figs. 9-13 and Pls. 4-6).[41] The length of the lateral north and south walls is 277 cm, from the entrance to the tomb at the east to the rear or west wall, or 245 cm from the end of the threshold to the west wall. Approximately in the middle of both the north and the south wall a small niche was excavated (Fig. 7, Pls. 4 and 5). The west end of the niche in the north wall is located 106 cm from the west wall of the tomb. It is 40.5 cm wide, 32.0 cm deep and 47.0 cm high. The niche is located 8.5 to 9.0 cm above the floor level (west to east). The west end of the niche in the south wall is located 104 cm from the west wall of the tomb. It is 42.0 cm wide, 30.0 cm deep and 48.5 cm high and located 7 to 8 cm (east to west) above the level of the floor. A line in red ink is drawn above (3 cm) and to the sides (2.0 to 2.5 cm) of both niches. The west or rear wall of the tomb is 87.5 cm wide. A niche is positioned almost in its very centre (Fig. 8). The niche is located 33.0 cm from the north wall and 31.5 cm from the south wall. It is 23.0 cm wide and has a total height of 57.5 cm, 12 cm of which sink below the floor level. A line in red ink is drawn above and on the sides of the niche (2.5 cm from the edge of the niche on the south side and above, and 3.0 cm from the edge of the niche on the north side).

The interior of all three niches was roughly worked and only partly smoothed. No traces of any mortar, plaster or walling up were discovered in these recesses. No object was found in the niches and their function remains open to discussion. The niches in

---

[38] The limestone ashlars that make up the walls of the burial chamber are on average between 25 and 35 cm thick. It was estimated that the floor in Iufaa's tomb had a thickness of at least 30-35 cm according to Bareš – Smoláriková, *Abusir XVII*, p. 53 (n. 126).

[39] Other burial chambers of the Saite-Persian shaft tombs were also built on top of a layer of sand: Udjahorresnet (Bareš, *Abusir IV*, pp. 62-63), Iufaa (Bareš – Smoláriková, *Abusir XVII*, p. 49 and figs. 10 and 11), the anonymous tomb R3 in Abusir (see Chapters 2.1 and 2.2 in this volume), as well as for instance Tjannehebu (E. Bresciani – S. Pernigotti – M.P. Giangeri-Silvis, *La tomba di Ciennehebu, capo della flotta del Re*, Pisa 1977, Tav. II) and Neferibra-sa-Neith (Drioton – Lauer, *ASAE* 51 (1951), p. 477) in Saqqara. The sand-bed foundation is a typical component of many constructions of the Saite period (see footnote 17), but its presence underneath the burial chambers also had religious connotations referring to the tomb of Osiris and the primeval hill. On this topic consult for instance E. Hornung, *The Ancient Egyptian Book of the Afterlife*, Ithaca – London 1999, p. 38; Stammers, *Elite Late Period Egyptian Tombs*, pp. 37-39 and Chapter 2.2 in this volume.

[40] Arnold, *Building in Egypt*, pp. 200-201. For parallels see the almost contemporary shaft tomb complexes of Neferibra-sa-Neith/Wahibremen and Hor in Saqqara and the nearby tomb of Udjahorresnet: Drioton – Lauer, *ASAE* 51 (1951), pp. 473, 479 and plates I, II, V, and IX; Lauer, *ASAE* 52 (1954), pp. 135-136 and plate II, and Bareš, *Abusir IV*, p. 50 and fig. 3.

[41] See Chapter 1.3 in this volume.

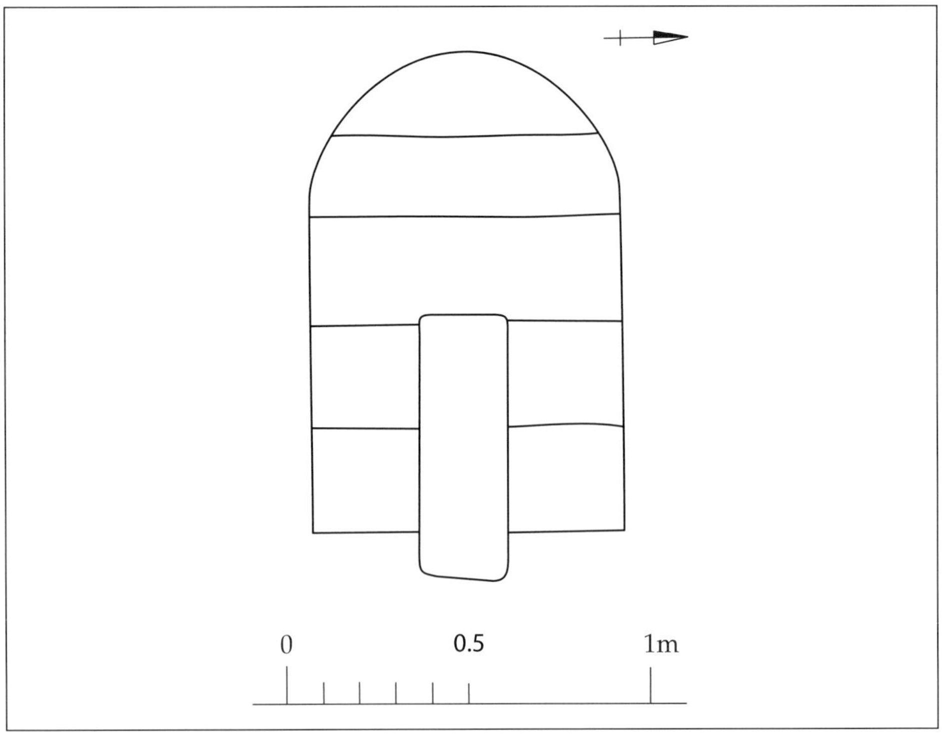

Fig. 8
The rear or west wall of the burial chamber

the lateral walls were perhaps intended to contain the so-called 'magical bricks'.[42] Similar recesses added in already existing walls were for instance also discovered in the burial chambers I and II in the so-called gallery of Padineith in the tomb of the Vizier Bakenrenef in Saqqara. In a number of these recesses the original magic bricks were still found untouched.[43] In the tomb of Udjahorresnet small irregular niches or recesses had also been cut and five fragments of the magical bricks discovered during the clearance of the sand and debris above the burial chamber.[44] The dimensions of these niches, ca. 15-20 cm high and wide and ca. 20 cm deep, are but half the size of the dimensions of the recesses in the tomb of Padihor. It is perhaps more likely that the niches in the south and north lateral walls of the tomb were intended to house the canopic jars – although not a single trace of these jars was found during the excavation of the tomb.[45] A similar situation occurred in the tomb of Udjahorresnet[46] and similar recesses

[42] In general on these 'magical bricks', consult M.S.H.G. Heerma van Voss, 'Ziegel (magische)', in W. Helck – E. Otto (eds.), *Lexikon der Ägyptologie VI*, Wiesbaden 1986, p. 1402; J. Monnet, 'Les briques magiques du Musée du Louvre', *RdE* 8 (1951), pp. 151-162; E. Thomas, 'The Four Niches and the Amuletic Figures in Theban Royal Tombs', *JARCE* 3 (1964), pp. 71-78; M.S.H.G. Heerma van Voss, 'An Egyptian Magical Brick', *JEOL* 18 (1964), pp. 314-317; L. Kákosy, 'Magical Bricks from TT 32', in J.H. Kamstra – H. Milde – K. Wagtendonk (eds.), *Funerary Symbols and Religion: Essays Dedicated to M.S.H.G. Heerma van Voss on the Occasion of his Retirement from the Chair in History of Ancient Religions at the University of Amsterdam*, Kampten 1988, pp. 60-72, and Roth – Roehrig, *JEA* 88 (2002), pp. 121-139. A dissertation dealing with magical bricks has been written by I. Régen, *Les quatres amuletes protectrices ou 'briques magiques'. Etude d'un ritual funéraire égyptien (chap. 151 A LdM sections g-h)*, Université Paul Valéry, Montpellier 1999 and should be published in the near future.

[43] E. Bresciani – S. an-Naggar – S. Pernigotti – F. Silvano, *La Galleria di Padineit, visir di Nectanebo I*, (Saqqara 1), Pisa 1983, pp. 44-45.

[44] Bareš, *Abusir IV*, pp. 51, 67-68, and fig. 49. The bricks might have been put directly into the tomb together with other parts of the burial equipment. In the tomb of Iufaa the magical bricks were for instance placed in the sand that filled the space between the sarcophagus and the walls of the burial chamber (Bareš – Smoláriková, *Abusir XVII*, pp. 63-64, and 82). In the tomb of Tjannehebu the same bricks were placed into a box in the tomb (Bresciani – Pernigotti – Giangeri-Silvis, *Ciennehebu*, p. 70 and pl. XXV).

[45] In Menekhibnekau's burial complex not a single trace of the canopic jars was discovered either. The absence of the jars is hard to explain given that they do not represent an obvious object for tomb robbers to remove. See Bareš – Janák – Landgráfová – Smoláriková, *ZÄS* 135 (2008), p. 108.

[46] Bareš, *Abusir IV*, p. 51. The dimensions of the niches in the lateral walls are 64×47 cm (north) and 78×50 cm (south).

also feature for instance in the lateral walls of the tombs of Hor and in the joint tomb of Neferibra-sa-Neith and Wahibremen in the temple area of Userkaf in Saqqara.[47] The function of the smaller niche in the rear or west wall of the burial chamber is unclear. In the burial chamber of Tjannehebu in Saqqara, the niche in the rear wall contained a vessel filled with embalming material.[48] Louise Gestermann has suggested that this might have also been the case in other burial chambers.[49] In other, large Late Period shaft tombs the niche in the rear wall had a functional purpose when the lid was being lowered onto the outer monumental sarcophagus.[50] A large-sized sarcophagus was never intended for the tomb of Padihor – who appears to have been buried in a wooden coffin – and would hardly have fitted in his burial chamber. The architects designing the burial chamber might have included the niche to give Padihor's chamber the same general outlook that most other burial chambers in Late Period shaft tombs had.

Padihor's tomb is one of almost two dozen Late Period (more precisely Twenty-Sixth and early Twenty-Seventh Dynasty) shaft tombs that have been identified[51] and documented in the greater Memphite area up to the present day.[52] Next to the already mentioned shaft tombs in the Late Period cemetery of Abusir (Udjahorresnet, Iufaa, Menekhibnekau, Padihor and 'R3'),[53] the heaviest concentration of tombs of this kind is found in nearby Saqqara, and especially in or around the pyramid complexes of the first and last Fifth Dynasty rulers, Userkaf and Unas respectively.[54] The burial complexes of Amuntefnakht (also called Haaibre-meriptah)[55] and Hekaemsaf[56] are located within the pyramid complex of Unas, while the shaft tombs of Tjannehebu,[57] Padine-

[47] Drioton - Lauer, *ASAE* 51 (1951), p. 476 and plates I and XII-XIII, and Lauer, *ASAE* 52 (1954), p. 134 and plate I. In the tomb of Neferibra-sa-Neith the niches have the following dimensions: 0.70×0.48×2.80 m.

[48] A. Barsanti, 'IV. Tombeau de Zannehibou. I. Rapport sur la découverte', *ASAE* 1 (1900), p. 267.

[49] Gestermann, *Sargtexte in spätzeitlichen Grabanlagen*, pp. 72 and 356 (n. 1482). A vessel with embalming materials was however found only in the niche in the tomb of Tjannehebu.

[50] Drioton – Lauer, *ASAE* 51 (1951), pp. 475-476, and Bareš, *Abusir IV*, p. 51.

[51] For a general definition of the Late Period 'shaft tomb', see for instance Bareš, in Hawass – Richards (eds.), *The Archaeology and Art of Ancient Egypt*, p. 87: 'The large Late Period shaft tombs ... (are) characterized by a massive vaulted burial chamber situated at the foot of a huge and deep shaft and accessible through a small lateral shaft and a horizontal corridor connecting the two shafts', or Stammers, *Elite Late Period Egyptian Tombs*, p. 26: 'The Saite-Persian Shaft Tomb has a deep central shaft, within which lies the burial chamber. Access to the burial chamber is by way of a smaller secondary shaft, from which a passage leads to the burial chamber, usually horizontally or at a slight incline'. See also Eigner, in K.A. Bard (ed.), *Encyclopedia of the Archaeology of Ancient Egypt*, esp. pp. 436-438, and Gestermann, *Sargtexte in spätzeitlichen Grabanlagen*, pp. 356-359.

[52] The inclusion of certain tombs in the spectrum of the Late Period shaft tombs, or their exclusion from it, is still open to debate and opinions vary. For a recent overview of tombs of this type, consult L. Bareš, 'The Social Status of the Owners of the Large Late Period Shaft Tombs', in M. Bárta – F. Coppens – J. Krejčí (eds.), *Abusir and Saqqara in the Year 2005. Proceedings of the Conference Held in Prague (June 27– July 5, 2005)*, Prague 2006, pp. 4-6. For a similar list see Stammers, *Elite Late Period Egyptian Tombs*, pp. 30, table 1, and 103-115.

[53] See already footnotes 2, and 5-8.

[54] In general on Saqqara in the Late Period, consult H.S. Smith, 'Saqqara. Late Period', in W. Helck – E. Otto (eds.), *Lexikon der Ägyptologie V*, Wiesbaden 1984, pp. 412-428 and J.D. Ray, 'Saqqara, Late Period and Graeco-Roman Tombs', in K.A. Bard (ed.), *Encyclopedia of the Archaeology of Ancient Egypt*, London-New York 1999, pp. 691-694. For an overview of the location of the tombs in Saqqara, see Stammers, *Elite Late Period Egyptian Tombs*, pp. 99 (map 5), and 101 (map 8).

[55] PM III^2, 650 and pl. LXI; Z.Y. Saad, 'Preliminary Report on the Royal Excavations at Saqqarah 1939–1940', *ASAE* 40 (1941), p. 693; Saad, *ASAE* 41 (1942), pp. 381-392; Z.Y. Saad, *Royal Excavations at Saqqara and Helwan (1941-1945)*, (CASAE 3), Cairo 1947, pp. 2-11; E. Drioton, 'Textes religieux des tombeaux saïtes', *ASAE* 52 (1954), pp. 105-122; D.A. Pressl, *Beamte und Soldaten. Die Verwaltung in der 26. Dynastie in Ägypten (664-525 v. Chr.)*, Frankfurt 1998, pp. 281-282; Gestermann, *Sargtexte in spätzeitlichen Grabanlagen*, pp. 59-65, and Stammers, *Elite Late Period Egyptian Tombs*, pp. 104, 130, and 164.

[56] PM III^2, 650 and pl. LXI; Barsanti, *ASAE* 5 (1905); G. Maspero, 'XIII. Les inscriptions du tombeau de Hikaoumsaf', *ASAE* 5 (1905); Pressl, *Beamte und Soldaten*, pp. 275-277, and Stammers, *Elite Late Period Egyptian Tombs*, pp. 109, 133, and 163-164.

[57] PM III^2, 648 and pl. LXI; Barsanti, *ASAE* 1 (1900), pp. 262-271; G. Maspero, 'IV. Tombeau de Zannehibou. II. Les inscriptions du tombeau de Zannehibou', *ASAE* 1 (1900); Bresciani – Pernigotti – Giangeri-Silvis, *Ciennehebu*; Pressl, *Beamte und Soldaten*, p. 317; Gestermann, *Sargtexte in spätzeitlichen Grabanlagen*, pp. 72-79, and Stammers, *Elite Late Period Egyptian Tombs*, pp. 108, 132-133, and 162.

se[58] and Psamtek[59] (the so-called 'Persian tombs'[60]) are found to the south and that of Padineith[61] to the south-east of it.[62] The joint tomb of the Twenty-Sixth Dynasty princess Khetbeneithyerboni[63] and two individuals called Psamtek in the vicinity of the monastery of Apa Jeremias, to the south-east of Unas' complex, might also have constituted a shaft tomb.[64] The location of this tomb is at present unknown. The joint tomb of Neferibra-sa-Neith and Wahibremen,[65] and the burial complex of Hor (also called Wahibre-em-akhet and later Neferibra-em-akhet)[66] are located, together with several other shaft tombs, in the pyramid complex of Userkaf.[67] Two other burials, of

---

[58] PM III^2, 649 and pl. LXI; Barsanti, *ASAE* 1 (1900), pp. 230-234; G. Maspero, 'IV. Tombeau de Péténisis. II. Les inscriptions du tombeau de Péténisis', *ASAE* 1 (1901); Pressl, *Beamte und Soldaten*, pp. 260-261; Gestermann, *Sargtexte in spätzeitlichen Grabanlagen*, pp. 86-94, and Stammers, *Elite Late Period Egyptian Tombs*, pp. 107-108, 131, and 163.

[59] PM III^2, 649 and pl. LXI; Barsanti, *ASAE* 1 (1900), pp. 161-166; G. Maspero, II. Les tombeaux de Psammétique et de Setariban. II. Les inscriptions de la chambre de Psammétique', *ASAE* 1 (1901); Pressl, *Beamte und Soldaten*, pp. 263-264; Gestermann, *Sargtexte in spätzeitlichen Grabanlagen*, pp. 80-85, and Stammers, *Elite Late Period Egyptian Tombs*, pp. 106-107, 130-131, and 162.

[60] A. Barsanti, 'Rapports de M. Alexandre Barsanti sur les déblaiements opérés autour de la pyramide d'Ounas pendant les années 1899-1901', *ASAE* 2 (1901), pp. 246-247, and 256.

[61] PM III^2, 649 and pl. LXI; Barsanti, *ASAE* 2 (1901), pp. 97-104; G. Maspero, 'VIII. Tombeau de Péténéith. II. Les inscriptions du tombeau de Péténéith', *ASAE* 2 (19021, pp. 104-111; S. Pernigotti, 'Saitica II', *EVO* 8 (1985), pp. 7-10; Pressl, *Beamte und Soldaten*, p. 297, and Stammers, *Elite Late Period Egyptian Tombs*, pp. 108, 131-132, and 163.

[62] See also the overview of the excavations taking place in and around the pyramid complex of Unas in A. Labrousse – J.-Ph. Lauer – J. Leclant, *Mission archéologique de Saqqarah II. Le temple haut du complexe funéraire du roi Ounas*, (BdE 73), Cairo 1977, pp. 1-11 and 31-32. Another shaft tomb of perhaps the same type was recently excavated by our Egyptian colleagues in the eastern part of the causeway of Unas, in the vicinity of the double mastaba of Niankhkhnum and Khnumhotep – according to Bareš, in Hawass – Richards (eds.), *The Archaeology and Art of Ancient Egypt*, p. 92, n. 3.

[63] The last word on this princess is yet to be said – see Gestermann, *Sargtexte in spätzeitlichen Grabanlagen*, pp. 99-100 for a general overview of the problematic identification of this personage. It has been suggested that she was the wife of Nekau II and the mother of Psamtek II, or the daughter of Psamtek II or Apries and the wife of either Apries or Amasis. See especially G. Vittmann, 'Zwei Königinnen der Spätzeit namens Chedebnitjebone', *CdE* 49 (1974); G. Vittmann, 'Die Familie der saitischen Könige', *Orientalia* 44 (1975), pp. 383-384, and Ray, in K.A. Bard (ed.), *Encyclopedia of the Archaeology of Ancient Egypt*, p. 693.

[64] According to Stammers, *Elite Late Period Egyptian Tombs*, p. 115. Very little is however known of this burial complex – consult: PM III^2, 670-671 and pl. LXII; A. Mariette, *Notice des principaux monuments exposés dans les galeries provisoires du Musée d'antiquités égyptiennes de S.A. le khédive à Boulaq*, Paris 1872, p. 157 (nr. 385); A. Mariette – G. Maspero, *Monuments divers recueillis en Egypte et en Nubie*, Paris 1872/1889, pp. 26 and 29 and pl. 77i and 95f; G. Daressy, 'Inscriptions du tombeau de Psamtik à Saqqarah', *RT* 17 (1895), pp. 17-25; J.-P. Corteggiani, 'Documents divers (I-VI)', *BIFAO* 73 (1973), pp. 151-153, and Gestermann, *Sargtexte in spätzeitlichen Grabanlagen*, pp. 95-100.

[65] PM III^2, 586-587 and pl. LVIII; C.M. Firth, 'Excavations of the Department of Antiquities at Saqqarah (October 1928 to March 1929)', *ASAE* 29 (1929), pp. 68-70; Drioton – Lauer, *ASAE* 51 (1951), pp. 470-490; Pressl, *Beamte und Soldaten*, pp. 234-235; Gestermann, *Sargtexte in spätzeitlichen Grabanlagen*, pp. 66-71, and Stammers, *Elite Late Period Egyptian Tombs*, pp. 104-106, 130, and 166.

[66] PM III^2, 587 and pl. LVIII; Saad, *ASAE* 41 (1942), pp. 391-393; Saad, *CASAE 3*, pp. 11-13; Lauer, *ASAE* 52 (1954); Drioton, *ASAE* 52 (1954), pp. 122-127, and Stammers, *Elite Late Period Egyptian Tombs*, pp. 103, 130, and 165-166.

[67] On the existence of other Saite shaft tombs in the area of the pyramid complex of Userkaf and the royal mother Neferhetepes, consult A. el-Khouli, 'Excavations at the Pyramid of Userkaf, 1976: Preliminary Report', *JEA* 64 (1978), p. 36; A. el-Khouli, 'Excavations at the Pyramid of Userkaf, 1979: Preliminary Report', *JEA* 66 (1980), pp. 46-47; A. el-Khouli, 'Excavations at the Pyramid of Userkaf', *JSSEA* 15 (1985), p. 87, and especially A. Labrousse – J.-Ph. Lauer, *Les complexes funéraires d'Ouserkaf et de Néferhétepès I. Texte*, (BdE 130/1), Cairo 2000, pp. 174-176, and figs. 12, 14 and 383. Six shaft tombs were excavated by C.M. Firth (according to Firth's notebook [1928-1930]), but only two – the aforementioned joint tomb of Neferibra-sa-Neith/Wahibremen and the burial complex of Hor – ever published. I am grateful to Prof. Ladislav Bareš for bringing this information to my attention.

Udjahor[68] and Hor-khebit,[69] were unearthed in Saqqara-North, presumably to the north-east or east of the pyramid complex of Djoser.[70] The exact position of these two tombs is at present unknown. Both burial complexes were not finished. Perhaps due to the untimely death of the tomb owners, the burial chamber in the tomb of Hor-khebit was left unfinished, while the sarcophagus of Udjahor was simply placed at the bottom of the main shaft.[71] The final resting place of Nesbanebdjed, discovered to the south-west of Unas' pyramid complex, consisted also of a sarcophagus at the bottom of a large shaft without any burial chamber.[72] Outside of the Saqqara-Abusir region, one more shaft tomb has been identified: the burial complex of Pakap (also called Wahibreemakhet) near the causeway of Khephren in Giza (LG 84, the so-called 'Campbell's tomb').[73]

In comparison with all other Late Period shaft tombs, the burial complex of Padihor contains all standard architectural components (a large main shaft with a constructed burial chamber at its bottom, a subsidiary shaft and a connecting corridor), but it appears by far the smallest tomb of its type excavated to the present day. The overview of the dimensions of the main and subsidiary shaft, connecting corridor and burial

---

[68] PM III², 503; A. Barsanti, 'Sur la découverte du puits d'Ouazhorou à Sakkarah', *ASAE* 3 (1902), pp. 209-212, and Stammers, *Elite Late Period Egyptian Tombs*, pp. 115 and 164.

[69] PM III², 588; Daressy, *ASAE* 4 (1903); D. Arnold, 'The Late Period Tombs of Hor-khebit, Wennefer and Wereshnefer at Saqqara', in C. Berger – B. Mathieu (eds.), *Etudes sur l'Ancien Empire et la nécropole de Saqqara dédiées à Jean-Philippe Lauer*, (Orientalia Monspeliensia IX), Montpellier 1997, pp. 31-33, and Stammers, *Elite Late Period Egyptian Tombs*, pp. 115 and 166.

[70] A number of large shaft tombs can be observed to the east of the Step Pyramid complex (Bareš, in Hawass – Richards (eds.), *The Archaeology and Art of Ancient Egypt*, p. 92, n. 3). The general disposition of Djoser's burial complex appears to have been an important source of inspiration for the designers of the Late Period shaft tombs. This idea was first suggested in J.-Ph. Lauer, *Les pyramides de Sakkarah*, (BiGen 3), Cairo 1972, pp. 12-13. It has been recently further developed in L. Bareš, 'Late Period Shaft Tombs, Step Pyramid and the Dry Moat?', in K. Daoud – S. Abd el-Fattah (eds.), *The World of Ancient Egypt. Essays in honor of Ahmed Abd el-Qader el-Sawi*, (Supplément aux Annales du Service des Antiquités de l'Egypte 35), Cairo 2006, pp. 31–33; Gestermann, in G. Moers – H. Behlmer – K. Demuss – K. Widmaier (eds.), *jn.t ḏr.w. Festschrift für Friedrich Junge*; K. Smoláriková, 'The Step Pyramid – A Constant Inspiration to the Saite Egyptians', in M. Bárta – F. Coppens – J. Krejčí (eds.), *Abusir and Saqqara in the Year 2005. Proceedings of the Conference Held in Prague (June 27– July 5, 2005)*, Prague 2006, and K. Smoláriková, 'The Embalmer's Cache as an Heir of the South Tomb', in P. Maříková Vlčková – J. Mynářová – M. Tomášek (eds.), *My Things Changed Things. Social Development and Cultural Exchange in Prehistory, Antiquity, and Middle Ages*, Prague 2009. See also Stammers, *Elite Late Period Egyptian Tombs*, pp. 31-32, and 86.

[71] The presence of an unfinished smaller shaft to the south of the main shaft of Udjahor suggests that it had most likely been the intention of the designers to construct a typical shaft tomb with a burial chamber at the bottom of the main shaft and a corridor connecting it with the smaller shaft – Barsanti, *ASAE* 3 (1902), p. 209. In the anonymous tomb R3 at Abusir the sarcophagus was simply placed at the bottom of a deep shaft, without any trace of a burial chamber – see Chapter 2.1 in this volume.

[72] PM III², 648 and pl. LXI; A. Barsanti, 'III. Le tombeau de Smendès', *ASAE* 1 (1900), pp. 189-190, and Stammers, *Elite Late Period Egyptian Tombs*, pp. 118-119. M. Stammers lists this tomb among a different type of Late Period tombs: 'shaft tombs' as opposed to 'Saite-Persian shaft tombs'. W. el-Sadeek, *Twenty-Sixth Dynasty Necropolis at Gizeh*, (Veröffentlichungen der Institute für Afrikanistik und Ägyptologie der Universität Wien 29, Beiträge zur Ägyptologie 5), Wien 1984, p. 162, and Bareš, in Bárta – Coppens – Krejčí (eds.), *Abusir and Saqqara in the Year 2005*, p. 5 consider, with some reserve, the tomb of Nesbanebdjed as belonging to the group of typical Late Period shaft tombs.

[73] PM III², 290-291 and plan III; K. R. Lepsius, *Denkmaeler aus Aegypten und Aethiopien* III, Berlin 1850, pl. 277 (d-f); K.R. Lepsius, *Denkmaeler aus Aegypten und Aethiopien. Text* I, Leipzig 1897, pp. 100-101; H. Vyse, *Operations Carried on at the Pyramids of Gizeh in 1837* I-II, London 1840, pp. 216-218 and 232-233 (vol. I) and 131–144 (vol. II); J.S. Perring, *The Pyramids to the Southward of Gizeh and at Abou Roash; also Campbell's tomb and a section of the rock of Gizeh from actual survey and admeasurements*, London 1842, pp. 21-24 and pl. XIX-XXII; el-Sadeek, *Twenty-Sixth Dynasty Necropolis at Gizeh*, pp. 126-132; C.-M. Zivie-Coche, *Giza au premier millénaire autour du temple d'Isis dame des pyramides*, Boston 1991, pp. 283-287; Pressl, *Beamte und Soldaten*, pp. 292-293, and Stammers, *Elite Late Period Egyptian Tombs*, pp. 28, 110 and 160. The tomb is named after Patrick Campbell (1779–1857), the British Consul-General in Egypt between 1833 and 1840 – W.R. Dawson – E.P. Uphill, *Who was who in Egyptology*, London 1995, p. 82.

Tomb owner	Burial shaft dimensions (m)	Burial shaft depth (m)	Subsidiary shaft dimensions (m)	Subsidiary shaft depth (m)	Corridor (length × width × × height/m)	Burial chamber (interior dimensions/m)
Padihor	**4.80 × 3.20**	**12.00**	**1.50 × 1.20**	**12.00**	**2.80 × 0.95 × 1.00**	**2.77 × 0.87 × 1.28**
'R3'	2.10 × 1.80	22.00	entrance corridor	no	no	no
Udjahorresnet	5.50 × 5.50	+ 20.00	2.50 × 2.50	17.00	10.50 × 1.10/40 × × 1.56/64	4.80 × 2.90 × 6.00
Iufaa	13.00 × 13.00	22.00	1.70 × 1.50	19.00	8.00 × 1.20 × 2.05	4.90 × 3.30 × 3.40
Menekhibnekau	12.50 × 12.00	20.00	1.10 × 1.00	20.00	8.00 × 1.10 × 1.26	5.00 × 3.20 × 3.85
Amuntefnakht	10.90 × 8.00	22.00	1.10 × 1.00	not given	not given	7.90 × 5.90 × ?
Hekaemsaf	10.80 × 8.70	28.00	not given	25.00	ca. 2.50 × ? × ?	5.20 × 3.13 × ?
Tjannehebu	13.00 × 10.00*	25.00-30.00	2.00 × 2.00	25.00-30.00	not given	not given
Padinese	8.00 × 7.10	+ 27.50	not given	27.50	3.00? × ? × ?	not given
Psamtek	ca. 10.00 - 11.00	ca. 20.00	1.40 × 1.30	25.00	5.00 × ? × ?	5.20 × 2.68 × 3.50
Padineith	4.50 × 3.00	+ 28.00	not given	28.00	not given	3.55 × 1.94 × 2.44
Neferibra-sa-Neith / Wahibremen	10.00 × 11.00	20.00-25.00	1.40 × 1.15	28.00	ca. 2.00 × ? × ? no separate corridor	3.85 × 1.87 × 3.95 not given
Hor	9.50 × 8.00	14.00	1.20 × 1.20	14.00	not given	? × ? × ca. 3.50
Udjahor	8.50 × 8.25	20.00	not given	unfinished (6.00)	no	no
Hor-khebit	8.00 × 8.50	ca. 20.00	no	no	no	9.55 × 8.10 × 8.60
Nesbanebdjed	3.00 × 2.50	8.00	no	no	no	no
Pakap	9.30 × 8.00	16.30	not given	not given	not given	4.50 × 3.35 × 5.80

Table I.
Overview of the known dimensions of Late Period Shaft Tombs

* Barsanti, *ASAE* 1 (1900), p. 262 has the following dimensions: 11.10 × 7.45 m.

chamber of all explored shaft tombs in Table I clearly illustrates the small size of Padihor's burial complex. The closest parallel, dimension-wise, to the tomb of Padihor is perhaps the burial complex of Padineith, located south-east of the pyramid temple of Unas.[74] In contrast to the nearby, larger burial complexes of Iufaa and Menekhibnekau, Padihor's tomb does not contain a second subsidiary shaft.[75] This second shaft is considered to be an imitation of the southern Saite entrance (the so-called Saite gallery)[76] to the nearby Step pyramid.[77] The absence of a second subsidiary shaft in Padihor's burial complex might be due to its reduced size, but the reason for the overall smaller dimensions of Padihor's tomb cannot be satisfactorily explained as yet. Only a single, mostly honorific, title is known for Padihor,[78] but that does not automatically imply that he had a lower social status (and hence smaller tomb) than the other owners of the Late Period shaft tombs in the Abusir-Saqqara region. The owner of the nearby tomb, Iufaa, has for instance also a single title preserved (*ḫrp ḥwwt* or 'Administrator of Palaces')[79] and his burial complex ranks amongst the largest discovered.[80] Although

[74] Although the shafts of Padineith's burial complex (+ 28m) reach twice the depth of Padihor's shafts (12 m).

[75] Bareš – Smoláriková, *Abusir XVII*, pp. 68-71; Bareš – Smoláriková – Strouhal, *ZÄS* 132 (2005), pp. 97-98, and Chapters 2.1 and 2.2 in this volume. Stammers' suggestion (*Elite Late Period Egyptian Tombs*, pp. 33-34) that all large Saite-Persian shaft tombs from the time of Pakap onwards – with the exception of Padihor – had a second subsidiary shaft does not hold. The burial complex of Udjahorresnet and anonymous tomb R3 in Abusir do not have the second subsidiary shaft either (see Chapter 2.1).

[76] C.M. Firth – J.E. Quibell, *The Step Pyramid*, with plans by J.-Ph. Lauer, Cairo 1935, Vol. I – text, pp. 90-91, Vol. II – plates: 12 and 22.

[77] Bareš – Bárta – Smoláriková – Strouhal, *ZÄS* 130 (2003), pp. 149-150; Smoláriková, in Bárta – Coppens – Krejčí (eds.), *Abusir and Saqqara in the Year 2005*, pp. 45-47; Stammers, *Elite Late Period Egyptian Tombs*, p. 33, and Gestermann, in Moers – Behlmer – Demuss – Widmaier (eds.), *jn.t ḏr.w*, pp. 201 and 203. See also footnote 70 and Chapter 2.2 in this volume on the influence of the outlook of the Step Pyramid on the layout of the shaft tombs.

[78] See Chapter 1.2.

[79] On the title of Iufaa consult Bareš – Smoláriková, *Abusir XVII*, pp. 92-93, and Bareš, in Bárta – Coppens – Krejčí (eds.), *Abusir and Saqqara in the Year 2005*, p. 9. In general on this title see E. Jelínková, 'Recherches sur le titre *ḫrp ḥwwt Nt* 'Administrateur des Domaines de la Couronne Rouge'', *ASAE* 50 (1950), pp. 321-362; E. Jelínková, 'Une titre saïte emprunté à l'Ancien Empire', *ASAE* 55 (1958), pp. 79-125, and R. el-Sayed, 'À propos du titre *ḫrp ḥwwt*', *RdE* 28 (1976), pp. 97-110.

[80] On this discrepancy, see also Bareš, in Bárta – Coppens – Krejčí (eds.), *Abusir and Saqqara in the Year 2005*, p. 17 (n. 118).

the excavation did not reveal a single item that would help date the construction of Padihor's tomb with any degree of certainty, it was most likely contemporary with the other shaft tombs constructed in Abusir during the late Twenty-Sixth to early Twenty-Seventh Dynasty.[81] The changing and unstable political situation in Egypt at the turn of the Twenty-Sixth to the Twenty-Seventh Dynasty[82] might have had impact on the scale of the tomb. Unsure what the future might bring, Padihor could have decided to commission a burial complex that contained all the essential elements of the other tombs, but on a much smaller scale than those of his predecessors. The excavation of other small and middle-sized shaft tombs, located along a north-west – south-east running line immediately to the east of Padihor's tomb,[83] might provide further information on the development of the Saite-Persian cemetery at Abusir and Padihor's place within the necropolis.

1.2. The owner of the tomb

1.2.1. Padihor

The name Padihor (*Pꜣ-di-Ḥr*),[84] commonly translated as 'The one who is given by Horus', occurs no less than 40 times in the inscriptions on the walls and ceiling of the burial chamber. The name is in all cases written vertically and, remarkably, no less than six variants of the writing of the name occur. The most typical form of the name (27 occurrences) consists of . The most common variant, occurring eight times, involves the use of the flying pintail duck (Gardiner G40) instead of the uniliteral sign *p* (Q3), while occasionally (4 occurrences) the forearm (D37) is used instead of the uniliteral sign *d* (D46). An overview of the various writings of the name of the tomb owner and their distribution over the columns on the walls and ceiling of the tomb is given in Table II.

It is interesting to observe that the three different writings of the name Padihor that use the falcon or Horus-hieroglyph (G5) instead of the face (D2) to write *ḥr* only occur in the columns on the ceiling of the burial chamber (five occurrences). It is impossible to say whether this is a mere coincidence or a deliberate choice of the priests (or owner?) designing the textual program to be applied to the walls of the burial chamber.[85] One can only wonder whether the limited use of the Horus-hieroglyph in Padihor's name only in the columns on the ceiling, representing the sky or heaven, might have been inspired by religious concepts or ideas. The three columns on the ceiling deal with various aspects of the renewal (PT utterance 249) and transformation of the king, among others into a supreme divine being (PT utterance 252) or a spirit (PT utterance 422), and his ascension into the sky to join the sun-god (PT utterance 251).[86] The representation of Horus on the ceiling of the tomb, suggestive of a falcon flying in the sky, might be related both to the idea of the renewal and continuation of life (Horus takes on the role of his father Osiris) and the concept of ascension. The correct execu-

---

[81] The pottery discovered in the nearby anonymous tomb R3 dates its construction to the end of the 6th century and the beginning of the 5th century BC, i.e. the reign of Darius I (522-486 BC). For the analysis of the pottery see Chapter 2.3 in this volume. Consult also the chronological overview in Stammers, *Elite Late Period Egyptian Tombs*, pp. 28-30 and table 1.

[82] In general on this period consult F.K. Kienitz, *Die politische Geschichte Ägyptens vom 7. bis zum 4. Jahrhundert vor der Zeitwende*, Berlin 1953, pp. 11-66, and A.B. Lloyd, 'The Late Period (664-332 BC)', in I. Shaw (ed.), *The Oxford History of Ancient Egypt*, Oxford 2000, pp. 383-385.

[83] See the plan in Bárta, in Bárta – Krejčí (eds.), *Abusir and Saqqara in the Year 2000*, p. 345, and the satellite image in M. Bárta – V. Brůna, *Satellite Atlas of the Pyramid Fields of Abusir, Saqqara and Dahshur*, Prague 2006, pp. 40 (pl. I) and 52 (pl. I) (= Plate I in this volume).

[84] The name also often occurs as 'Pedehor'.

[85] A single occurrence of the name on the ceiling that is not written with the falcon-hieroglyph (but the most typical form of the name, in column 2) leaves the matter open to debate.

[86] The inscriptions contain passages from the Pyramid Texts. For more information on these texts, see Chapter 1.3.6.

tion of the funerary rites and the well-chosen design of the burial complex, with the right choice of texts, would have allowed the Osiris Padihor to ascend the heavens and live on in the netherworld.

Table II.
The various writings of the name Padihor and their location on the walls of the tomb.

Writing	Location
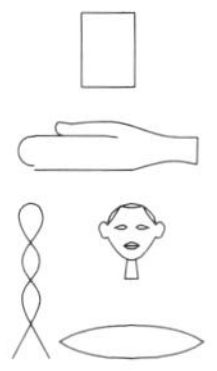	27 occurrences - west wall, columns 7, 8 (twice), 9, 11 (twice) and 12 - north wall, columns 1, 2, 3, 5, 6, 7, 9, 19, 20, 21, 21/22,[87] 22, 23 (twice), 24, 24/25, 27, 28 (twice)[88] - ceiling, column 2
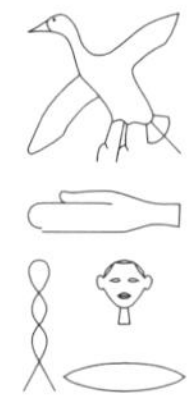	7 occurrences - west wall, column 2 and 4 - north wall, columns 11, 13/14 and 15 - east wall, column 12 - south wall, column 2
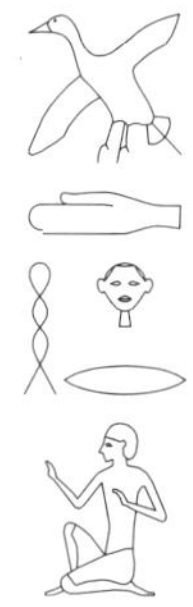	1 occurrence - south wall, column 29
	3 occurrences - ceiling, column 3 (thrice)
	1 occurrence - ceiling, column 1
	1 occurrence - ceiling, column 2

On some of the remaining fragments of the shabtis, discovered during the excavation of the burial complex, (part of) the name of the tomb owner is also still visible

[87] The use of 'xx/xx' indicates that the writing of the name begins at the bottom of one column and continues at the top of the next column.
[88] The second time the final elements of the name have not been written, most likely due to lack of space in the final column of this inscription. See Figure 10.

(Figs. 14-15 and Pls. 8-9).[89] The most common writing makes use of the forearm (D37) and the falcon (G5), but other variants occur (for instance the use of the face for writing *ḥr* – D2).

The name Padihor appears to have been known in another context in the Saite-Persian cemetery at Abusir prior to the excavation of the man's burial complex. A similar name features on a blue-green faience scarab that was discovered near the opening of the small access shaft to the east of the enclosure wall of the burial complex of Udjahorresnet.[90] On the bottom of the 11 mm long scarab the name *Pꜣ-di-Ḥr-p* or 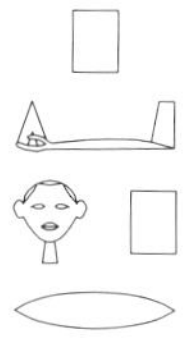 is written in incised relief. The name can be read as Padihor(-en)-Pe (*Pꜣ-di-ḥr(-n)-py* or 'the one who Horus of Pe has given').[91] The scarab was however discovered in the immediate vicinity of Padihor's burial complex and hence most likely belongs to his burial equipment. The small object might have been lost by the tomb robbers when they were leaving the burial complex.[92]

The name Padihor very frequently occurs throughout the Late Period and the Ptolemaic era.[93] Among the Twenty-Sixth and early Twenty-Seventh Dynasty 'contemporaries' of the Padihor who had his burial complex built in Abusir, belong for instance the following individuals:[94]

a. Padihor, the father of Hor-khebit, who is buried in a shaft tomb in Saqqara.[95]

b. Padihor, a general in the army of Psamtek I, whose statue is currently in the *National Archaeological Museum* of Athens.[96]

c. Padihor, head of draughtsmen, married to Thesmutperet and father of Wahibra-Nebpehty. The latter was the owner of TT191 in the Assasif and a contemporary of Psamtek I.[97]

d. Padihor, chamberlain of the divine adoratrice, son of Wahibra-Nebpehty and grandson of the aforementioned Padihor.[98]

e. Padihor, the mayor of Abydos, features on a partly preserved lintel from the small temple of Abydos, dated to the reign of Psamtek I.[99]

---

[89] For more information and a detailed description of the shabtis discovered during the excavation of Padihor's burial complex, consult Chapter 1.4.

[90] Bareš, *Abusir IV*, pp. 68 (excav. no. 97/H/89), 71 (fig. 2 – for the location of the small shaft) and plate 14, fig. 50.

[91] On this name consult H. Ranke, *Die ägyptischen Personennamen I. Verzeichnis der Namen*, Glückstad 1935, p. 125, no. 8, and E. Lüddeckens – W. Brusch – G. Vittmann – K.-Th. Zauzich, *Demotisches Namenbuch. Band I, Lieferung 5. p3-ty-wp-w3.wt – pa-nfr*, Wiesbaden 1985, p. 331.

[92] Fragments of several shabtis of Padihor were also recovered on the bedrock in the immediate vicinity of the main shaft and might have also been left behind by the tomb robbers – excavation nos. 99/R/01 and 131/R/01a (bottom fragment).

[93] See for instance Ranke, *Die ägyptischen Personennamen I*, p. 124, nos. 18 and 19, and Lüddeckens – Brusch – Vittmann – Zauzich, *Demotisches Namenbuch. Band I, Lieferung 5*, pp. 322-323.

[94] The following list is by no means exhaustive and only aims to illustrate the very common usage of the name throughout the Twenty-Sixth Dynasty and early Twenty-Seventh Dynasty. In the study of J.F. Aubert – L. Aubert, *Bronzes et Or Egyptiens*, Paris 2001 (see index), a number of bronze statuettes, mostly dated to the Twenty-Sixth Dynasty, are mentioned on which the name of Padihor is also inscribed.

[95] PM III², 588 (with no reference to its source). On the tomb of Hor-khebit, see already Chapter 1.1 and note 69.

[96] V.I. Chrysikopoulos, 'The Statue of Padihor, General of the Army of Psammetichus I, at the National Archaeological Museum of Athens', in P. Kousoulis – K. Magliveras (eds.), *Moving Across Borders. Foreign Relations, Religion and Cultural Interactions in the Ancient Mediterranean*, (OLA 159), Leuven 2007, pp. 157-168 (Athens no. 3).

[97] PM I, p. 297. A limestone block statue of presumably the same Padihor, father of Wahibra-Nebpehty, was on sale at a Sotheby's auction (Sotheby's, New York, The Breitbart Collection of Ancient Glass, Egyptian, Western Asiatic and Classical Antiquities, June 20th, 1990, no. 15). The statue was dated late in the reign of Psamtek I.

[98] PM I, p. 297.

[99] PM V, 70.

f. Padihor, son of Irethorreru and Nyny[...] and the owner of a painted limestone stela from Abydos dated to the early Twenty-Sixth Dynasty and currently in the *British Museum*, London.[100]

g. Padihor, father of a no longer identifiable daughter, who was the owner of an early Twenty-Sixth Dynasty round-topped wooden stela from Thebes, currently in the *Egyptian Museum*, Cairo.[101]

h. Padihor, father of Djedjehutefankh. The son is the owner of a round-topped stone donation stela dated to the 11th year of Nekau II. The stela is part of the collection of the *Oriental Institute Museum*, Chicago, IL (#13943).[102]

i. Padihor, husband of Djed-Hor and father of Irethorreru. The latter is the owner of a mid Twenty-Sixth Dynasty round-topped wooden stela from Thebes currently in the *Museo Civico Archeologico* in Bologna.[103]

j. Padihor, husband of Theshapperet and father of Padineith, whose Twenty-Sixth Dynasty stela is part of the Egyptian collection of the *Koninklijke Musea voor Kunst en Geschiedenis*, Brussel.[104]

k. Padihor, the father of Neith-Igeret, is mentioned on the round-topped Twenty-Sixth Dynasty limestone stela of Pasenenkhonsu from Akhmim, currently in the *Egyptian Museum*, Cairo.[105]

l. Padihor, father of Meshwahoreru. The daughter is the owner of a late Twenty-Sixth Dynasty round-topped wooden stela from Thebes, currently in the *National Archaeological Museum* in Athens (no. 189).[106]

m. Padihor, son of Tutu, is mentioned on the remains of a naophorous statue that is partly in the *Acerbi* collection (Mantua), the *British Museum* (BM 178), London, and the *Brooklyn Museum*, New York.[107] According to the inscription on the base of the statue, this Padihor was a priest of Osiris and Neith in Sais. The statue is dated to the end of the Twenty-Sixth or the beginning of the Twenty-Seventh Dynasty.

n. Padihor, father of Tutu, whose statuette was discovered in Sais (*Egyptian Museum* Cairo, JE 31912 = CG 712).[108] According to S. Pernigotti, the Padihor mentioned on the statuette might be the same as the owner of the naophorous statue mentioned above.[109]

o. Padihor, son of Padihorpakhered, is mentioned on a stela attested with the burial of Apis XLIII in the Serapeum. The Padihor in question was most likely a contemporary of Darius I.[110]

p. Padihor, father of Pedesek (or Peresek), who was the owner of a limestone stela dated to the early Twenty-Seventh Dynasty. The stela originated in Memphis and is currently in the *Louvre*, Paris.[111]

---

[100] P. Munro, *Die spätägyptischen Totenstelen*, (AF 25), Glückstad 1973, p. 288 (BM 640).

[101] Munro, *Totenstelen*, p. 112 (Cairo A 9445).

[102] A. Leahy, 'Two Donation Stelae of Necho II', *RdE* 34 (1982-1983), pp. 84-90, E. Teeter, *Ancient Egypt. Treasures from the Collection of the Oriental Institute, University of Chicago*, (OIMP 23), Chicago 2003, pp. 86-87 [44], 129 [44], and 136 [44], and D. Meeks, 'Les donations aux temples dans l'Égypte du Ier millénaire avant J.-C.', in E. Lipinski (ed.), *State and Temple Economy in the Ancient Near East* II, (OLA 6), Leuven 1979, p. 676 [26.2.11].

[103] E. Bresciani, *Le stele egiziane del Museo Civico Archeologico di Bologna*, Bologna 1985, pp. 96-97, and Munro, *Totenstelen*, pp. 226-227.

[104] PM III^2, 735, and H. De Meulenaere, 'Trois stèles inédites des Musées Royaux d'Art et d'Histoire', *CdE* 48 (1973), pp. 47-51.

[105] The stela was discovered in Akhmim in 1994 and ended up in a private collection in New York before being returned to Egypt in 2004. See New York Times, February 23, 2004 (archive at www.nytimes.com).

[106] B. Pörtner, *Aegyptische Grabsteine und Denksteine aus Athen und Konstantinopel*, Strasbourg 1908, p. 11 [30], and Munro, *Totenstelen*, p. 226. The stela probably originated in Thebes.

[107] L. Donatelli, *La raccolta egizia di Giuseppe Acerbi*, Mantova 1983, pp. 44-45 (no. 12); Pernigotti, *EVO* 8 (1985), pp. 10-14, and H. De Meulenaere, 'E Pluribus Una', *BIFAO* 87 (1987), pp. 135-140.

[108] PM IV, 47; L. Borchardt, *Statuen und Statuetten von Königen und Privatleuten* III *Catalogue Général des Antiquités Égyptiennes du Musée du Caire, Nos 654-950*, Berlin 1930, p. 50, and R. el-Sayed, *Documents relatifs à Sais et ses divinités*, (BdE 69), Cairo 1975, pp. 284-285 (no. 105).

[109] Pernigotti, *EVO* 8 (1985), pp. 13-14.

[110] PM III^2, 803 (IM.4004).

[111] Munro, *Totenstelen*, p. 335 (Louvre C 294).

None of the presently known bearers of the name Padihor from the Twenty-Sixth or early Twenty-Seventh Dynasty can be identified with the owner of the shaft tomb in the Saite-Persian cemetery at Abusir with any degree of certainty. Numerous other bearers of the name Padihor are frequently encountered throughout the Late Period and in all parts of Egypt.[112]

The burial complex of Padihor reveals hardly any information on his parentage. Only the name of Padihor's mother is known: *Nḏm-B3st.t-n-irt* or Nedjem-bastet-en-iret. The name occurs twice in the inscriptions on the walls of the burial chamber: once on the south wall of the tomb (column 2) and once on its ceiling (column 1) (Figs 11 and 13). Both texts mention that Padihor was 'born of Nedjem-bastet-en-iret (*ms n Ndm-b3st.t-n-ir.t*). To our knowledge, the name of the mother has not been attested anywhere else yet.[113]

Writings of the name Nedjem-bastet-en-iret.

The name of Padihor's father is not mentioned a single time on the walls of the tomb or on any other object associated with his burial complex. In the nearby tomb of Iufaa the father's name was not attested either, in contrast with the burial chambers of

[112] These include, among the individuals listed in Ranke, *Die ägyptischen Personennamen I*, p. 124, nos. 18 and 19, and Lüddeckens – Brusch – Vittmann – Zauzich, *Demotisches Namenbuch. Band I, Lieferung 5*, pp. 322-323 and many others, the following:
a. Padihor, son of Irwahen, is mentioned in an inscription on a statue of Harpocrates, dated to the Late Period or early Ptolemaic times (*Egyptian Museum*, Cairo, CG 38174).
b. Padihor, owner of a Late Period coffin from Akhmim (*Egyptian Museum*, Cairo, JE 26032).
c. Padihor, owner of a Late Period stela from Abydos, currently in the *Egyptian Museum*, Cairo.
d. Padihor, prophet of Montu and owner of a Late Period wooden shrine from TT511, currently in the *Metropolitan Museum of Art*, New York (M.M.A. 26.3.234).
e. Padihor, the father of Paditjesirnetjer, who dedicated a statue of Neith, dated to the Late Period/Ptolemaic era (*Cairo Museum* CG 38951 (= JE 28821 and 29167)).
f. Padihor, god's father of Thoth and son of Nebetudjat, whose naophorous statue is dated to the Thirtieth Dynasty or early Ptolemaic Period (*Egyptian Museum*, Cairo, CG 722).
g. Padihor, father of Bek(en)renes, whose coffin was found in the tomb of Imen-kha in Gurna (BM 15654). The tomb is dated to the Twenty-Fourth Dynasty.
h. Padihor, father of [...]esi, whose coffin was likewise found in the tomb of Imen-kha. The coffin is currently in the Museum Castle at Norwich.
i. Padihor, official of the estate of Amun and married to Tabes. Their Third Intermediate/Late Period coffins were found in WV 22 (the tomb of Amenhotep III).
j. Padihor, father of Ira'hor, whose canopic jars are dated to the Late Period. (*Museo Gregoriano*, Vatican, no. 141-4).
k. Padihor(?), son of Pefneferu, has an inscription on the Apis-stela of Pedesi, dated to the Late Period (*Louvre*, IM. 2784).
l. Padihor, owner of a Late Period offering table from the Sacred Animal Necropolis, North Saqqara (*Egyptian Museum*, Cairo, JE 91143 [272]).
m. Padihor is mentioned with other quarrymen in a Late Period inscription in the Wadi Hammamat (PM VII, 336).
n. Padihor, son of Ta(ese) and owner of a Thirtieth Dynasty shabti in the *Fitzwilliam Museum*, Cambridge, USA (accession no. E.3.1979 and reference number 63461).
o. Padihor, son of Dinefbastet and owner of a Late Period statue in the *Walters Art Museum*, Baltimore, USA (no. 54.544).

[113] The name is for instance not attested in Ranke, *Personennamen* or Lüddeckens, *Demotisches Namenbuch*.

Udjahorresnet (Peftjauemauineith)[114] and Menekhibnekau (Gemenefhorbak)[115] where it is mentioned several times. A similar situation occurs in other Twenty-Sixth Dynasty shaft tombs: the name of the father is for instance not given in the tombs of Amuntefnakht and Tjannehebu in Saqqara. The reason behind the absence of the name of the father in these tombs cannot be adequately explained at present.[116]

1.2.2. The title *rḫ nswt*; 'king's acquaintance'.

Only a single title of Padihor is mentioned in the inscriptions in his burial chamber: *rḫ nsw.t* or 'king's acquaintance'.[117] The title occurs twice in the columns on the ceiling of the tomb (columns 1 and 2 and Fig. 13), written as  and  respectively.

The title *rḫ nswt* or 'king's acquaintance' is prolifically attested throughout the Old Kingdom,[118] but occurs also in other periods of ancient Egyptian history well into Ptolemaic and Roman times.[119] In the Old Kingdom the title was most likely honorific in nature, while during the Middle Kingdom it seems to be associated mainly with the domain of the treasury.[120] The title is only sporadically attested during the New Kingdom,[121] but very common from the Twenty-Fifth Dynasty onwards. Throughout the Late Period the title is, once again, for the most part honorific in meaning, although it could also have a religious connotation. The title occurs occasionally amidst a series of priestly titles, especially titles of priests active in the cult of Sokar or Osiris.[122]

---

[114] Bareš, *Abusir IV*, pp. 52 and 60-61.

[115] Bareš – Janák – Landgráfová – Smoláriková, *ZÄS* 135 (2008), pp. 108-109 (also on the plausible relation between this Gemenefhorbak and the individual with the same name buried in the nearby tomb of Iufaa). Bareš – Smoláriková, *Abusir XVII*, p. 94 (n. 37) remark that in Abusir the names of the fathers are not preserved for tomb owners with a minimum of official titles (Padihor and Iufaa each had only a single title mentioned in their burial complex). Given the limited number of burial complexes excavated, it is at present impossible to say whether this is a mere coincidence.

[116] Various explanations and theories are listed and cited in Bareš – Smoláriková, *Abusir XVII*, p. 94, but none of these suggestions are convincing or applicable to all Late Period shaft tombs in which the name of the father has been omitted from the walls of the tomb and the burial equipment.

[117] Wb. II, p. 446-447, and R. Hannig, *Die Sprache der Pharaonen. Grosses Handwörterbuch Ägyptisch-Deutsch (2800–950 v. Chr.)*, (Kulturgeschichte der Antiken Welt), Mainz 1995, p. 475. It is not my intention to reopen the discussion on the reading of the title (*rḫ-nswt*, *iry-iḫ.t-nswt* or *iry-ḫ-nswt*). A very good historical overview of the various readings and interpretations of the title and arguments for the reading *rḫ-nswt* (or *rḫ(.t)-n(.t)-nswt*) can be found in M. Baud, *Famille royale et pouvoir sous l'Ancien Empire égyptien* I, (BdE 126/1), Cairo 1999, pp. 107-118. Important studies and notes on various aspects of the title include H. De Meulenaere, 'Un titre memphite méconnu', in *Mélanges Mariette*, (BdE 32), Cairo 1961, pp. 285-286; H. Brunner, 'Der Bekannte des Königs', *SAK* 1 (1974), pp. 55-60, and M. Bárta, 'The Title "Property Custodian of the King" during the Old Kingdom Egypt', *ZÄS* 126 (1999), pp. 79-90. In general on the titles and status of the owners of Late Period shaft tombs, see Bareš, in Bárta – Coppens – Krejčí (eds.), *Abusir and Saqqara in the Year 2005*, and Stammers, *Elite Late Period Egyptian Tombs*, pp. 69-82 and 181-188.

[118] On the occurrence of the title in the Old Kingdom and beyond, see D. Jones, *An Index of Ancient Egyptian Titles, Epithets and Phrases of the Old Kingdom* I, (BAR International Series 866), Oxford 2006, pp. 327-328.

[119] G. Gorre, '*Rḫ-nswt*: titre aulique ou titre sacerdotal "spécifique"?', *ZÄS* 136 (2009), pp. 8-18. The article was brought to my attention by Ladislav Bareš.

[120] H.G. Fischer, *Egyptian Titles of the Middle Kingdom: A Supplement to Wm. Ward's Index*, New York 1985, pp. 36 and 93 referring to W.A. Ward, *Index of Egyptian Administrative and Religious Titles of the Middle Kingdom, with a glossary of words and phrases used*, Beirut 1982 (no mention of the title); S. Quirke, *Titles and Bureaux of Egypt 1850–1700 BC*, London 2004, p. 60, and Stammers, *Elite Late Period Egyptian Tombs*, pp. 78 and 184.

[121] A. al-Ayedi, *Index of Egyptian Administrative, Religious and Military Titles of the New Kingdom*, Ismailiya 2006, p. 308. See also W. Helck, *Zur Verwaltung des Mittleren und Neuen Reiches*, Leiden 1958, pp. 279-280, and H. Kees, 'Zur Familie des 3. Amonspropheten Amenophis', *ZÄS* 84 (1959), pp. 58-59.

[122] H. De Meulenaere, 'Le clergé abydénien d'Osiris à la Basse Epoque', in P. Naster – H. De Meulenaere – J. Quaegebeur (eds.), *Miscellanea in Honorem Joseph Vergote*, (OLP 6/7), Leuven 1975–1976, p. 138; I. Guermeur, 'Glanures (3-4)', *BIFAO* 106 (2006), pp. 116-117; Gorre, *ZÄS* 136, pp. 15-18, and L. Coulon, 'Les uraei gardiens du fétiche abydénien. Un motif osirien et sa diffusion à l'époque saïte', in D. Devauchelle (ed.), *La XXVIe dynastie. Continuité ou rupture. Actes du colloque de l'Université de Lille-III. 26-27 novembre 2004*, in press.

The title commonly occurs in the Twenty-Fifth and Twenty-Sixth Dynasties, but it is not attested for any of the other owners of the burial complexes in the Saite-Persian cemetery at Abusir. Among Padihor's contemporaries in the greater Memphite area, at least another six individuals are known to have carried the title *rḫ nsw.t* or 'king's acquaintance':[123] Nesdjehuty,[124] Shepensenut,[125] Ptahirdis,[126] Rames,[127] Hor-Neferibra-sa-Neith[128] and Harbes.[129] With the exception of Ptahirdis, several other titles have been attested for these individuals next to 'king's acquaintance'.[130] Ptahirdis, like Padihor, only had the single honorific title *rḫ nswt.*

Udjahorresnet, who was buried near Padihor in Abusir, owned a very similar but more extended version of the title: *rḫ nswt mꜣꜥ mry=f* or 'true king's acquaintance, who loves him'.[131] The title does not appear among the inscriptions in the burial complex, but features twice in Udjahorresnet's biographical text on his naophorous statue, currently kept in the *Museo Gregoriano* in Vatican City.[132] This title was also held by numerous individuals throughout the Twenty-Fifth and Twenty-Sixth Dynasties,[133] such as Djedptahiufankh and Padihor, both generals in the army of Psamtek I,[134] and by other 'contemporaries' like Tefnakht, Nesnasiut, Petamenope and Panehsi, to name but a few.[135] The title, like the shorter version *rḫ nswt* attested for Padihor, is generally considered to be honorific in the Late Period.[136]

The almost complete absence of biographical information in the inscriptions from the burial chamber of Padihor, with the exception of the mother's name and a single honorific title, means that little more definite can be said about the owner of this burial complex beyond the information obtained by the anthropological and palaeopathological analysis of the remains of his body.

---

123 Stammers, *Elite Late Period Egyptian Tombs*, pp. 78-79 and 184.

124 Nesdjehuty's tomb is located in the vicinity of the monastery of Apa Jeremias in Saqqara: PM III², 669-670, and J.E. Quibell, *Excavations at Saqqara, 1908-09, 1909-10. The Monastery of Apa Jeremias*, Cairo 1912, pp. 30-33.

125 Shepensenut's intrusive burial was discovered in mastaba G7130B among a cluster of tombs in and around the temple of Isis at Giza: Zivie-Coche, *Giza au premier millénaire*, pp. 271-272.

126 Ptahirdis was buried in a rock cut tomb in the vicinity of the sphinx at Giza: PM III¹, p. 291, and Zivie-Coche, *Giza au premier millénaire*, p. 288.

127 Rames' tomb was discovered in Matareya: H. Gauthier, 'A travers la Basse Egypte. VII: Tombeau d'un certain Rames à Materia', *ASAE* 21 (1921), pp. 197-203.

128 Hor-Neferibra-sa-Neith was buried in a vaulted chamber tomb in Heliopolis: S. Bickel – P. Tallet, 'La nécropole Saïte d'Héliopolis. Etude preliminaire', *BIFAO* 97 (1997), pp. 82-83.

129 Only a block of the tomb of Harbes has been discovered in Heliopolis: Bickel – Tallet, *BIFAO* 97 (1997), pp. 68-76, and Stammers, *Elite Late Period Egyptian Tombs*, pp. 141-142 and 155.

130 The attestations include priestly (e.g. *it-nṯr* and *ḥry-ḥb* with Rames), administrative (e.g. *wdpw Ꞽwnw* with Rames or *sš-nswt* with Hor-Neferibra-sa-Neith), military (e.g. *mḥ ib ḫnt mnfyt* with Hor-Neferibra-sa-Neith or *imy-r-sšw mšꜥ nw šmꜥw mḥw* with Nesdjehuty) and honorific (e.g. *rpꜥ* and *ḥꜣty-ꜥ* with Hor-Neferibra-sa-Neith and Shepensenut) titles.

131 Bareš, *Abusir IV*, pp. 32-33, and Bareš, in M. Bárta – F. Coppens – J. Krejčí (eds.), *Abusir and Saqqara in the Year 2005*, p. 8. For more information on the title, consult Zivie-Coche, *Giza au premier millénaire*, p. 112 (with several references to literature dealing with the topic), and H. De Meulenaere – I. De Strooper, 'Notes de prosopographie thébaine. Cinquième série', *CdE* 73 (1998), p. 253 (n. 24). For the occurrence of the title in the Old Kingdom, also consult the overview in Jones, *Index*, p. 330.

132 G. Botti – P. Romanelli, *Le sculture del Museo Gregoriano Egizio*, Vatican 1951, pp. 32-40 and plates xxvii-xxxi; G. Posener, *La première domination Perse en Égypte. Recueil d'inscriptions hiéroglyphiques*, Cairo 1936, pp. 1-26, and Bareš, *Abusir IV*, pp. 31-38. The title occurs twice: in the eighth column, on the right side of the chest, and in the sixteenth column on the left side of the statue's chest.

133 See for instance the overview in H. De Meulenaere, 'La statue du général Djed–ptah–iouf–ankh (Caire JE 36949)', *BIFAO* 63 (1965), p. 20 (n. a) with additions by el-Sayed, *Documents relatifs à Sais*, pp. 81-82.

134 Chrysikopoulos, in P. Kousoulis – K. Magliveras (eds.), *Moving Across Borders*, p. 161.

135 H. Ranke, 'Statue eines hohen Beamten under Psammetich I', *ZÄS* 44 (1907), pp. 43-44; G. Daressy, 'Samtaui-Tafnekht', *ASAE* 18 (1918), p. 30; G. Loukianoff, 'Les statues et les objets funéraires de Pedamenopet', *ASAE* 37 (1937), p. 221; A. el-Sawi – F. Gomaa, *Das Grab des Panehsi, Gottesvaters von Heliopolis in Matariya*, (ÄAT 23), Wiesbaden 1993, esp. p. 125 (for the title), and Bickel – Tallet, *BIFAO* 97 (1997), p. 80. Stammers, *Elite Late Period Egyptian Tombs*, pp. 78 and 154-155 records only the title *rḫ-nswt* for Panehsi.

136 Stammers, *Elite Late Period Egyptian Tombs*, p. 78.

1.2.3 The remains of Padihor.

The detailed anthropological and palaeopathological study of the remains of Padihor by Eugen Strouhal and Alena Němečková has already been published in relation to the five individuals discovered in the nearby tomb of Iufaa in the volume *Abusir XVII*.[137] There is little point in reprinting the entire chapter in this volume; hence only a summary of the main results of the analysis will be presented.

The remains of the scattered burial of Padihor[138] were discovered on three separate locations in the burial complex: a) in the clearance of the west half of the sand filling of the subsidiary shaft (fragments of the skull and postcranial bones), b) in the small area between the burial chamber and the wall of the main shaft (more fragments of the skull and vertebrae) and c) in the heap of sand that sloped down from the entrance into the burial chamber (other postcranial bones). In all three locations the human remains were accompanied by numerous fragments of completely rotten wood with small remains of black paint (most likely the remains of a wooden coffin) and fragments of blackened resin.

The fragments that survived of Padihor's skeleton include from the calvarium half of the squama frontalis, postero-medial quarter of the right parietale, antero-lateral quarter of the left parietale, anterior edge of the right temporale connected with part of the sphenoid and the squama occipitalis, together with the anterior third of the mandibular body from R M_1 to L P_1. Of the postcranial skeleton remained vertebrae C_2, C_7-T_6, L_{1-2}, ribs, sacrum S_{1-3}, scapulae, L clavicle, and all arm bones, hip bones and leg bones (some entirely, others with defects).

The study of the human remains by E. Strouhal and A. Němečková indicated that Padihor was 28 to 32 years old at the time of his death. His living stature was reconstructed to the height of 173.1 cm. His remains indicated a moderately progressed degenerative osteoarthritis in his right shoulder joint and both hip joints, possibly caused by strenuous walking over long distances. A strong slanting attrition on the anterior side of his lower frontal teeth might have been caused by a habitual activity (pathological mastication during sleep) or by their use for a particular type of work. The skull did not show any evidence of brain removal, while the absence of stains by resin on the preserved bones suggests that no resinous filling was applied. The analysis also indicated that Padihor was no relation of any of the persons buried in the nearby tomb of Iufaa.

1.3. The inscriptions

1.3.1. Introduction

The entire burial chamber of Padihor received a textual programme: inscriptions, in text columns, feature on the west face of the lintel above the entrance, the north and south lateral walls, the west rear wall and the central part of the ceiling (Figs. 9-13, Pls. 4-6). The inscriptions were executed in incised relief with a few exceptions. The individual text columns are usually not separated from one another by an engraved or painted line; instead, the entire text is often demarcated above and below with a red

[137] E. Strouhal – A. Němečková, 'Iufaa and the others. Anthropological and palaeopathological analysis', in Bareš – Smoláriková, *Abusir XVII*, pp. 253-281. Preliminary reports were published as E. Strouhal, 'The Relation of Iufaa to Persons found beside his Shaft-tomb at Abusir', in F. Coppens (ed.), *Abusir and Saqqara in the Year 2001. Proceedings of the Symposium (Prague, September 25th – 27th 2001), Archiv Orientální* 70.3 (2002), pp. 403-414; E. Strouhal, 'Relation of Iufaa to Persons found beside his Shaft-tomb at Abusir', *Anthropologie* 40/1 (2002), pp. 37-50; E. Strouhal – A. Němečková – M. Kouba, 'Palaeopathology of Iufaa and Other Persons found beside his Shaft Tomb at Abusir (Egypt)', *International Journal of Osteoarchaeology* 13 (2003), pp. 332-334, and 338, and E. Strouhal – A. Němečková, 'Paleopathological Find of a Sacral Neurilemmoma from Ancient Egypt', *AJPA* 125 (2004), pp. 320-322.

[138] Excavation no. 132/R/01.

line. The texts are, similar to all other large shaft tombs of this era, for the most part copies of various (excerpts of) utterances from the Pyramid Texts (PT) (on the north and west walls and on the ceiling) and of a number of spells from the Coffin Texts (CT) (on the south wall). The use of both Pyramid Texts[139] and Coffin Texts[140] and still other religious texts,[141] such as the Book of the Dead (BD),[142] in the burial chambers of the large Late Period shaft tombs has already been discussed extensively.[143] On top of a transcription, translation and analysis of the texts from Padihor's burial chamber,

[139] In general: W. Schenkel, 'Zur Frage der Vorlagen spätzeitlicher "Kopien"', in J. Assmann – E. Feucht – R. Grieshammer (eds.), *Fragen an die altägyptische Literatur. Studien zum Gedenken an Eberhard Otto*, Wiesbaden 1977, pp. 440-441, and Stammers, *Elite Late Period Tombs*, pp. 63-68. For the use of the Pyramid Texts in the Saite (and early Persian) tombs, consult T.G. Allen, *Occurrences of Pyramid Texts with Cross Indexes of Those and Other Egyptian Mortuary Texts*, (SAOC 27), Chicago 1950, pp. 12-47; G. Soukiassian, 'Textes de pyramides et formules apparantés. Remarques à propos des tombes saïtes', *L'Egyptologie en 1979: Axes prioritaires des recherches II*, (Colloques internationaux du CNRS 595), Paris 1982, pp. 55-61; M. Patanè, *Les variantes des textes de pyramides à la Basse Epoque*, Genève 1992; R. Buongarzone, 'Testi religiosi di epoca saitica e Testi delle piramidi', *EVO* 16 (1993), pp. 23-30; N. Guilhou – B. Mathieu, 'Cent dix ans d'étude des Textes des Pyramides (1882–1996)', in C. Berger – B. Mathieu (eds.), *Etudes sur l'Ancien Empire et la nécropole de Saqqâra dédiées à Jean-Philippe Lauer*, (Orientalia Monspeliensia 9), Montpellier 1997, pp. 233-244; Gestermann, *Sargtexte in spätzeitlichen Grabanlagen*, pp. 368-378, and R.B. Hussein, *The Saite Pyramid Text Copies in the Memphite and Heliopolitan Shaft-Tombs: A Study of their Selection and Layout*, Brown University 2009 (unpublished PhD thesis). I am very grateful to Dr. Hussein for providing me with a copy of his PhD thesis. His detailed study points out, especially in the lists on pp. 187-192 (regarding the tombs of Amuntefnakht, Psamtek, and Padinese), the numerous mistakes and inaccuracies found in the previous, mostly early 20th century, publications of the PT texts from the Saite tombs at Saqqara, and highlights the need to proceed very carefully when making textual comparisons on the basis of the presently published material. It also identifies a need for a new publication and study of most inscriptions from the Late Period shaft tombs from Saqqara, which Dr. Hussein hopes to undertake in the future (*personal communication, Prague, September 3, 2009*).

[140] The basic work on the occurrence of Coffin Texts in Late Period tombs is Gestermann, *Sargtexte in spätzeitlichen Grabanlagen*. See also R. Buongarzone, 'Su alcuni testi della tomba di Bakenrinef. A proposito di una redazione saitica', *EVO* 14-15 (1991–1992), pp. 31-42; L. Gestermann, 'Zu den spätzeitlichen Bezeugungen der Sargtexte', *SAK* 19 (1992), pp. 117-132, and L. Gestermann, "Neue" Texte in spätzeitlichen Grabanlage von Saqqara und Heliopolis', in M. Minas – J. Zeidler (eds.), *Aspekte spätägyptische Kultur. Festschrift für Erich Winter zum 65. Geburtstag*, (Aegyptiaca Treverensia 7), Mainz 1994, pp. 89-95.

[141] For instance the representation of standing women as the personifications of the twelve hours of the day and of the night on the lateral walls of the tomb of Menekhibnekau – see Bareš – Janák – Landgráfová – Smoláriková, *ZÄS* 135 (2008), p. 106, and L. Bareš, 'Personifications of the Day- and Night-Hours in the Tomb of Menekhibnekau at Abusir – A Preliminary Notice', in P. Maříková Vlčková – J. Mynářová – M. Tomášek (eds.), *My Things Changed Things. Social Development and Cultural Exchange in Prehistory, Antiquity, and Middle Ages*, Prague 2009, pp. 16-24. In general on this type of representation, fairly common at that time (although not in the decoration of the monumental shaft tombs), see E. Graefe, 'Das Stundenritual in thebanischen Gräbern der Spätzeit (Über den Stand der Arbeit an der Edition)', in J. Assmann – E. Dziobek – H. Guksch – F. Kampp (eds.), *Thebanische Beamtennekropolen. Neue Perspektiven der archäologischen Forschung. Internationales Symposium Heidelberg 9.-13.6.1993*, (SAGA 12), Heidelberg 1995, pp. 85-93, and R. Buongarzone, 'La funzionalita dei testi nel contesto architettonico della tomba di Bakenrenef', *EVO* 13 (1990), pp. 88-90.

[142] For instance chapters 144 and 148 on the south and north walls of the tomb of Menekhibnekau respectively – see Bareš – Janák – Landgráfová – Smoláriková, *ZÄS* 135 (2008), pp. 106-107, or numerous chapters on the walls of the as yet unpublished external and internal sarcophagus of Iufaa (BD chapters 1B, 5, 26, 27, 28, 29, 30, 51, 57, 64, 69, 70, 72, 89, 100, 148, 157 and 158) – Bareš, in Györy (ed.), *Aegyptus et Pannonia III*, pp. 2-5.

[143] Next to the publications already mentioned in the previous footnotes, see also P. Lacau, 'Textes religieux écrits sur les sarcophages', in J.E. Quibell, *Excavations at Saqqara (1906-1907)*, Cairo 1908, pp. 21-61; Drioton, *ASAE* 52 (1954), and Bresciani – Pernigotti – Giangeri-Silvis, *Ciennehebu*, pp. 28-29. See also the important general overviews in Gestermann, *Sargtexte in spätzeitlichen Grabanlagen*, pp. 368-387, and Stammers, *Elite Late Period Egyptian Tombs*, pp. 171-180.

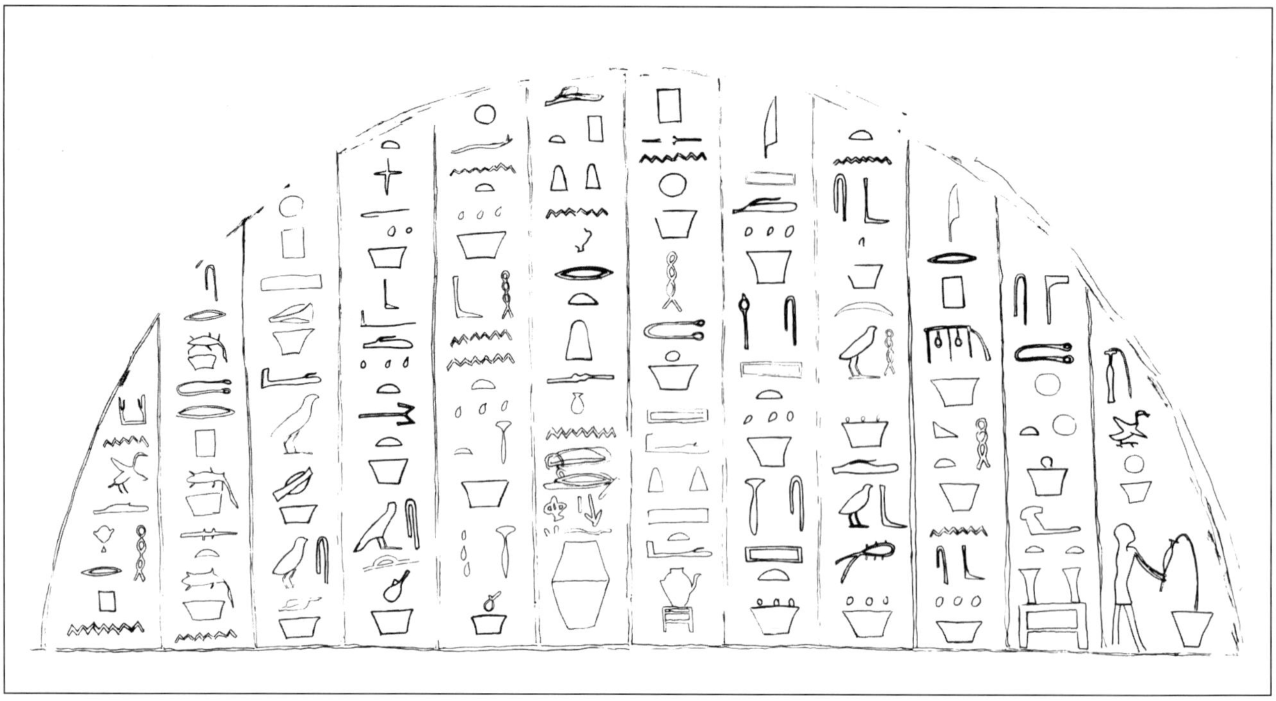

Fig. 9
The lintel above the entrance into the burial chamber

the present chapter also provides a comparison with similar texts in other tombs within the greater Memphite area.[144]

1.3.2 The lintel above the entrance: offering list (Fig. 9 and Pl. 6a)

The inscription on the west face of the lintel above the entrance to the tomb of Padihor is an offering list.[145] The list, read from south to north, is not depicted in its usual tabular form, but consists of 12 text columns of varying height. The individual columns are separated by engraved lines. A red line demarcates the entire inscription and is on average located 2.0-2.5 cm from the edge of the lintel. The block was not smoothed before the inscription was engraved upon it and a lot of chiselling marks are still clearly visible on its surface.

The offering list in tabular form is an integral part of the wall decoration of the burial chambers of most Late Period monumental shaft tombs and can be traced

[144] The inscriptions of the following tombs have been consulted and will be referred to in this chapter: the Twenty-Sixth Dynasty shaft tombs of Amuntefnakht, Padineith, Padinese, Hekamesaf, Psamtek ('the physician'), Psamtek ('the treasurer'), Hor, Udjahor, Neferibre-sa-Neith and Tjannehebu in Saqqara, the Twenty-Sixth dynasty shaft tomb of Pakap in Giza, and the late Twenty-Sixth – early Twenty-Seventh Dynasty shaft tombs of Udjahorresnet and Iufaa, and the wooden coffin of Nekau, buried in a small chamber in the west wall of the west subsidiary shaft of Iufaa's burial complex in Abusir. Next to the inscriptions from the shaft tombs, inscriptions from contemporary burial complexes of other types have also been consulted, such as the tomb of Bakenrenef in Saqqara, the tomb of Tjery in Giza, and the tombs of Wahibra-Tjeset, Udjahormehnet and Panehsi in Heliopolis. A distinction needs to be made between inscriptions from the tomb of Psamtek, buried to the south of the pyramid temple of Unas (= Psamtek 'the physician' – see already footnote 59) and those from the burial place of his namesake Psamtek, buried in a joint tomb with yet another individual named Psamtek and the princess Khetbeneithyerboni near the monastery of Apa Jeremias in Saqqara (= Psamtek the 'treasurer' – see already footnote 64). For a similar distinction between both individuals, consult Hussein, *Saite Pyramid Text Copies*, p. 24. References to the various publications of the inscriptions from these tombs will be given in individual footnotes in relation to the occurrence of specific texts in Padihor's burial chamber.

[145] In general consult W. Barta, *Die altägyptische Opferliste von der Frühzeit bis zur griechisch-römischen Epoche*, (MÄS 3), Berlin 1963, and G. Lapp, *Die Opferformel des Alten Reiches unter berücksichtigung einiger späterer Formen*, (SDAIK 21), Mainz 1986, esp. pp. 118-150.

back to the type found within the pyramid of Unas.[146] The list occurs in the burial chambers of Amuntefnakht (south wall), Hor (south wall), Hekaemsaf (south wall), Iufaa (south wall), Tjannehebu (west wall), Psamtek 'the physician' (west wall), Padineith (west wall), Padinese (east wall), and Udjahorresnet (east wall).[147] Despite the impression given by its geographical distribution (east, west or south wall), the location of the offering list on the walls of the tomb appears to have been preordained: it is almost without exception located on the right side of the deceased.[148] The only exceptions are two tombs in Abusir – those of Udjahorresnet and Padihor – where the text is located at the foot of the deceased (in both cases on the east wall).[149] The reason for this diversion from the general pattern in these two tombs cannot be satisfactorily explained at present. In several burial chambers a sequence of PT utterances 267-269-270 features opposite the offering list (to the left of the deceased). In Padihor's tomb a similar combination of PT utterances is found on the north wall (also to the left).[150]

The list on the lintel of Padihor's burial chamber is the smallest one so far attested in a Late Period shaft tomb; it contains only about half the amount of products (35) usually attested.[151] The various items on the list are not ordered by type as strictly as is the case in other offering lists and the common tabular form of the list was replaced by a continuous text which contains a selection of 35 offerings, including (various types of) natron, incense, ointment, eye paints, wine, beer, fruit, cakes and bread, and pieces of meat and poultry (geese).

---

[146] Gestermann, *Sargtexte in spätzeitlichen Grabanlagen*, p. 375, and Hussein, *The Saite Pyramid Text Copies*, p. 99. See also Barta, *Altägyptische Opferliste*, offering list type A (fig. p. 181). The offering list most likely represents a tabular form of PT utterances 108-171. On this topic, consult also J. Baines, 'Modelling Sources, Processes, and Locations of Early Mortuary Texts', in S. Bickel – B. Mathieu (eds.), *Textes des Pyramides. Textes des Sarcophages. D'un monde à l'autre*, (BdE 139), Cairo 2004, pp. 15-41.

[147] Maspero, *ASAE* 1 (1900), pp. 171-172; 237-238, and 272-273; Maspero, *ASAE* 2 (1901), pp. 105-106; Maspero, *ASAE* 5 (1904), pp. 81-82; Drioton, *ASAE* 52 (1954), opposite pp. 114 and 122; Bresciani – Pernigotti – Giangeri Silvis, *Ciennehebu*, pp. 37-39; Bareš, *Abusir IV*, pp. 53-54, and Bareš, in Györy (ed.), *Aegyptus et Pannonia III*, p. 3. The list also occurs in the tombs of Bakenrenef in Saqqara and Wahibra-Tjeset in Heliopolis: K.R. Lepsius, *Denkmaeler aus Aegypten und Aethiopien* III, Berlin 1850, bl. 260c; H. Gauthier, 'Tombe d'époque saïtique à Héliopolis', *ASAE* 27 (1927), pp. 13-14, and M.C. Betro – F Silvano, 'Progetto visir. La simulazione nel restauro della tomba di Bekenrenef a Saqqara (L 24)', *EVO* 14-15 (1991–1992), pp. 5-8. In the tombs of Amuntefnakht, Padineith, and Tjannehebu the PT series 223–25–32 (the concluding offering spell, a censing spell and a libation spell) features on the same wall, while in the tomb of Psamtek 'the physician' it has been reduced to PT 25-32 – Soukiassian, *L'Egyptologie en 1979*, p. 60; Stammers, *Elite Late Period Egyptian Tombs*, pp. 63-64, and Hussein, *Saite Pyramid Text Copies*, pp. 136 and 175. In Padihor's burial chamber PT 25 features on the opposite west wall (at the head of the deceased), while PT 32 and 223 do not occur – see Chapter 1.3.5.

[148] This is the case in the burial chambers of Hor, Amuntefnakht, Hekaemsaf, Tjannehebu, Psamtek ('the physician'), Padineith, Padinese and Iufaa – see also Stammers, *Elite Late Period Egyptian Tombs*, pp. 63-64. The location of several texts on the walls of the burial chambers seems to have been directed by the position of the deceased (head, foot, left, right) rather than by geography (see for instance the sequence of PT utterances engraved on the north wall of Padihor's burial chamber – Chapter 1.3.3). On this topic, consult already Bresciani – Pernigotti – Giangeri-Silvis, *Ciennehebu*, pp. 27-29, and Soukiassian, *L'Egyptologie en 1979*, p. 57.

[149] It is also the case in the tomb of Wahibra-Tjeset in Heliopolis: Gauthier, *ASAE* 27 (1927), pp. 13-14. PT 213-214 feature at the head of the deceased in Udjahorresnet's tomb and PT 213 and 593 feature at the same position in Wahibra-Tjeset's tomb.

[150] See Chapter 1.3.3. The sequence occurs in the burial chambers of Amuntefnakht, Psamtek 'the physician', Padineith, and Tjannehebu. The exterior of the unpublished basalt inner sarcophagus of Iufaa contains the combination PT 267-269 (north side) and PT 270-271-272 (south side).

[151] For example: the tabular offering list has 88 compartments in the tombs of Psamtek 'the physician', Tjannehebu and Amuntefnakht and 90 compartments in Padinese's tomb.

(1) *ḥsmny*[152] (2) *snṯr* (*ḥr*) *ḫt ḥ3tt* (3) *irp ḥnk.t nbs* (4) *t-nbs wꜥḥ d3b* (5) *išd sḫt-ḥd.t sḫt-w3ḏ.t* (6) *psn ḥṯ3 šꜥwt šꜥwty* (7) *dpt nḥr sḫn*[153] *iꜥw-r3? f3j šns?*[154] (8) *ḫnf ḥbnnwt t-w3ḏ/w3d.t w3ḏw* (9) *t-imy-t3 bd t-rtḥ msdmt*[155] (10) *ḫps ꜥw swt* (11) *sr ṯrp st n* (12) *k3 n P3-di-ḥr pn*

(1) Water vessel, (2) incense (upon) fire, *ḥ3t.t*-oinment, (3) wine, beer, *nbs*-fruit(cake), (4) *nbs*-bread, *wꜥḥ*-fruit(cake), figs, (5) *išd*-fruit(cake), *sḫt-ḥd.t*-fruitcake, *sḫt-w3ḏ.t*-fruitcake, (6) *psn*-bread, *ḥṯ3*-bread, *šꜥwt*-cake, the *šꜥwty*-basin, (7) *dpt*-cake/bread, *nḥr*-bread, *sḫn*-bread, breakfast?, bringing the offering?, (8) *ḫnf*-cake/bread, *ḥbnnwt*-bread, *w3ḏ*-bread/*w3ḏ.t*-fruit, green eye paint (9) 'country' bread, *bd*-natron, *rtḥ*-bread, black eye paint, (10) a *ḫps*-foreleg, *ꜥw*-meat (from a small stock animal), a *swt*-piece of meat, (11) a *sr*-goose, a *ṯrp*-goose and a *st*-goose for (12) the *ka*[156] of this Padihor.

1.3.3 The north wall: PT 268 and 269 (Fig. 10 and Pls. 4a-b)

The inscription on the north lateral wall of the tomb consists of 28 text columns orientated from west to east. The top and bottom of the text are demarcated by a line drawn in red ink. These lines are located 22.50 and 92.00 cm above the ground level respectively, giving the text columns an average length of 69.50 cm. The individual columns are not divided from one another by a line in ink or an engraving; a single text column measures on average 7.0–7.5 cm in width.

The inscription consists of a sequence of two PT utterances: PT 268 and 269. The combination of these two utterances is, within the text corpus of the Late Period shaft tombs, unique to the burial chamber of Padihor. In the shaft tombs surrounding Unas' pyramid in Saqqara, namely the tombs of Amuntefnakht (north wall), Padineith, Psamtek 'the physician', and Tjannehebu (east wall),[157] one finds the very similar combination of PT 267–269–270 instead.[158] The exterior of the unpublished basalt inner sarcophagus of Iufaa contains the combination PT 267-269 (north side) and PT 270-271-272 (south side). PT utterance 268 is however presently attested only in the burial chamber of Padihor.

---

[152] Given the determinative of the person pouring water, I prefer the reading *ḥsmny* ('waschkrug') to the reading *ḥsmn* ('natron') – Wb III, pp. 162-163; R. Hannig, *Die Sprache der Pharaonen. Grosses Handwörterbuch Ägyptisch-Deutsch (2800–950 v. Chr.)*, (Kulturgeschichte der Antiken Welt 64), Mainz 2006 (4. überarbeitete Auflage), pp. 604-605, and Barta, *altägyptische Opferliste*, p. 38.

[153] The inscription was corrected in black ink after it had been engraved on the wall. The determinative of the word originally written as a piece of meat (a flat F51?) or a rib (F42?) was amended to low and very broad bread (X4?) – Wb III, pp. 470-471. See also Plate 7a, Chapter 1.3.7 and Table III for a more in-depth study of these corrections. In general on these corrections, consult Bareš, in Régen – Servajean, *Verba Manent*, pp. 51-56.

[154] The inscription was corrected in black ink after it had been engraved on the wall. The uniliteral sign *r* (D21) was replaced by the sign of an eye touched up with paint (D5) or perhaps rather by the sign of a mouth from which corn sprouts forth (D154). The accompanying vertical stroke (Z1) was altered by adding the signs *sn* (T22) and *ḥr* (D2). Below another sign resembling the viper *f* (I9) was added and turned in the opposite direction. See also Plate 7a, Chapter 1.3.7 and Table III. The reading of this particular passage is complicated and inconclusive. The first sign, combined with the vertical stroke, might have been intended as D154 for *iꜥw-r3* or 'breakfast' (Wb I, p. 39, and Hannig, *Grosses Handwörterbuch*, p. 28), while the following signs could be interpreted as *f(3j) šns* or 'bringing the offering' (Wb IV, pp. 516-517, and Hannig, *Grosses Handwörterbuch*, p. 898). The presence of the *ḥr*-sign in this passage is difficult to explain, but perhaps it was intended to represent a type of bread (X2).

[155] The outline of a hand, the uniliteral sign *d* (D46), was added in black ink below the engraved uniliteral signs *s* (S29) and *m* (G17).

[156] On the concept of ka, consult in general U. Schweitzer, *Das Wesen des Ka im Diesseits und Jenseits der alten Ägypter*, (ÄF 19), Glückstadt 1956; P. Kaplony, 'Ka', in W. Helck – E. Otto (eds.), *LdÄ* III, Wiesbaden 1980, pp. 275–282; A. Bolshakov, 'Ka', in D. Redford (ed.), *The Oxford Encyclopedia of Ancient Egypt* II, Oxford–New York 2001, pp. 215–217; L.D. Bell, 'Ancient Egyptian Personhood (Anthropology/Psychology): The Nature of Humankind, Individuality and Self–identity', in H. Beinlich – J. Hallof – H. Hussy – C. von Pfeil (eds.), *5. Ägyptologische Tempeltagung, Würzburg, 23.–26. September 1999*, (ÄAT 33/3), Wiesbaden 2002, pp. 41-42; J. Janák, *Staroegypstká kniha mrtvých. Kapitola 105*, (Pontes Pragenses 29), Prague 2003, pp. 30-38; J. Janák, 'Journey to the Resurrection. Chapter 105 of the Book of the Dead in the New Kingdom', *SAK* 31 (2003), pp. 193-210 and J. Janák, *Staroegyptské náboženství I. Bohové na zemi a v nebesích*, (Oikúmené 151), Prague 2009, pp. 211-224.

a) PT 268 (§370-375): *ḏd-mdw ỉꜥ sw Wsỉr Pꜣ-di-ḥr ḫꜥ Rꜥ psḏ*[159] *psḏ.t* (2) *wr.t kꜣ.t Nbty m-ḫnty ỉtr.t nḥm Wsỉr Pꜣ-di-ḥr p*(3)*ꜥ.t m ꜥ.t ỉm=f ḫfd Wsỉr Pꜣ-di-ḥr wrrt m-ꜥ* (4) *psḏ.ty ꜣṯ sw S.t snḳ sw Nb.t-ḥ.t šsp sw* (5) *Ḥr r ḏbꜥ.wy.f swꜥb=f Wsỉr Pꜣ-di-ḥr m š* (6) *sꜣby sfḫ kꜣ n Wsỉr Pꜣ-di-ḥr m š dwꜣty sk*[160]*=f* (7) *ỉwf n Wsỉr Pꜣ-di-ḥr n ḏ.t=f m nw ḥr rmn.wy* (8) *Rꜥ m ꜣḫ.t šsp=f psḏ tꜣ.w*[161] *wn=f ḥr nṯr.w* (9) *sḫp=f kꜣ n Wsỉr Pꜣ-di-ḥr n ḏ.t=f r ḥ.t-ꜥꜣ ỉr*[162](10) *n=f ꜥrrw.t ṯss n=f ḥmꜣṯ.t sšm Wsỉr* (11) *Pꜣ-di-ḥr ỉḫmw-skw*[163] *ḏꜣ=f r sḫ.t-ỉꜣrw ḫn* (12) *sw ỉmyw ꜣḫ.t sḳd sw ỉmyw ḳb*(13)*ḥw mnḫ.t Wsỉr Pꜣ-*(14)*di-ḥr mnḫ.t n sꜣw-ꜥ=f* (15) *ḫn.t Wsỉr Pꜣ-di-ḥr ḫnt* (16) *spr kꜣ=f r=k*

b) PT 269 (§376-382): *ḏd-mdw wdỉ*[164] *sḏt* (17) *wbn sḏt*[165] *wdỉ* (18) *snṯr ḥr sḏt w*(19)*bn snṯr*[166] *ỉy sṯi=k r Wsỉr Pꜣ-di-ḥr* (20) *snṯr ỉy sṯi Wsỉr Pꜣ-di-ḥr <r=k>*[167] *snṯr ỉy* (21) *sṯi=ṯn*[168] *r Wsỉr Pꜣ-di-ḥr nṯr.w ỉy sṯi Wsỉr Pꜣ-di-*(22)*ḥr r=ṯn nṯr.w*[169] *Wsỉr Pꜣ-di-ḥr ḥnꜥ=ṯn nṯr.w wn*[170](23)*=ṯn ḥnꜥ Wsỉr Pꜣ-di-ḥr nṯr.w ꜥnḫ Pꜣ-di-ḥr ḥnꜥ=ṯn* (24) *nṯrw ꜥnḫ=ṯn ḥnꜥ Pꜣ-di-ḥr nṯr.w mr ṯn Pꜣ-di-*(25)*ḥr mr sw nṯr.w ỉy pꜣḳ ỉy pꜣd pr m* (26) *mꜣs.t Ḥr ỉy prw ỉy ḥfdw ỉy šw*

---

[157] Two other large shaft tombs are located in this general area around Unas' pyramid. The sequence of utterances is completely absent in Hekaemsaf's tomb (Maspero, *ASAE* 5 (1904), while in Padinese's tomb only PT utterance 270 occurs – Maspero, *ASAE* 1 (1900), pp. 258-259. Padinese's tomb contains the sequence PT 213-222 instead, which was replaced by PT 267-270 in the other tombs according to Hussein, *Saite Pyramid Text Copies*, pp. 102-103, and 159-160. The combination PT 213-222 also occurs on Iufaa's outer sarcophagus, in the inner cavity (bottom). I am grateful to Prof. Ladislav Bareš for providing me with a copy of all inscriptions from the as yet unpublished burial chamber and sarcophagi of Iufaa.

[158] Maspero, *ASAE* 1 (1900), pp. 175-177 (Psamtek 'the physician'), and 274-276 (Tjannehebu); Bresciani – Pernigotti – Giangeri-Silvis, *Ciennehebu*, pp. 35-36 (Tjannehebu); Maspero, *ASAE* 2 (1901), pp. 107-108 (Padineith), and Drioton, *ASAE* 52 (1954), pp. 118-119 (Amuntefnakht). See also Hussein, *Saite Pyramid Text Copies*, p. 179 (table 1a). On the transmission of PT 269, see also A. Grimm, 'Ein Zitat aus den Pyramidentexten in einem ptolemäischen Ritualtext des Horus-Tempels von Edfu. Edfu III, 130, 14-15 = Pyr. 376b (Spr. 269). Zur Tradition altägyptischer Texte. Voruntersuchungen zu einer Theorie der Gattungen', *GM* 31 (1979), pp. 35-45.

[159] The uniliteral sign *s* (S29) was mistakenly written with the uniliteral sign *i* (M17).

[160] The uniliteral sign *k* (V31) was written mistakenly with the biliteral sign *nb* (V30).

[161] In the PT the two lands (*tꜣ.wy*) are mentioned instead of the lands (*tꜣ.w*): Sethe, *Pyramidentexte* I, p. 194.

[162] The verb is written as *itrw* instead of *ir*, known from other versions of the PT (Sethe, *Pyramidentexte* I, p. 194).

[163] The uniliteral sign *k* (V31) was, once more, written mistakenly with the biliteral sign *nb* (V30).

[164] The verb *wdi* is more commonly written with the sign of the hand (D46). This verb is either missing in this passage or was written with the signs Z9 and X1, and the fire (*sḏt*) only with the sign of the brazier (Q7). See parallels in Sethe, *Pyramidentexte* I, p. 195; Maspero, *ASAE* 1 (1900), p. 175 (Psamtek 'the physician'); Maspero, *ASAE* 1 (1900), p. 275 (Tjannehebu); Maspero, *ASAE* 2 (1901), p. 107 (Padineith); Drioton, *ASAE* 52 (1954), p. 118 (Amuntefnakht), and the exterior of Iufaa's basalt inner sarcophagus.

[165] The expression *wbn sḏt* is missing from this passage in the tombs of Psamtek 'the physician', Padineith and Amuntefnakht, but it occurs in Tjannehebu's and Iufaa's inscriptions.

[166] The passage in Tjannehebu's tomb still continues with the expression *ij snṯr* or 'the incense has come'.

[167] See parallels in Sethe, *Pyramidentexte* I, p. 196; Maspero, *ASAE* 1 (1900), p. 275 (Tjannehebu); Maspero, *ASAE* 2 (1901), p. 108 (Padineith); Drioton, *ASAE* 52 (1954), p. 118 (Amuntefnakht), and on Iufaa's sarcophagus.

[168] The passage in the tomb of Psamtek 'the physician' has *sṯi-nṯr* instead – Maspero, *ASAE* 1 (1900), p. 176.

[169] The inscription was 'corrected' in black ink after it had been engraved on the wall. The biliteral *mr*-sign (U6) was drawn twice – first with its point to the east, then to the west – over the last *nṯr*-sign (R8), and a new *nṯr*-sign was drawn immediately to the west of the engraved sign. The reason for this unnecessary correction cannot be explained – the engraved writing was correct and clearly follows the original PT 269 version. See also Chapter 1.3.7, Table III and Pl 7b for a more in-depth study of these corrections.

[170] The presence of these two signs (N29) is rather unusual in combination with the verb *wnn* ('to be'). The signs figure more commonly in similar sounding words, such as *wnm* ('to eat') and *wnmyt* ('fire') – Wb I, pp. 320-321. A similar writing of the verb is found in all other occurrences of this text in the large shaft tombs – see Maspero, *ASAE* 1 (1900), p. 176 (Psamtek 'the physician'); Maspero, *ASAE* 1 (1900), p. 275 (Tjannehebu); Maspero, *ASAE* 2 (1901), p. 108 (Padineith) and Drioton, *ASAE* 52 (1954), p. 119 (Amuntefnakht). In the inscription on Iufaa's sarcophagus the previous passage also opens with *wn*, written exactly the same way: *wn Ꞽwfꜥꜣ ḥnꜥ=ṯn nṯr.w*.

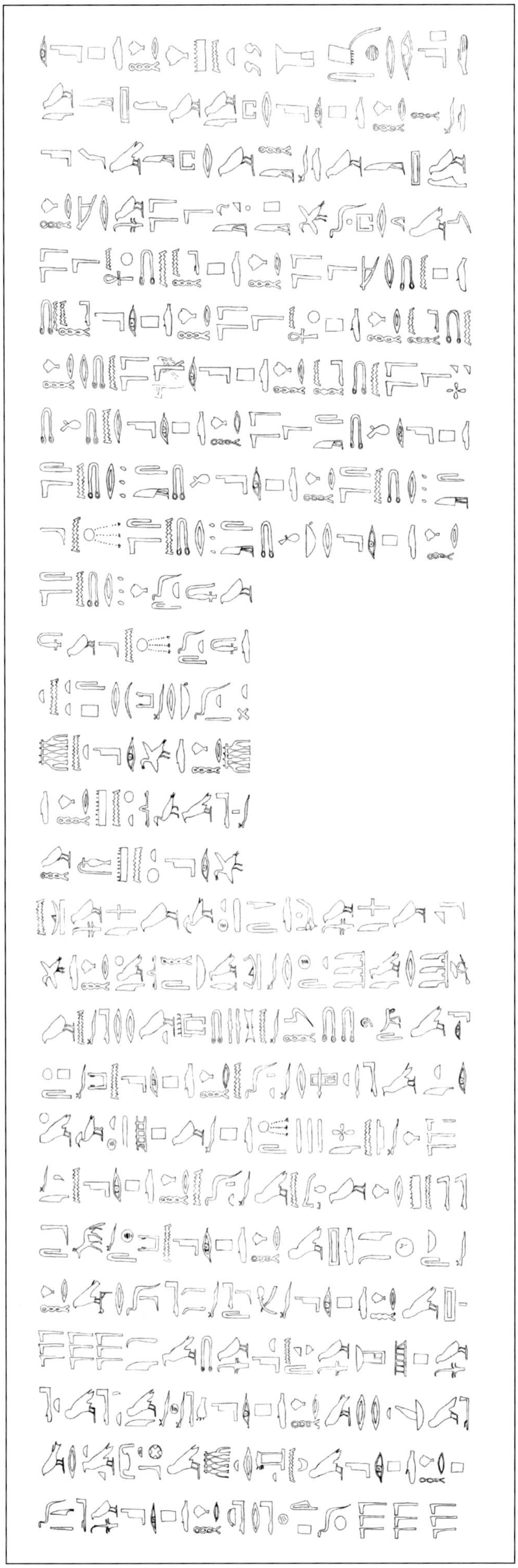

Fig. 10
The north wall of the burial chamber

(27) *iy šw*[171] *pr Wsir P3-di-ḥr ḫfd* (28) *Wsir P3-di-ḥr ḥr mnty Nb.t-Ḥ.t*[172] *im3ḫ r Wsir P3-di-<ḥr>*[173]

a) PT 268 (§370-375):[174] 'Recitation: the Osiris Padihor will wash himself when Ra appears and the Great Ennead (2) shines. Should the Ombite become high at the head of the shrine the Osiris Padihor will seize (3) the elite as a limb in/of himself, and the Osiris Padihor will seize the wereret-crown (the white crown)[175] from the hands of (4) the Dual Ennead. Isis will nurture him, Nephthys will suckle him, Horus will receive him (5) at his two fingers. He will purify the Osiris Padihor in the 'Jackal (6) Lake',[176] releasing the *ka* of the Osiris Padihor in the 'Duat-Lake',[177] and he will wipe (7) the flesh of the Osiris Padihor[178] and of his body, with that what is on both shoulders (8) of Ra in the horizon, which he receives when the lands shine and when he reveals the gods' faces. (9) He will conduct the *ka* of the Osiris Padihor to his body at the 'Great Enclosure'.[179] (10) The portals will act for him, the *ḥm3t.t*[180] will be tied on for him, the Osiris (11) Padihor will lead the 'imperishable stars'.[181] He will cross the 'Field of Rushes,[182] (12) those that are in the horizon rowing him, those that are in the 'Cool Waters' (the firmament)[183] sailing him. (13) The Osiris Pa-(14)dihor will become truly excellent/functional, and his arm will not be feeble. (15) The Osiris Padihor will become truly foremost, (16) and his *ka* will reach him'.

b) PT 269 (§376-382):[184] 'Recitation: the fire (17) has been set, the fire has arisen. (18) The incense has been set on the fire, (19) the incense has arisen. Your scent has come to the Osiris Padihor, (20) incense; the scent of the Osiris Padihor has come <to you>, incense. Your scent (21) has come to the Osiris Padihor, gods; the scent of the Osiris Padihor has come (22) to you, gods. The Osiris Padihor will be with you, gods; you

---

[171] In the Pyramid Texts these three sentences (*iy prw iy ḫfdw iy šw*) are usually repeated twice: Sethe, *Pyramidentexte* I, p. 197. The repetition of the first two sentences is missing in Padihor's inscription, but the passage is complete in Amuntefnakht's and Iufaa's texts. In the text of Psamtek 'the physician' these three sentences are not repeated at all, and in Padineith's text the entire passage has been reduced to a single *iy šw*. In Tjannehebu's text the first two sentences are repeated, while the third sentence is not.

[172] In older versions of the spell (Sethe, *Pyramidentexte* I, p. 197) one reads 'NN will go up (*pr*) on Isis' thighs, NN will climb (*ḫfd*) on Nephthys' thighs'. The reference to the thighs of Isis is missing in Padihor's inscription, but the inscription is complete in the tombs of Psamtek 'the physician', Tjannehebu, Padineith, and Amuntefnakht and on the exterior of Iufaa's basalt sarcophagus.

[173] The sign of the hand (D46) was engraved in the opposite direction from the rest of the text. The final part (*ḥr*) of the name Padihor has not been written out, most likely due to a lack of space in the last text column.

[174] For various previous translations of PT 268, consult Faulkner, *Pyramid Texts*, pp. 76-77, and especially Allen, *Pyramid Texts*, p. 49.

[175] Abd el Monem Joussef Abubakr, *Untersuchungen über die ägyptischen Kronen*, Hamburg – Glückstadt – New York 1937, pp. 30-31.

[176] The *š s3by* refers to a portion of the night or morning sky according to Allen, *Pyramid Texts*, p. 434.

[177] The *š dw3ty* refers to a portion of the night sky according to Allen, *Pyramid Texts*, p. 429.

[178] The original PT utterance reads 'the flesh of the ka of the Osiris N' instead – Sethe, *Pyramidentexte* I, p. 194.

[179] The *ḥw.t-ꜥ3.t* is a designation of the solar temple in Heliopolis according to Allen, *Pyramid Texts*, p. 427. See also Wb III, p. 4.

[180] An expression for the coil of the red crown: Abubakr, *die ägyptischen Kronen*, p. 53.

[181] Wb. I, p. 125; W. Barta, 'Funktion und Lokalisierung der Zirkumpolarsterne in den Pyramidentexte', *ZÄS* 107 (1980), pp. 1-4, and Allen, *Pyramid Texts*, p. 434.

[182] R. Weill, *Le Champ des Roseaux et le Champ des Offrandes*, Paris 1936; D. Bidoli, *Die Sprüche der Fangnetze in den altägyptischen Sargtexten*, ADAIK 9 (1976), pp. 26-44; H.M. Hays, 'Transformation of Context: The Field of Rushes in Old and Middle Kingdom Mortuary Literature', in S. Bickel – B. Mathieu (eds.), *Textes des Pyramides. Textes des Sarcophages. D'un monde à l'autre*, (BdE 139), Cairo 2004, pp. 175-200, and Allen, *Pyramid Texts*, p. 436.

[183] S.A. Mercer, *The Pyramid Texts in Translation and Commentary* IV, New York – London – Toronto 1952, pp. 53-54, and Allen, *Pyramid Texts*, p. 428.

[184] For various previous translations of PT 269, consult Faulkner, *Pyramid Texts*, pp. 77-78; Bresciani – Pernigotti – Giangeri-Silvis, *Ciennehebu*, pp. 35-36, and Allen, *Pyramid Texts*, pp. 49 and 175.

will be (23) with the Osiris Padihor, gods. Padihor[185] will live with you, (24) gods; you will live with Padihor, gods. Padihor will love you,[186] (25) may you love him, gods. The *p3k*-wafer has come, the knee-cap that comes from (26) the knee of Horus,[187] has come. The 'one that emerges' has come, the 'one that flies up' has come, the 'one that soars up' has come, (27) the 'one that soars up' has come. The Osiris Padihor will emerge, (28) the Osiris Padihor will go up on the thighs of Nephthys, the *im3ḫw* near Osiris, Padi(hor)'.[188]

The sequence of PT 268 and the shortened version of PT 269, found on the north wall of Padihor's burial chamber, appears to have performed the same function as the more common sequence PT 267–269–270 in the tombs of Amuntefnakht, Tjannehebu, Psamtek and Padineith and on Iufaa's inner sarcophagus. The general theme of these texts concerns the reconstitution of the body of the deceased and the resurrection, transformation and departure of the deceased from the Duat or his ascension into the heavens.[189] The location of Padihor's inscription, i.e. on the left hand side of the deceased (with his head towards the west), is identical with the text's location on the walls of the other four tombs at Unas' pyramid complex.[190] In these four tombs the sequence faces a series of offering spells on the opposite wall.[191] This is not the case in Padihor's tomb where the offering list is located on the lintel above the entrance (east wall), and a sequence of Coffin Texts was engraved on the opposite, south wall.

2.3.3. The south wall: CT 151, 625, 208, 716 and 352 (Fig. 11, Pls. 5a-b)

The inscription on the south lateral wall of the tomb consists of 29 text columns, one more than the opposite north wall, and is orientated from west to east. The top and bottom of the text is demarcated by a line drawn in red ink. The lines are located 22.50 and 93.00 cm respectively above the ground level, giving the text columns an average length of 70.50 cm. The columns measure on average 7.0–7.5 cm in width and are not divided from one another by a line in ink or an engraving.

The inscription on the right side of the deceased consists of a combination of five spells from the Coffin Texts in the following sequence: CT 151–625–208–716–352. These particular CT spells regularly occur on the walls of other Late Period tombs, although not necessarily in the same sequence.[192] In contrast with the previously analysed PT utterances, the location

---

[185] The noun 'Osiris' is left out twice in front of Padihor in this passage. This is not the case in the same passage of the text in the tombs of Tjannehebu, Padineith and Amuntefnakht. In the tomb of Psamtek 'the physician' the noun 'Osiris' is left out in the passages with the verbs *wn*, *ꜥnḫ* and *mr*. In the inscription on Iufaa's inner sarcophagus the noun 'Osiris' is never written before the name of the tomb owner.

[186] The term *nṯr.w* was omitted from Padihor's text, but it features in the same passage in the tombs of Psamtek 'the physician', Tjannehebu, Padineith and Amuntefnakht, and on Iufaa's sarcophagus. See also Sethe, *Pyramidentexte* I, p. 196.

[187] Compare with E. Otto, *Das ägyptische Mundöffnungsritual* I, (ÄA 3), Wiesbaden 1960, pp. 144-145 (scene 64): pellets of natron come from the knee of Horus. The shape of the kneecap (hemiglobular) might perhaps refer to the shape of the pellet.

[188] The final passage of PT utterance 269 (§381-382) has not been copied on the north wall of Padihor's burial chamber. It does feature in the tombs of Psamtek 'the physician' (Maspero, *ASAE* 1 (1900), pp. 176-177), Tjannehebu (Maspero, *ASAE* 1 (1900), pp. 275-276), Padineith (Maspero, *ASAE* 2 (1901), p. 108), Amuntefnakht (Drioton, *ASAE* 52 (1954), p. 119), and on the exterior of Iufaa's basalt sarcophagus.

[189] On the ascension aspect in the Pyramid Texts, consult W.M. Davis, 'The Ascension-Myth in the Pyramid Texts', *JNES* 36/3 (1977), pp. 161-179.

[190] The inscriptions are located on the north (Amuntefnakht and Padihor) and east (Psamtek 'the physician', Padineith and Tjannehebu) walls respectively, but always on the left hand side of the deceased. On the exterior of the inner sarcophagus of Iufaa, the sequence occurs partly on the left side and partly on the right side. It needs to be noted that when considering the position of the texts with regard to the disposition of the body in Iufaa's tomb, one might have to take into consideration that the original entrance (from the east) was changed to the opposite side (west) for reasons unknown. It is still unclear whether this change had an effect on the position of the inscriptions in relation to the body of the deceased – see Bareš – Smoláriková, *Abusir XVII*, pp. 52-54.

[191] See also Hussein, *Saite Pyramid Text Copies*, p. 160. Next to the offering spells, the sequence PT 223–25–32 often features on the opposite wall – Soukiassian, *L'Egyptologie en 1979*, p. 60, and Stammers, *Elite Late Period Egyptian Tombs*, pp. 63-64. See already footnotes 147 and 149.

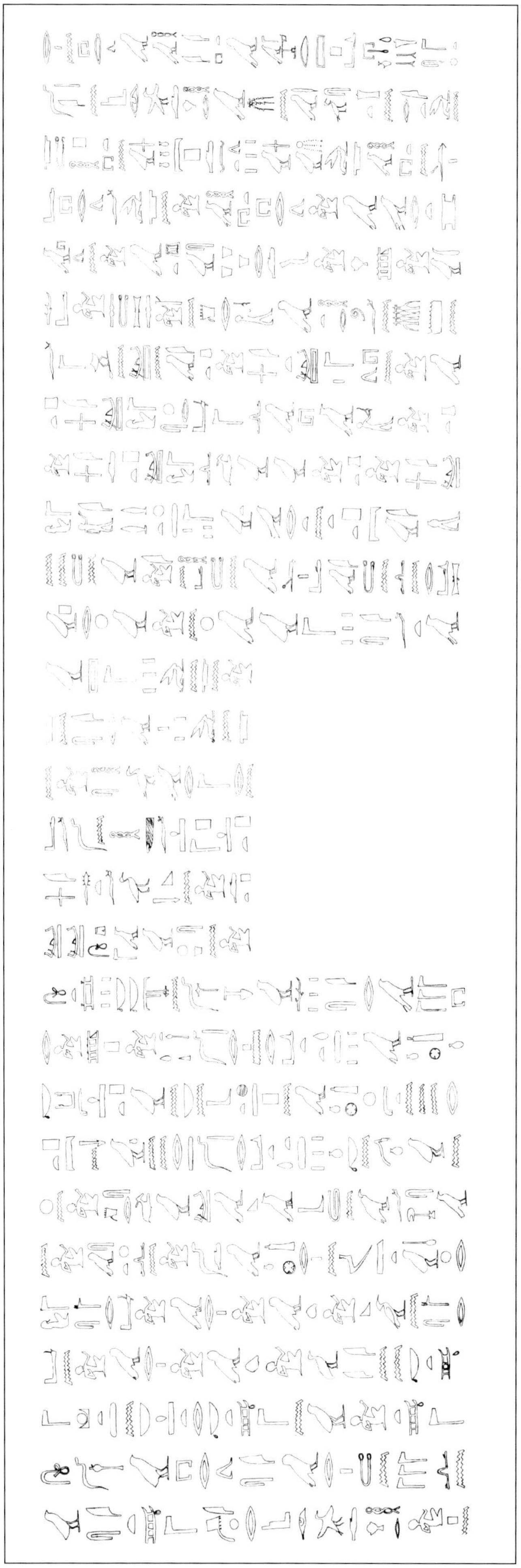

Fig. 11
The south wall of the burial chamber

of the CT spells on the walls of the burial chamber does not appear to have been governed by any geographical rules or the disposition of the body of the deceased. The CT spells occur in the Late Period tombs of the Memphite necropolis as follows: Amuntefnakht (CT 151-625 on the north wall/right side, CT 208-716 on the south wall/left side); Neferibra-sa-Neith (CT 151-625-208-716 on the east wall/feet); Padinese (CT 151-625-208-716-352 on the south wall/feet); Tjannehebu (CT 151-625 on the south wall/feet, CT 716 on the east wall/right side); Psamtek 'the treasurer' (CT 151-625 on the west wall/head, CT 352 on the east wall/feet); Panehsi (CT 151-625-208 on the west wall/head); Wahibra-Tjeset (CT 151 on the east wall/right side, CT 625-352 on the west wall/left side); Tjery (CT 151-625-352 on the north wall of Chamber 2), and Bakenrenef (CT 151-625-208-716 on the west wall of Room D). The closest parallel, as concerns the sequence of the spells as well as the orthography, is found on the unpublished south half of the outside of Iufaa's anthropomorphic basalt sarcophagus. The sequence consists of CT 151–625–208–716 located below a series of protective deities and forms the beginning of the inscriptions on the south half, starting at the head of the sarcophagus.[193] The final spell engraved on the south wall of the tomb of Padihor, i.e. CT 352, is also present on the south side of the exterior of Iufaa's sarcophagus, separated from the preceding inscriptions by a series of other spells.

a) CT151:[194] (1) *rꜣ n pr m ḥꜣy.t m ẖr.t-nṯr r šsp pr.t-ḫrw*[195] (2) *ḏd-mdw*[196] *ꞽn Wsꞽr Pꜣ-dꞽ-ḥr ms n Ndm-bꜣst.t-n-ꞽr.t wn* (3) *ṯpḥ.t n ꞽmyw Nw pḏ nmt.t (n)*[197] *ꞽmyw ꞽꜣḫ.w wn ḥꜣy.t n wꜥ* (4) *pr=f wn n=ꞽ ḥꜣy.t*[198] *pr(.n)=ꞽ*[199] *m wr.t* (5) *ḥꜣ.n=ꞽ m ẖꜣsw*[200] *rd=ꞽ ḥr špṯw* (6) *ꜥ=ꞽ sṯs*[201] *nḏr*[202] *m ḥtr n ḫnty-mnꞽ.t*(7)*=f ẖn.n<=ꞽ> m ns.t=ꞽ ꞽm.t dp.t-nṯr hꜣ.n=ꞽ m* (8) *ns.t ꞽm.t dp.t-nṯr ḫsr n mhꜣ=ꞽ*[203] *ns.t*(9)*=ꞽ ꞽmy.t dp.t-nṯr n ꞽw.w=ꞽ ns.t=ꞽ ꞽmy.t dp.t-*(10)*nṯr*

b) CT 625:[204] *ꞽ ḏꜣḏꜣ.t tw wr.t n.t p.t*[205] *ꞽw ꞽn.*(11)*n=ṯn wꞽ*[206] *ḥnꜥ=ṯn m wꜥ ꞽm=ṯn n*[207] *rdꞽ<=ꞽ> ṯs* (12) *pw rḫ.w=ꞽ*[208] *n ḫm.w nṯr.w ꞽsf.tyw* (13) *nṯr.w wn n=ꞽ*[209] (14) *ꜥꜣ n ꞽsr.tyw wn* (15) *n=ꞽ*

---

[192] References to other Late Period tombs in which the same spells occur will be provided separately for each spell in the footnotes. See also the overview in Stammers, *Elite Late Period Egyptian Tombs*, pp. 63-65, and Gestermann, *Sargtexte in spätzeitlichen Grabanlagen* I, pp. 353-354; 378-380, and 390-397.

[193] Bareš, in Györy (ed.), *Aegyptus et Pannonia III*, pp. 4-5. See also the photo of the sarcophagus in Verner – Benešovská, *Unearthing Ancient Egypt*, p. 191.

[194] CT 151 also occurs in the tombs of Amuntefnakht, Neferibra-sa-Neith, Padinese, Tjannehebu, Psamtek 'the treasurer' and Bakenrenef in Saqqara; Tjery in Giza, and Wahibra-Tjeset and Panehsi in Heliopolis. For an overview of the various inscriptions, their locations in the tombs and references to their publications, consult Gestermann, *Sargtexte in spätzeitlichen Grabanlagen* II, pp. 1-11. The spell also features on the south side of the exterior of Iufaa's inner sarcophagus.

[195] The title is completely absent in Amuntefnakht's version of the text. In almost all other Late Period versions, the text ends with *n=f* or 'for you', while Wahibra-Tjeset's version has *ꞽn Wsꞽr N* or 'by the Osiris N'.

[196] The expression *ḏd-mdw* is missing in the version of the text in the tombs of Bakenrenef, Neferibra-sa-Neith, Tjannehebu, Padinese, Psamtek 'the treasurer' and Iufaa.

[197] The genitive *n* is written out in the text version of Amuntefnkaht and Tjannehebu, while all other versions, including Padihor's, have a direct genitive construction.

[198] This expression is found in all Late Period texts, but is missing in the older versions. See Gestermann, *Sargtexte in spätzeitlichen Grabanlagen* II, pp. 4-5.

[199] All other Late Period versions have the *sḏm.n.f*-form. The suffix *=ꞽ* is missing in the versions of Neferibra-sa-Neith, Psamtek 'the treasurer' and Panehsi.

[200] The inscription was corrected in black ink after it had been engraved on the wall. The engraved uniliteral sign *p* (Q3) was changed to the correct sign of the butcher's block (T28) in black ink. See also Chapter 1.3.7.

[201] Compare with a similar expression in PT 625 (§1763c): *rd=f ḥr sꜣḥ ꜥ n N m sṯs*.

[202] Only Amuntefnakht's text has *nḏr=ꞽ*; the suffix *=ꞽ* is not written in any of the other Late Period versions, but it is typical of the older versions.

[203] The versions of Bakenrenef, Panehsi, Psamtek 'the treasurer', Iufaa and Tjannehebu read *mhw*, while those of Wahibra-Tjeset, Amuntefnakht, Neferibra-sa-Neith, and Padinese feature the younger variant of the word *mhꜣ*. See Wb II, p. 113.

[204] CT 625 also occurs in the Late Period tombs of Panehsi and Wahibra-Tjeset in Heliopolis, Tjery in Giza, and of Amentefnakht, Bakenrenef, Neferibre-sa-Neith, Tjannehebu, Psamtek 'the treasurer' and Padinese in Saqqara. For an overview of the various inscriptions, their locations in the tombs and references to their publications, consult Gestermann, *Sargtexte in spätzeitlichen Grabanlagen* II, pp. 151-161. The first lines of the spell also feature on the south side of the outside of Iufaa's sarcophagus, following immediately after CT 151.

ḥsꜣ wr rmn(16)*=f ḏnḥ=f*[210] *Ḥtp ḥtp.w* (17) *im ḫ.t=f bꜣḳ n=i dp*(*w*)*.ti*[211] (18) *Gwꜣ wsḫ*(*.w*) *n=i* (19) *wꜣ.wt kkw nḏ* (*wi*) *smꜣ.w isr.tyw pr*(20)*=i šsp=i*[212] *t=ḥḏ*

c) CT 208:[213] *ḏd-mdw rꜣ n rd.t t m Ỉwnw*[214] (21) *ink kꜣ ḥtp.w nb*[215] *ḫ.t 5*[216] *m Ỉwnw 3 r* (22) *p.t*[217] *snnw r tꜣ*[218]

d) CT 716:[219] *ḏd-mdw rd.t t*[220] *ink nw nḫn* (23) *sḏr.w iwy m-ḳꜣb n*[221] *mw.t=f sḫꜣ*(24)*.n=i smḫ.t.n=i*[222] *ḏd<=i>*[223] *m Ỉwnw*

---

[205] For slightly different reproductions of this passage in the tombs of Panehsi, Psamtek 'the treasurer', Wahibra-Tjeset, Neferibra-sa-Neith and Amuntefnakht, consult Gestermann, *Sargtexte in spätzeitlichen Grabanlagen* I, p. 324, n. 1337, and II, pp. 152-153.

[206] In a slight majority of the Late Period versions – in the tombs of Bakeneref, Wahibra-Tjeset, Amuntefnakht, Tjannehebu, Padinese and Psamtek 'the treasurer' – one finds the pronoun *nwi*. In the tombs of Iufaa, Pahnesi and Neferibra-sa-Neith, like in Padihor's version, *wi* occurs instead.

[207] Padinese and Neferibra-sa-Neith have *nn* instead.

[208] Padihor's version is the only Late Period example in which the suffix *=i* has been written out, following the Middle Kingdom examples of this passage.

[209] Panehsi, Padinese and Amuntefnakht have *wn=i* or 'I opened' instead.

[210] The suffix *=f* is only present in the versions of Padihor, Iufaa, Amuntefnakht and Tjery.

[211] A similar orthography is found in the versions of Bakenrenef, Wahibra-Tjeset, Nefreribra-sa-Neith, Padinese and Iufaa. Panehsi, Tjanehebu and Psamtek 'the treasurer' have *dp*(*w*)*.t* instead.

[212] Psamtek 'the treasurer' has a slightly different version: *pr.n=i šsp.n=i* or 'I have come and I have received'.

[213] The opening lines of CT 208 also occur in the Late Period tombs of Panehsi in Heliopolis, and Amuntefnakht, Bakenrenef, Neferibra-sa-Neith and Padinese in Saqqara. For an overview of the various inscriptions, their locations in the tombs and references to their publications, consult Gestermann, *Sargtexte in spätzeitlichen Grabanlagen* II, pp. 43-48. The first lines of the spell also feature on the south side of the inside of the Iufaa's inner sarcophagus, following the sequence 151–625. CT 208 is very similar to CT 729, while PT 409 is an early variant of CT 208 – Gestermann, *Sargtexte in spätzeitlichen Grabanlagen* I, pp. 183-185.

[214] The very same variant of the opening passage of this spell occurs in the inscriptions in the tombs of Bakenrenef, Neferibra-sa-Neith, Padinese and Iufaa. In Panehsi's tomb it still continues with the expression *ḏd-mdw in Wsir N mꜣꜥ-ḫrw* or 'recitation by the Osiris N, justified of voice'. In Amuntefnakht's tomb the spell starts solely with *ḏd-mdw in N* or 'recitation by N'.

[215] In the tombs of Bakenrenef, Pahnesi, Padinese and Iufaa, *nb* is written with the same phonetic complements. In the tomb of Neferibra-sa-Neith the *nb*-sign (V30) was by mistake written with the uniliteral sign *k* (V31).

[216] In all Late Period variants the numeral 5 from the hieratic text has been written as *pn*.

[217] In numerous Middle Kingdom versions of the spell, this sentence still continues with *ḫr Ḥr* or 'for Horus' – Gestermann, *Die Überlieferung* II, p. 46.

[218] The version of this sentence in the tomb of Padihor is free of orthographic mistakes, as are the occurrences of the same sentence in the tombs of Panehsi, Amuntefnakht and Neferibra-sa-Neith. In the tombs of Bakenrenef and Padinese the sign for *tꜣ* was replaced by the door–sign (O31) and the uniliteral sign *n* (N35) respectively. The text on Iufaa's sarcophagus is more corrupted and ends as follows: 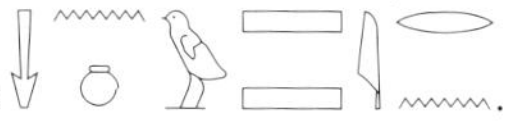. In numerous Middle Kingdom versions of the spell, this sentence still continued with *ḫr ꜥꜣ* or 'for the great one' – Gestermann, *Sargtexte in spätzeitlichen Grabanlagen* II, p. 46.

[219] CT 716 also occurs in the Late Period tombs of Amentefnakht, Bakenrenef, Tjannehebu, Neferibra-sa-Neith and Padinese in Saqqara. For an overview of the various inscriptions, their locations in the tombs and references to their publications, consult Gestermann, *Sargtexte in spätzeitlichen Grabanlagen* II, pp. 163-166. The spell also features on the south side of the inside of Iufaa's sarcophagus, where it follows after spells CT 151–625–208.

[220] Amuntefnakht has only *ḏd-mdw* or 'recitation' and no title of the spell. The plural strokes accompanying the bread sign also occur in the rendering of this spell in the tombs of Iufaa, Bakenrenef and Neferibra-sa-Neith, but not in the tombs of Amuntefnakht, Padinese and Tjannehebu.

[221] Only the inscription of Padinese features a direct genitive. *m-ḳꜣb* is written incorrectly in the text from the tomb of Bakenrenef.

[222] This passage reads similar in the tombs of Neferibra-sa-Neith and Tjannehebu – the latter without the first person suffix accompanying the second verb. Padinese has *sḫꜣ.n.i smḫ.n=i* or 'I have forgotten and I have remembered', while Bakeneref and Iufaa have *sḫꜣ.t.n=i smḫ.t.n=i* and Amuntefnakht features *sḫꜣ.t.n=i smḫ.n<=i>*.

[223] The older versions of CT 716 have *ḏd* followed by a suffix – Gestermann, *Sargtexte in spätzeitlichen Grabanlagen* II, p. 165.

e) CT 352:[224] *rꜣ n mꜣꜥ ḫrw ḫr* (25) *nṯr*[225] *wsr=ỉ*[226] *m rꜣ=ỉ m fnḏ=ỉ ꜥḳ.n<=ỉ>*[227] *wsr*(26)*.n=ỉ m rꜣ=ỉ m fnḏ=ỉ*[228] *(n)ꜣy n<=ỉ> n nb tm*[229] (27) *ꜣḫ.t n nb/n=k*[230] *ḥtp r=k tm (ỉ)n (ṯ)w*[231] *tm.w*[232] (28) *wꜣḏ.w pr*[233] *ỉs m rꜣ=ṯn nṯr.w n<=ỉ> wỉ* (29) *ỉs tm*[234] *ỉmꜣḫw Wsỉr Pꜣ-dỉ-ḥr pn*

a) CT151:[235] (1) 'Spell for going out of the tomb in the necropolis and for receiving an invocation offering. (2) Recitation by the Osiris Padihor, born of Nedjembasteteniret: (3) the cavern[236] for those that are in the Nun is opened, the strides of those that are in the sunlight are stretched out, open is the tomb for the 'One' (god)[237] (4) that he may come out, open is the tomb for me. I went forth from the 'Great Water', (5) after I had descended into the *ḫꜣsw*-marshes. My foot is on the step, (6) my arm raised up, having seized his cord/lashings of *Ḫnty-mnỉ.t=f*.[238] (7) <I> will sail in my seat, which is in the divine bark. I will descend to (8) the seat that is in the divine bark of the 'Dispeller'.

---

[224] CT 352 also occurs in the Late Period tombs of Wahibra-Tjeset in Heliopolis, Tjery (very fragmentary) in Giza, and Padinese and the two individuals named Psamtek ('the treasurer and his namesake), buried in the joint tomb with princes Khedbeneithyerboni, in Saqqara. For an overview of the various inscriptions, their locations in the tombs and references to their publications, consult Gestermann, *Sargtexte in spätzeitlichen Grabanlagen* II, pp. 105-109. The spell also occurs on the south side of the inside of Iufaa's sarcophagus, but it does not follow directly after the previous sequence of CT spells 151–625–208–716. CT 352, together with passages from CT 353 and 355, also occurs in the Book of the Dead, chapter 57 – see for instance E. Hornung, *Das Totenbuch der Ägypter*, Düsseldorf 2000, pp. 448-449.

[225] In the tombs of Padinese and Iufaa, the text starts with *ḏd-mdw*, while with Wahibra-Tjeset and Psamtek 'the treasurer' the expression *ḏd-mdw* follows only after the title of the spell. In addition, Wahibra-Tjeset has *ỉn N* or 'by N' at the end of the title of the spell.

[226] All other Late Period versions of this text, including Iufaa, have *wsr.n=ỉ* instead.

[227] The other Late Period versions, including Iufaa, read *ꜥḳ.n=ỉ* – Gestermann, *Sargtexte in spätzeitlichen Grabanlagen* II, p. 107.

[228] Most Late Period versions of this passage are riddled with mistakes to a degree, with the exception of the inscriptions in the tombs of Padihor, Iufaa and Wahibra-Tjeset. For an overview of the various mistakes, consult Gestermann, *Sargtexte in spätzeitlichen Grabanlagen* I, p. 254, n. 1180, and Gestermann, *Sargtexte in spätzeitlichen Grabanlagen* II, p. 107.

[229] In this reading, all Late Period versions would thus mistakenly have the uniliteral sign *k* (V31) instead of *nb* (V30). A plausible different reading, suggested by Gestermann, *Sargtexte in spätzeitlichen Grabanlagen* I, p. 254, n. 1181, might be *nꜣy n=ỉ nnk tm* or 'this belongs to me, to me belongs everything'. The presence of the *nṯr*-determinative at the end of this particular passage rather suggests the reading *nb tm* and can be construed as a reference to Atum – see B. Altenmüller, *Synkretismus in den Sargtexten*, (GOF IV/7), Wiesbaden 1975, p. 28. The Psamtek 'the treasurer' version has *nḥy n nb tm* or 'A prayer/praying to the lord of completeness' instead.

[230] Padihor, Iufaa, Wahibra-Tjeset and Padinese have *n nb*, while the two Psamteks have *n=k* instead. The Middle Kingdom version of this spell differs extensively and reads *ỉ.n=sn nṯr.w ipw/ipn ꜣḫ.w* (see CT IV, 391b).

[231] The version of Padihor is the only inscription where the uniliteral sign *ṯ* (V13) is missing. See also E. Edel, *Altägyptische Grammatik* II, Roma 1964, p. 423, §845, anm. 1.

[232] Only in the passages from Iufaa and Wahibra-Tjeset is *tm* not followed by the *nṯr*-determinative. In the Psamtek version *tm* is replaced by *psḏ.t*.

[233] The suggestion of Gestermann, *Sargtexte in spätzeitlichen Grabanlagen* I, p. 255, n. 1189 to connect *pri* with the previous sentence and to see the verb *nis* as the beginning of the next passage is only tenable for some of the Middle Kingdom versions of this text. *nis* is not present in any of the Late Period versions – unless one would assume that the uniliteral sign *n* (N35) has been omitted from every single example. See also Gestermann, *Sargtexte in spätzeitlichen Grabanlagen* I, pp. 257-258, dev. 7-9 for an overview.

[234] On this passage, consult also M. Gilula, 'An Adjective Predicative Expression of Possession in Middle Egyptian', *RdE* 20 (1968), pp. 57-58. The Psamtek version ends with *wsr* instead of *tm*.

[235] For various previous translations of CT 151, consult Faulkner, *Coffin Texts* I, pp. 130-131, Barguet, *Textes des sarcophages*, pp. 133-134, Bresciani – Pernigotti – Giangeri-Silvis, *Ciennehebu*, pp. 30-31, el-Sawi – Gomaa, *Panehsi*, p. 24, and Gestermann, *Sargtexte in spätzeitlichen Grabanlagen* I, pp. 144-151.

[236] On the various possible meanings of the term *tpḥ.t*, 'holes of various kinds', consult H. Willems, *The Coffin of Heqata (Cairo JdE 36418). A Case Study of Egyptian Funerary Culture of the Early Middle Kingdom*, (OLA 70), Leuven 1996, p. 314, n. 1898.

[237] The god Shu appears to have been intended: Gestermann, *Sargtexte in spätzeitlichen Grabanlagen* I, p. 147, n. 846.

[238] On this divinity, consult Gestermann, *Sargtexte in spätzeitlichen Grabanlagen* I, pp. 142-143.

I will not neglect my seat (9) that is in the divine bark, and I will not let my place, which is in the divine bark, become stranded'.

b) CT 625:[239] (10) 'Oh this great *ḏꜣḏꜣ.t*-council of heaven, you have brought (11) me among/to you as one of you. I will not give this utterance (12) that I know to one who does not know the gods or the enemies/sinners (13) of the gods. Open for me (14) is the door leaf of the *isr.tyw*, open (15) for me are the *ḥsꜣ*-waters/the flood[240] of the 'great one'; he carries (16) his wing of Hetep ('the contended one'),[241] when that what is in his body is satisfied. (17) Bright are for me both barks (18) of *Gwꜣ*,[242] and broad are for me (19) the roads of darkness.[243] The branches of the two tamarisks/the *isr.tyw* safeguard (me) (20) that I may come forth and receive the white bread'.

c) CT 208:[244] 'Recitation: spell for placing bread in Heliopolis. (21) I am the 'bull of offerings',[245] lord of five provisions/portions in Heliopolis: three are for (22) heaven, two are for the land'.[246]

d) CT 716:[247] 'Recitation: bringing bread. I am this[248] child,[249] (23) sleeping helplessly[250] in the inside of his mother. I have remembered (24) that what I had forgotten and (thus) <I> will speak in Heliopolis'.[251]

---

[239] For various previous translations of CT 625, consult Faulkner, *Coffin Texts* I, p. 208; Barguet, *Textes des sarcophages*, p. 104; Bresciani – Pernigotti – Giangeri-Silvis, *Ciennehebu*, p. 31; el-Sawi – Gomaa, *Panehsi*, pp. 25-26; el-Sadeek, *Gizeh*, p. 33, and Gestermann, *Sargtexte in spätzeitlichen Grabanlagen* I, pp. 324-327.

[240] On the translation of the term: a) el-Sadeek, *Gizeh*, p. 33 suggested 'slime', most likely based on Wb III, 160: 'Schleim, Teig'. b) Bresciani – Pernigotti – Giangeri-Silvis, *Ciennehebu*, p. 31 translated it as 'grande volatile' instead, undoubtedly inspired by the following passage of the spell. c) el-Sawi – Gomaa, *Panehsi*, p. 26 translated it as 'grossen *ḥsꜣ*-Gott'. d) The determinative rather suggests some sort of water, as Faulkner *Coffin Texts* I, p. 208 ('flood') and Gestermann, *Sargtexte in spätzeitlichen Grabanlagen* I, p. 352 ('gewässer') have suggested. See in this regard also PT utterance 509.

[241] *Ḥtp* is known as a god since the Pyramid Texts: PT utterance 603. Faulkner *Coffin Texts* I, p. 208 translated this passage as 'he supports the comfortable(?) wing' – using a version of the spell in which only one *ḥtp*-sign is present and is not determined by the *nṯr*-sign.

[242] There is no doubt that the day and night barks are meant, but the exact meaning of the term *gwꜣ* remains unclear. Faulkner *Coffin Texts* I, p. 208 translated it as 'him who is tied up', Barguet, *Textes des sarcophages*, p. 104 'les barques de Celui-qui-est-amarré', while el-Sawi – Gomaa, *Panehsi*, p. 26 interpreted it as an adjective ('schmale'). Consult also Bidoli, ADAIK 9 (1976), p. 81 and E. Otto, 'Sprüche auf altägyptischen Särgen', *ZDMG* 102 (1952), p. 189.

[243] Alternative translation: 'May both barks of *gwꜣ* be bright for me, may the roads of darkness be broad for me' – see already Faulkner *Coffin Texts* I, p. 208.

[244] For various previous translations of CT 208, consult Faulkner, *Coffin Texts* I, p. 169, Barguet, *Textes des sarcophages*, p. 398, el-Sawi – Gomaa, *Panehsi*, p. 27, and Gestermann, *Sargtexte in spätzeitlichen Grabanlagen* I, pp. 188-191.

[245] *kꜣ-ḥtp* is also often a reference to Osiris as the 'appeased ka' in scenes in Ptolemaic temples, for instance: R. Mond – O.H. Myers, *The Bucheum II. The Inscriptions*, London 1934, p. 25, Edfou V, 293, 11-12, or Dendara VIII, 21, 17. See also Schweitzer, *Wesen des Ka*, pp. 42–43, and S. Cauville, *La théologie d'Osiris à Edfou*, (BdE 91), Cairo 1983, p. 140, n. 3.

[246] In all Late Period examples only the first part of CT 208 features. In examples from the Old Kingdom and the Middle Kingdom the text still continues and refers to the day and night barks bringing the offerings and the disgust of the deceased at faeces and urine – Gestermann, *Sargtexte in spätzeitlichen Grabanlagen* II, pp. 46-48.

[247] For various previous translations of CT 716, consult Faulkner, *Coffin Texts* I, p. 271, Barguet, *Textes des sarcophages*, p. 608, Bresciani – Pernigotti – Giangeri-Silvis, *Ciennehebu*, p. 40, and Gestermann, *Sargtexte in spätzeitlichen Grabanlagen* I, pp. 332-333.

[248] Edel, *Altägyptische Grammatik* I, Roma 1954, p. 88, §196-197.

[249] On *nḫn*, 'child', in general, consult E. Feucht, *Das Kind im alten Ägypten. Die Stellung des Kindes in Familie und Gesellschaft nach altägyptischen Texten und Darstellungen*, Frankfurt – New York 1995, pp. 527-534.

[250] Wb I, 47: 'der Schiffslose', but also 'jem. ausschliessen von etw.'. Barguet, *Textes des sarcophages*, p. 608 translated it as 'abandonné', which is hard to correlate with the context of the sentence. I follow Faulkner, *Coffin Texts* I, p. 271 and Gestermann, *Sargtexte in spätzeitlichen Grabanlagen* I, p. 333 who suggested the translation 'helpless/hilflos'.

[251] An alternative translation is plausible in the case of the text in the tombs of Tjannehebu and Amuntefnakht, where the suffix is missing: *smḫ.t.n<=i>*. In the case of Tjannehebu the sentence could for instance be interpreted as *sḫꜣ.n=i smḫ.t n ḏd m Ỉwnw* or 'I have remembered that what the one that speaks in Heliopolis had forgotten'. See already Bresciani – Pernigotti – Giangeri-Silvis, *Ciennehebu*, p. 40, and Gestermann, *Sargtexte in spätzeitlichen Grabanlagen* I, pp. 332-333.

e) CT 352:[252] 'Spell for being justified of voice before a (25) god. I have might over my mouth and over my nose. <I> have entered because (26) I have might over my mouth and over my nose. This belongs to me, it belongs to the lord of completeness. (27) It is useful for the lord/you. Be content, Atum, you are complete (28) and green/youthful, which comes out of your mouth, gods. (29) To me belongs the completeness, the *imꜣḫw*, this Osiris Padihor'.

The five CT spells on the south wall of Padihor's burial chamber complement the PT utterances engraved on the opposite wall.[253] Thematically, the opening spells – CT 151 and CT 625 which are often combined in Late Period tombs – focus on the resurrection of the deceased: his possibility to move about freely and reach beyond the confines of the tomb, his journey to the watery regions of the sky and his arrival in the netherworld. These passages are further complemented by three smaller CT spells: CT 208 and 716; in case of the latter it is only its title, ensuring a continuous flow of offerings for the deceased, equating the deceased with the unborn child (CT 716), and delivering on the wish of the deceased to be justified (*mꜣꜥ-ḫrw*) and complete (CT 352).

1.3.5. The west wall: PT 77, 78, 81 and 25 (Fig. 12, Pl. 6b)

The inscription on the west or rear wall consists of 12 columns of texts. A line in red ink separates the 12 columns from the edges of the wall. The individual columns are not separated from each other by an engraving or a line drawn in ink. The average width of each column is 6.50 cm. Near the bottom of the wall a line in black ink separates the 12 text columns from a 8 cm high frieze depicting vessels containing various ointments and other offerings (five objects to the south and six to the north of the central niche). An engraved line located 22 cm above the floor level marks the bottom of the frieze.

The text on the west wall contains a sequence of (parts of) four utterances from the Pyramid Texts: PT 77 (§52), 78 (§54), 81 (§56-57) and 25 (§17-18). These spells are found on the walls of most large shaft tombs of this era, but in most cases the sequence PT 77-78-81 does not occur on the same wall as PT 25. This utterance, a censing spell, is usually located on the wall to the right of the deceased, often in combination with the tabular offering list.[254] This is the case in the tombs of Amuntefnakht (south wall), Padineith (west wall), Tjannehebu (west wall), Psamtek 'the physician' (west wall), and Padinese (west wall).[255] The utterance is located to the left of the deceased in the tombs of Psamtek 'the treasurer' and Udjahorresnet (both on the north wall),[256] and on the exterior of Iufaa's inner sarcophagus (north side). In the tombs of Padinese and Hekaemsaf PT 25 occurs at the head of the deceased in combination with other utterances from the PT 72-81 series.[257] A similar situation occurs on the west wall at the head of the deceased in Padihor's burial chamber, where PT 25 is combined with PT 77-78-81. These three utterances form part of a much larger popular sequence (PT 72-81) that deals with the presentation of ointments, eye paints and linen.[258] In several other large shaft tombs, especially those located in and around the pyramid temple of Unas in Saqqara (a-f, below), this sequence often occurs at the head of the deceased on the walls of the burial chamber:[259]

---

[252] For various previous translations of CT 352, consult Faulkner, *Coffin Texts* I, p. 284, Barguet, *Textes des sarcophages*, p. 289, and Gestermann, *Sargtexte in spätzeitlichen Grabanlagen* I, pp. 252-255.

[253] Hussein, *Saite Pyramid Text Copies*, pp. 163-164.

[254] See already Chapter 1.3.2.

[255] Maspero, *ASAE* 1 (1900), pp. 173 (Psamtek 'the physician'); 239; 246 (Padinese), and 273 (Tjannehebu); Maspero, *ASAE* 2 (1901), p. 107 (Padineith); Drioton, *ASAE* 52 (1954), p. 115 (Amuntefnakht), and Bresciani – Pernigotti – Giangeri-Silvis, *Ciennehebu*, p. 39 and plate XII (Tjannehebu).

[256] Daressy, *RT* 17 (1895), p. 18 (Psamtek 'the treasurer'), and Bareš, *Abusir IV*, pp. 52-53 (Udjahorresnet).

[257] Maspero, *ASAE* 1 (1900), pp. 252-253 (Padinese), and Maspero, *ASAE* 5 (1904), p. 79 (Hekaemsaf).

[258] Hussein, *Saite Pyramid Text Copies*, pp. 98 and 138 on the occurrence of this series of spells in Late Period shaft tombs – especially in the tombs surrounding the pyramid of Unas.

[259] Maspero, *ASAE* 1 (1900), p. 180 (Psamtek 'the physician'); Maspero, *ASAE* 2 (1901), pp. 109-110 (Padineith); Drioton, *ASAE* 52 (1954), pp. 112-113 (Amuntefnakht), and Bresciani – Pernigotti – Giangeri-Silvis, *Ciennehebu*, pp. 33-34 and plate IX (Tjannehebu).

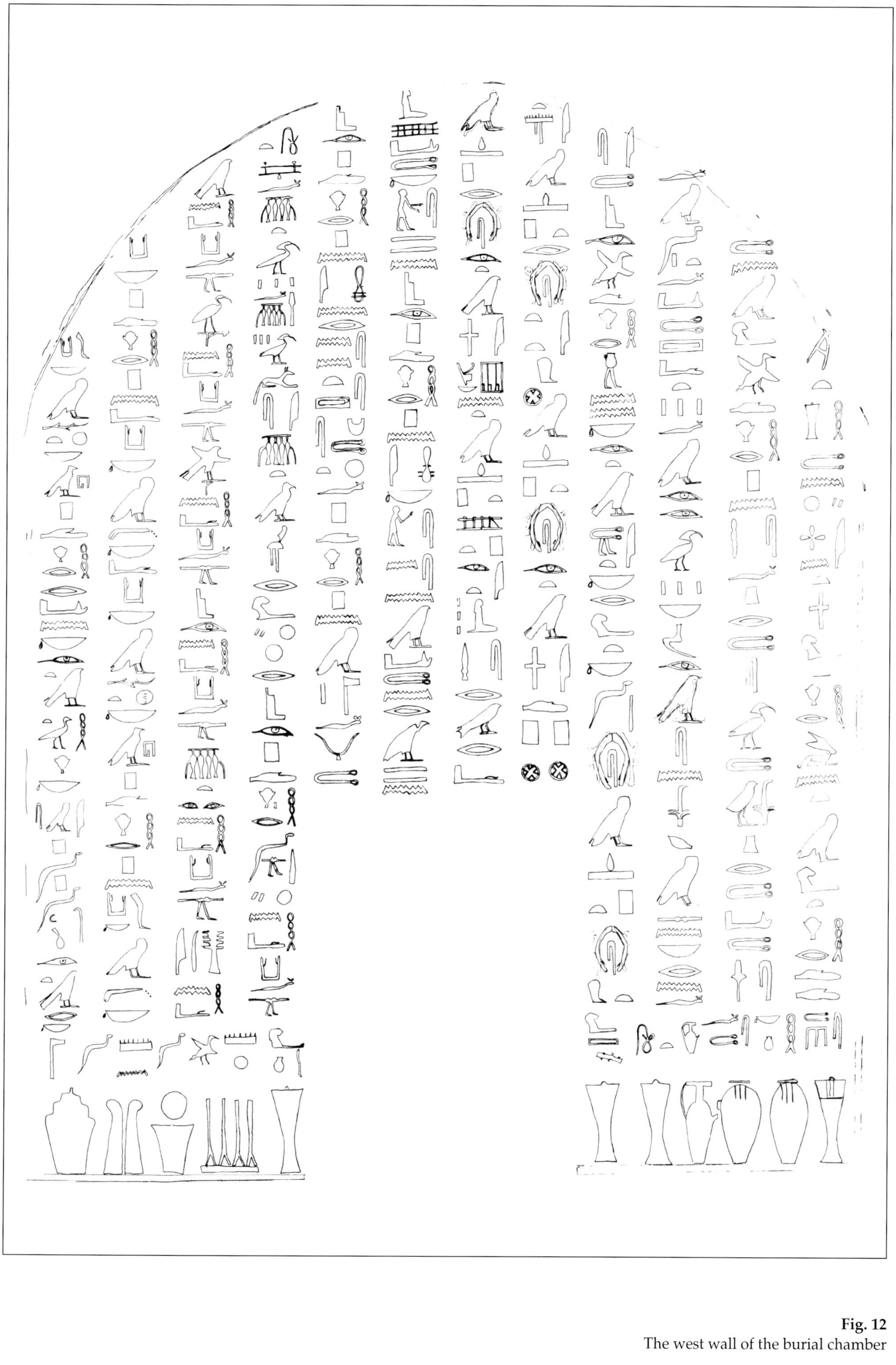

Fig. 12
The west wall of the burial chamber

a. Amuntefnakht: the complete sequence PT 72-81 at the head of the deceased (west wall).

b. Padineith: the complete sequence PT 72-81 at the head of the deceased (north wall).

c. Psamtek 'the physician': PT sequence 72-79 and PT 81 at the head of the deceased (north wall).

d. Tjannehebu: PT sequence 72-79 and PT 81 at the head of the deceased (north wall).

e. Padinese: PT 25 and PT sequence 72-79 and PT 81 at the head of the deceased (north wall).

f. Hekaemsaf: PT 25, and PT sequence 72-77[260] and PT 81 at the head of the deceased (west wall).

The passage also occurs elsewhere in large Late Period shaft tombs:[261]

g. Hor: PT sequence 72-78 and PT 81 at the foot of the deceased (east wall).

h. Psamtek 'the treasurer': PT 77-78 and 81 on the left side of the deceased (north wall).

i. Iufaa: only PT 81 figures, in two locations: on the east wall of the burial chamber (head) and on the outside bottom of the inner basalt sarcophagus.

The overview illustrates that the occurrence of PT 77-78-81, and to a lesser degree of PT 25, on the west wall of Padihor's burial chamber, at the head of the deceased, appears to follow the general disposition of these PT utterances on the walls of most other large Late Period shaft tombs.

a) PT 77:[262] (1) *mrḥ.t sp-2 ṯnỉ*[263] (2) *ṯn m ḥꜣ.t Pꜣ-dỉ-ḥr pn snḏm=f ḫr=t*[264] *sꜣḫ=ṯ sw ḫr=t dỉ=ṯ sḫm*(3)*=f m ḏ.t=f dỉ=ṯ šꜥw=f m ỉrty ꜣḫw nbw mꜣꜣ*[265]*=sn sw*[266] *sḏm=sn nbw*[267] *rn=f ỉsṯ*

b) PT 78:[268] (4) *Wsỉr Pꜣ-dỉ-ḥr ỉn.n<=ỉ> n=k ỉr.t-Ḥr ỉṯ=k*(sic)[269] *r hꜣ.t=k*

c) PT 81:[270] *ḏd-mdw rs*[271] *m ḥtp rs Tꜣy.t* (5) *m ḥtp rs Tꜣyt.t m ḥtp rs*[272] *ỉr.t-Ḥr ỉmy Dp* (6) *m*[273] *ḥtp*[274] *rs ỉr.t-Ḥr ỉmy ḥw.t-N.t*[275] *m ḥtp šsp ỉrywt sḫkr wrꜥ*[276] (7) *dỉ=ṯ ks tꜣ.wy*[277] *n Wsỉr Pꜣ-*

260 PT 78 is not present on the walls of Hekaemsaf's burial chamber.

261 Daressy, *RT* 17 (1895), p. 19 (Psamtek 'the treasurer'), and Drioton, *ASAE* 52 (1954), pp. 123-124 (Hor).

262 PT utterance 77 also occurs in the tombs of Amuntefnakht, Tjannehebu, Hekaemsaf, Hor, Padineith, Padinese, Psamtek 'the physician' and Psamtek 'the treasurer' in Saqqara.

263 The interrogative adverb *ṯnỉ* is written mistakenly in front of *sp-2*. The opening passage of this utterance was abbreviated in Padihor's inscription to its most basic form. For the complete reading, see Sethe, *Pyramidentexte* I, p. 29 (*mrḥ.t mrḥ.t ṯnỉ wn=t ỉmy ḥꜣt Ḥr ṯnỉ wn=t ỉmy ḥꜣt Ḥr*) and Padinese, Psamtek 'the treasurer' and Hekaemsef's version. A more abbreviated version is found with Psamtek 'the physician', Hor, Tjannehebu, Amuntefnakht, and Padineith.

264 The PT version reads originally: *snḏm=ṯ n=f ḫr=ṯ* or 'you shall make (it) pleasant for him, wearing you' (Sethe, *Pyramidentexte* I, p. 29). For a similar reading see Psamtek 'the treasurer', Hor, Tjannehebu, Amuntefnakht, and Padineith's version. A version similar to Padihor's is found in the tombs of Padinese, Psamtek 'the physician' and Hekaemsaf.

265 The text was corrected in black ink after it had been engraved on the wall: the sign of the Horus falcon (G5) was changed to the correct sign of the vulture (G1) in the verb *mꜣꜣ*. See also Chapter 1.3.7, Table III, and Pl. 7c.

266 The version in the tomb of Psamtek 'the treasurer' reads *mꜣꜣ=sn n=f ḫr=ṯ*. Most other versions are varieties of this expression.

267 *nbw* only occurs in Padihor's version.

268 PT utterance 78 also occurs in the tombs of Amuntefnakht, Tjannehebu, Hor, Padineith, Padinese, Psamtek 'the physician', and Psamtek 'the treasurer' in Saqqara.

269 The original PT version features *ỉṯ=f* or 'that he took/seized/acquired' instead (Sethe, *Pyramidentexte* I, p. 30). The version in the tombs of Amuntefnakht, Psamtek 'the physician', Padinese and Padineith reads *ỉṯ.n=f*.

270 PT utterance 81 also occurs in the tombs of Amuntefnakht, Tjannehebu, Hekaemsaf, Hor, Padineith, Padinese, Psamtek 'the physician', and Psamtek 'the treasurer' in Saqqara. The utterance also features on the east wall of the tomb of Iufaa and on the outside bottom part of his sarcophagus.

271 The engraved hieroglyphs were corrected in black ink: the erroneous combination of the sign of the embracing arms (D32) and the uniliteral sign *s* (S29) was corrected by adding the sign T13 twice on both sides of the *s*-sign to create symmetry. The same correction was repeated four more times in columns 4 (once), 5 (twice) and 6 (once), always correcting the reading to *rs*. See also Chapter 1.3.7, Table III and Pl. 7c-d. In the original PT version and in all other Late Period copies – with the exception of Padineith where it is missing – one finds *rs=ṯ* or 'may you awake in peace' instead – Sethe, *Pyramidentexte* I, p. 31. In general on this expression, consult H. Goedicke, '*Rs m ḥtp*', *SAK* 34 (2006), pp. 187-204 who translates the expression as 'awake from rest/inertia'.

272 In the original PT version the verb *rs* is not repeated in front of this and, sometimes, also the next passage – Sethe, *Pyramidentexte* I, p. 31. It is present in the Late Period versions.

di-ḥr pn mi ks=sn n Ḥr di=ṯn nr t3.wy n (8) *Wsir P3-di-ḥr pn mi nr=sn n Stš*[278] *ḥms=ṯ*[279] *ḫft P3-di-ḥr pn m nṯry=f wp=ṯ* (9) *w3.t=f ḫnt 3ḫw ꜥḥꜥ=f ḫnt 3ḫw inpw is ḫnt imntyw*[280] *r-ḥ3ty*[281] *sp-2 ḫr Wsir P3-di-ḥr*

d) PT 25:[282] *ḏd-mdw sbi sp-2*[283] *ḥnꜥ k3=f sbi* (10) *Ḥr ḥnꜥ k3=f*[284] *sbi Ḏḥwty ḥnꜥ k3=f sbi nṯr ḥnꜥ k3=f sbi Wsir ḥnꜥ k3=f sbi ḫnty-ir.ty ḥnꜥ k3=f sbi ḏd=ṯ* (11) *ḥnꜥ k3=k*[285] *<h3>*[286] *P3-di-ḥr pn ꜥ-k3=k m-b3ḥ=k ꜥ-k3=k m-ḫ.t=k h3 P3-di-ḥr rd-k3=k m-b3ḥ=k* (12) *rd-k3=k m-ḫ.t=k*[287] *h3 P3-di-ḥr rdi<.n=i> n=k ir.t-Ḥr ḥtm ḥr=k im=s pḏpḏ sṯy ir.t-Ḥr r=k*

a) PT 77:[288] (1) 'Ointment, ointment where should you be? On the forehead of Horus. You are on the forehead of Horus, but <I> will place (2) you on the forehead of this Padihor making him feel pleasant, wearing you. You shall make him excellent

---

273 The poorly engraved hieroglyph of the owl (uniliteral sign *m* or G17) was accentuated in black ink. See also Chapter 1.3.7, Table III, and Pl. 7d.

274 The uniliteral *t*-sign (X1) was not written on this occasion.

275 The term follows the original PT version, but during the Twenty-Sixth or Saite Dynasty, it might have also evoked the meaning *Ḥw.t-N.t* of the 'Mansion of Neith': the temple of Neith in Sais and Sais itself. The presence of the goddess Tayt in the previous passage in addition also provides a link with the domain of Neith in Sais: R. el-Sayed, *Documents relatifs à Sais et ses divinités*, (BdE 69), Cairo 1975, pp. 180-199.

276 Wb I, p. 332. The determinative of the irrigated land (N24; *sp3t*) is unusual and most likely refers to another word for a carrying chair: *sp3* (Wb. III, p. 441). In the versions in the tomb of Amuntefnakht, Psamtek 'the physician', Padinese, Padineith, Iufaa, Tjannehebu and Psamtek 'the treasurer', one reads *wrḥꜥ* (sic) instead.

277 The version in the tomb of Psamtek 'the treasurer' has *mw* or 'water' instead, while in the tombs of Amuntefnakht, Psamtek 'the physician', Tjannehebu, and Hor one reads *t3.w* instead of *t3.wy*.

278 The name Seth was replaced by Geb in the version of Amuntefnakht, Padineith, Psamtek 'the physician' and Hor, and is missing in Hekaemsaf's version. On the bottom of Iufaa's inner sarcophagus the name was replaced by the sign of the falcon on the standard (G7), while in Tjannehebu's version it was replaced by the Horus-falcon (G5). The name of the god Seth only occurs in the version of Padinese and Psamtek 'the treasurer'. On this topic, see J. Kahl, 'Religiöse Sprachensensibilität in den Pyramidentexten und Sargtexten am Beispiel des Namens des Gottes Seth' in S. Bickel – B. Mathieu (eds.), *Textes des Pyramides. Textes des Sarcophages. D'un monde à l'autre*, (BdE 139), Cairo 2004, pp. 219-246. The central stroke in the uniliteral *š*-sign (N38) was added in black ink.

279 The poorly engraved hieroglyph of the rope (uniliteral sign *ṯ* or V13) was accentuated in black ink.

280 On the bottom of Iufaa's inner sarcophagus one still finds: *ꜥnḏty is ḫnty spw.t i3b.t* or 'Andjety who is at the head of the eastern nomes'. For the occurrence of this epithet of the god Andjety, see already PT 224 (§220) and 650 (§1833). In general: E. Otto, 'Anedjti', in W. Helck – E. Otto (eds.), *Lexikon der Ägyptologie I*, Wiesbaden 1975, pp. 269-270.

281 The version in the tombs of Amuntefnakht, Hekaemsaf, Padinese, Psamtek 'the physician', Iufaa and Psamtek 'the treasurer' reads *ḏd-mdw sp-4 r-ḥ3ty sp-2 ḫr Wsir*. The name of the tomb owner is usually not written after *Wsir*, with the exception of the versions of Iufaa and Padinese. This passage is missing in the tombs of Padineith and Hor. The inscription in Tjannehebu's tomb is similar to Padihor's version.

282 PT utterance 25 also occurs in the tombs of Amuntefnakht, Tjannehebu, Hekaemsaf, Padineith, Padinese, Psamtek 'the physician' and Psamtek 'the treasurer' in Saqqara. It also features in the tomb of Udjahorresnet in Abusir and on the outer north half of the sarcophagus of Iufaa.

283 All other Late Period versions, with the exception of Iufaa and Padinese, have *sbi sbi* instead.

284 In the original PT version 25 the text continues with *sbi Stš ḥnꜥ k3=f* or 'Seth has gone with his ka' (see Sethe, *Pyramidentexte* I, p. 17). This passage is also missing in all other Late Period versions. The omission of this passage might be due to the position Seth occupied in Late Egyptian religion as primarily a god of chaos and enemy of the gods. Perhaps it was therefore undesirable to include a reference to him in this passage – although he does feature in the previous utterance (see west wall, column 8). See also H. te Velde, 'Seth', in W. Helck – E. Otto (eds.), *Lexikon der Ägyptologie V*, Wiesbaden 1984, p. 910; H. Bonnet, *Reallexikon der ägyptischen Religionsgeschichte*, Berlin 1952, pp. 711–712; H. Kees, *Horus und Seth als Götterpaar* II, (MVAG 29/1), Leipzig 1924, pp. 82–87, and H. te Velde, *Seth, God of Confusion. A Study of his Role in Egyptian Mythology and Religion*, (PdÄ 6), Leiden 1967, pp. 138-151, esp. p. 148.

285 The uniliteral sign *k* (V31) was written mistakenly with the biliteral sign *nb* (V30).

286 Compare with Sethe, *Pyramidentexte* I, p. 18. The expression *h3 NN* is repeated four times in this passage.

287 This expression is not present in Padineith's version of the text.

288 For various previous translations of PT 77, consult Faulkner, *Pyramid Texts*, p. 18, Bresciani – Pernigotti – Giangeri-Silvis, *Ciennehebu*, p. 33, and Allen, *Pyramid Texts*, p. 22.

(*'akhify'*),[289] wearing you; you shall make that he has control over (3) his body; you shall place his ferocity/terror of him in the eyes of all the *Akhu* when they shall look at him and in all those that hear his name as well'.

b) PT 78:[290] (4) 'Osiris Padihor, I have brought for you the eye of Horus, that you (sic) seized, for your forehead'.

c) PT 81:[291] 'Recitation: Awake in peace/from rest! Awake Tayt (5) in peace! Awake those of Tayt-town[292] in peace! Awake the eye of Horus that is in Dep (6) in peace! Awake the eye of Horus that is in the enclosures of the *Nt*-crown[293] in peace! The one that the female companions receive, who adorn the one of the sedan chair. May you make that the Two Lands bow before this Osiris Padihor like they bow before Horus, (and) may you make that the Two Lands fear (8) this Osiris Padihor like they fear Seth. May you sit opposite this Padihor in his divinity, and may you open (9) his path at the head of the *Akhu*, that he may stand at the head of the *Akhu* as Anubis at the front of the Westerners. To the front! To the front with the Osiris Padihor!'

d) PT25:[294] 'Recitation: one who has gone has gone with his *ka*.[295] (10) Horus has gone with his *ka*, Thoth has gone with his *ka*, the god has gone with his *ka*, Osiris has gone with his *ka*, Khenty-Irty[296] has gone with his *ka*, (and) you have also gone with (11) your *ka*. <Oh> this Padihor! Your *ka*'s arm is in front of you; your *ka*'s arm is behind you. Oh this Padihor! Your *ka*'s foot is in front of you; (12) your *ka*'s foot is behind you. Oh Padihor! I have given you the eye of Horus: provide your face with it and let the scent of Horus's eye disseminate to you'.

Underneath the four PT utterances, a frieze with 11 objects is located consisting of the following (from north to south):

1. *sṯy-ḥb*	Festival oil/perfume
2. *ḥknw*	*ḥknw*-ointment
3. *sfṯ*	*sfṯ*-ointment
4. *n(y-)ẖnm*	*n(y-)ẖnm*-ointment
5. *twꜣwt*	*twꜣwt*-ointment
6. *ḥꜣtt n.t ʿš*	*ḥꜣtt n.t ʿš*-ointment
7. *ḥꜣtt n.t ṯḥnw*	*ḥꜣtt n.t ṯḥnw*-ointment

[289] 'Akhify' (*sꜣḫ*, the causative of *ꜣḫ*) or helping the deceased to become an 'akh', enabling eternal life. On this concept, see for instance E. Otto, 'Ach', in W. Helck – E. Otto (eds.), *Lexikon der Ägyptologie I*, Wiesbaden 1975, pp. 49-52; G. Englund, *Akh – une notion religieuse dans l'Egypte pharaonique*, (BOREAS. Uppsala Studies in Ancient Mediterranean and Near Eastern Civilizations 11), Uppsala 1974; J. Assmann, 'Death and Initiation in the Funerary Religion of Ancient Egypt', in J.P. Allen – J. Assmann – A.B. Lloyd – R.K. Ritner – D.P. Silverman (eds.), *Religion and Philosophy in Ancient Egypt* (YES 3), New Haven 1989, p. 136; J.P. Allen, 'The Cosmology of the Pyramid Texts', in J.P. Allen – J. Assmann – A.B. Lloyd – R.K. Ritner – D.P. Silverman (eds.), *Religion and Philosophy in Ancient Egypt* (YES 3), New Haven 1989, p. 20; K. Jansen-Winkeln, ''Horizont' und 'Verklärheit': Zur Bedeutung der Wurzel *ꜣḫ*', *SAK* 23 (1996), pp. 201-215; Bell, in H. Beinlich – J. Hallof – H. Hussy – C. von Pfeil (eds.), *5. Ägyptologische Tempeltagung*, pp. 38-42; Janák, *Staroegyptská Kniha mrtvých*, pp. 27-29; J. Janák, 'Migratory Spirits. Remarks on the Akh Sign', in M. Cannata (ed.), *Current Research in Egyptology 2006*, Oxford 2007, pp. 116-119 and Janák, *Staroegyptské náboženství*, pp. 238-250.

[290] For various previous translations of PT 78, consult Faulkner, *Pyramid Texts*, p. 19; Bresciani – Pernigotti – Giangeri-Silvis, *Ciennehebu*, p. 34, and Allen, *Pyramid Texts*, p. 22.

[291] For various previous translations of PT 81, consult Faulkner, *Pyramid Texts*, p. 19; Bresciani – Pernigotti – Giangeri-Silvis, *Ciennehebu*, p. 34, and Allen, *Pyramid Texts*, p. 22.

[292] Wb V, p. 231: 'Name der Stadt der Weberei in Unter-ägypten'. This may be a reference to Sais and the temple domain of Neith in Sais. On the association of Tayt and linen with Sais, see already footnote 275.

[293] A name for the red crown of Lower Egypt – Abubakr, *die ägyptischen Kronen*, p. 54

[294] For various previous translations of PT 25, consult Faulkner, *Pyramid Texts*, pp. 4-5; Bresciani – Pernigotti – Giangeri-Silvis, *Ciennehebu*, p. 39, and Allen, *Pyramid Texts*, pp. 19 and 28.

[295] On this reading, see Bareš, *Abusir IV*, p. 53, n. 286.

[296] Wb III, p. 306, and E. Brunner-Traut, 'Chenti-irti', in W. Helck – E. Otto (eds.), *Lexikon der Ägyptologie I*, Wiesbaden 1975, pp. 926-930: The falcon-headed god of Letopolis.

8. *mnḫ.t*	Linen
9. *pꜣḏ*	*pꜣḏ*-cake
10. *mnḏ.ty*	*mnḏ.ty*-feathers
11. *nṯry*	Natron

The frieze at the bottom of the west wall contains the seven sacred oils (no. 1-7),[297] linen (no. 8), a cake (no. 9), feathers (no. 10), and natron (no. 11). Similar but more extensive friezes, which almost always include the black and green eye paints[298] and sometimes a larger variety of linen, are also found at the head of the deceased in the tombs of Amuntefnakht (west wall), Hekaemsaf (west wall), Padinese (north wall), Tjannehebu (north wall), Psamtek 'the physician' (north wall), and Padineith (north wall), while in the tomb of Hor a similar frieze is located at the feet of the deceased (east wall).[299]

The utterances and frieze with objects on Padihor's west wall provide the deceased with ointments, linen and censing as a means or instruments for reaching the afterlife. The combination of unguents, linen and censing on the rear wall of the tomb reflects a long tradition – a similar combination of offerings was used in a large variety of cultic activities that resulted in regeneration and rejuvenation. These activities were not limited to the funerary sphere; they occur also in the temple (whether during the daily temple ritual when the statue was awoken anew[300] or during the preparation of the statues of the gods in the *wabet* for their rejuvenation at the time of the New Year and on other occasions throughout the year)[301] and in the renewal of kingship (whether during the sed-festival of the king[302] or during the renewal of the kingship of the gods in Ptolemaic and Roman temples).[303] The preparatory rites, which the pharaoh, the statues of the deities or the deceased underwent before the actual act of renewal or rejuvenation took place, all involved a very similar set of clothing rites: the presentation of linen, unguents and ointments that represented the idea of renewal and, at times, also the presentation of a set of amulets to provide protection in a weakened state or condition. Anointed and clothed, the deceased was ready to join the gods - a theme eloquently expressed on the ceiling of Padihor's burial chamber.

---

[297] E.V. Pischikova, 'Representations of Ritual and Symbolic Objects in Late XXVth Dynasty and Saite Private Tombs', *JARCE* 31 (1994), pp. 63-77; Y. Harpur, *Decoration in Egyptian Tombs of the Old Kingdom: Studies in Orientation and Scene Content*, London-New York 1987, pp. 24-25; 28-30; 63-64; 75, and 119, and J. Bourriau, 'Salbgefässe', in W. Helck – E. Otto (eds.), *Lexikon der Ägyptologie V*, Wiesbaden 1984, pp. 362-366. See also Barta, *Die altägyptische Opferliste*, pp. 90-91; S. Tawfik, 'Die Alabasterpaletten für die sieben Salböle im Alten Reich', *GM* 30 (1978), pp. 77-87; B. Vachala, 'Neue Salbölpaletten aus Abusir', *ZÄS* 108 (1981), pp. 61-67; B. Vachala, 'Neue Salbölpaletten aus Abusir – Addendum', *ZÄS* 109 (1982), p. 171 and M. Verner – Callender, V.G., *Djedkare's Family Cemetery (Abusir VI)*, Prague 2002, pp. 33-34. On the use of these oils in the ritual of 'the opening of the mouth', see Otto, *Das ägyptische Mundöffnungsritual*, pp. 121-122.

[298] PT 79, dealing with the green and black eye paint, is missing on Padihor's west wall, but is usually included in the inscriptions at the head of the deceased – see Hussein, *Saite Pyramid Text Copies*, p. 98-99.

[299] Maspero, *ASAE* 1 (1900), pp. 180; 251 and 253; Maspero, *ASAE* 2 (1901), pp. 109-110; Maspero, *ASAE* 5 (1904), p. 79; Drioton, *ASAE* 52 (1954), pp. 112 and 123, and Bresciani – Pernigotti – Giangeri-Silvis, *Ciennehebu*, plates VIII-IX.

[300] F. Coppens, *The Wabet. Tradition and Innovation in Temples of the Ptolemaic and Roman Period*, Prague 2007, pp. 207-208.

[301] Coppens, *The Wabet*, and F. Coppens, 'Linen, Unguents and Pectorals. Instruments of Regeneration in Ptolemaic and Roman Temples', in M. Dolinska – H. Beinlich (eds.), *8th Egyptological Tempeltagung. Interconnections between Temples*, (Königtum, Staat und Gesellschaft Früher Hochkulturen 3/3), Wiesbaden (in press).

[302] U. Rummel, 'Weihrauch, Salböl und Leinen. Balsamierungsmaterialien als Medium der Erneuerung im Sedfest', *SAK* 34 (2006), pp. 381–407.

[303] Coppens, *The Wabet*, pp. 154-155, and 208; F. Coppens – H. Vymazalová, 'Long Live the King! Notes on the Renewal of Divine Kingship in the Temple', in L. Bareš – F. Coppens – K. Smoláriková (eds.), *Social and Religious Development of Egypt in the First Millennium BCE*, Prague 2010 (in press).

1.3.6. The ceiling: PT 249, 251, 252 and 422 (Fig. 13)

In the centre of the ceiling of the burial chamber three text columns have been engraved. The text runs from north to south and from west to east. The text columns are 240 cm long and the entire text was about 24-25 cm wide, meaning each column was ca. 7.5-8.0 cm wide on average. The three text columns were separated from one another by lines in red ink, traces of which can still be observed on the ceiling. The columns of text combine four passages from various utterances of the Pyramid Texts: the final passage of utterance 249 (§266),[304] the first part of utterances 251 (§269) and 252 (§272) and the very end of utterance 422 (§764).

The occurrence of columns of text on the ceiling of a burial chamber is not very common in Late Period large shaft tombs. The ceiling is often left undecorated, or at most provided with the portrayal of a starry sky or painted blue to represent heaven.[305] The burial chamber of Menekhibnekau, one of Padihor's neighbours and contemporaries in Abusir, is a rare exception. It also features three text columns in the very centre of the ceiling (BD 100 and another short but as yet unidentified passage), surrounded by a starry sky and depictions of the tomb owner in adoration before the solar barque.[306]

The same passage of PT utterance 249 (§266), the central column on Padihor's ceiling, is found regularly in other large Late Period shaft tombs, but there it is almost always engraved in the middle of the lid of the monumental rectangular sarcophagus. This is the case on the sarcophagi of Amuntefnakht, Hor, Udjahor, Neferibra-sa-Neith, Tjannehebu and Psamtek 'the physician' in Saqqara,[307] Pakap in Giza,[308] and also Udjahormehnet in Heliopolis.[309] The same text passage also features on the outside of the lid of the wooden coffin of Nekau, interred in a small burial chamber in the west wall of the west subsidiary shaft of Iufaa's burial complex in Abusir.[310] It also occurs on the top of the vaulted roof on the outside of the burial chamber of Hor.[311] It has been suggested that a shroud discovered on the top of the monumental sarcophagus of Tjannehebu contained this passage of PT utterance 249, together with passages of PT utterances 422 (§753-754) and 468 (§894-895), but this seems to refer to the aforementioned inscription on the monumental sarcophagus of Tjannehebu instead.[312] The final passage of utterance 422 (§764) features at the very end of the third text column on Padihor's ceiling.

---

304 See also BD 147.

305 For instance: the ceiling of the tombs of Psamtek 'the physician' (Barsanti, *ASAE* 1 (1900), pp. 163-165); Padinese (Barsanti, *ASAE* 1 (1900), pp. 321-322), and Padineith (Barsanti, *ASAE* 2 (1901), p. 98).

306 Bareš – Janák – Landgráfová – Smoláriková, *ZÄS* 135 (2008), pp. 106-107.

307 Barsanti, *ASAE* 1 (1900), p. 163 (Psamtek 'the physician'); Barsanti, *ASAE* 1 (1900), pp. 267-268 (Tjannehebu); Barsanti, *ASAE* 3 (1902), p. 210 (Udjahor); Saad, *ASAE* 41 (1941), p. 391 (Hor); Saad, *ASAE* 41 (1941), p. 385; Drioton, *ASAE* 52 (1954), p. 105 (Amuntefnakht), and Drioton, *ASAE* 51 (1951), p. 485 (Neferibra-sa-Neith). The occurrence of this specific PT utterance is not noted in Stammers, *Elite Late Period Egyptian Tombs*, p. 175 (overview of funerary texts in Late Period tombs in the greater Memphite area) although he does mention the text on p. 130 (without identifying it as PT 249).

308 el-Sadeek, *Twenty-Sixth Dynasty Necropolis at Gizah*, pp. 130-131. The same text also occurred on a large block that covered Pakap's sarcophagus.

309 Bickel – Tallet, *BIFAO* 97 (1997), p. 90, fig. 7. PT utterance 249 (§266) is not mentioned in the article, but it is clearly visible on the photograph of the anthropoid sarcophagus. See also Stammers, *Elite Late Period Tombs*, pp. 126 and 142 for more information on the tomb.

310 Bareš – Smoláriková, *Abusir XVII*, pp. 120-121 (fig. 37).

311 Saad, *ASAE* 41 (1941), p. 393; Drioton, *ASAE* 52 (1954), p. 122, and Bresciani – Pernigotti – Giangeri-Silvis, *Ciennehebu*, p. 20.

312 PM III^2, p. 648; Allen, *Occurrences of Pyramid Texts*, p. 72, and Gestermann, *Sargtexte in spätzeitlichen Grabanlagen*, pp. 77 and 372. The text of Barsanti, *ASAE* 1 (1900), p. 267 however states that 'sous l'étoffe, une large bande d'hiéroglyphes apparaissait, gravée, en trois lignes, sur toute la longueur du corps, du Nord au Sud, c'est-à-dire de la tête aux pieds' – a clear reference to the three columns engraved on the lid of the sarcophagus. Barsanti does not mention that the shroud was inscribed. See also Bresciani – Pernigotti – Giangeri-Silvis, *Ciennehebu*, pp. 45-46 for a similar opinion.

Fig. 13
The ceiling of the burial chamber

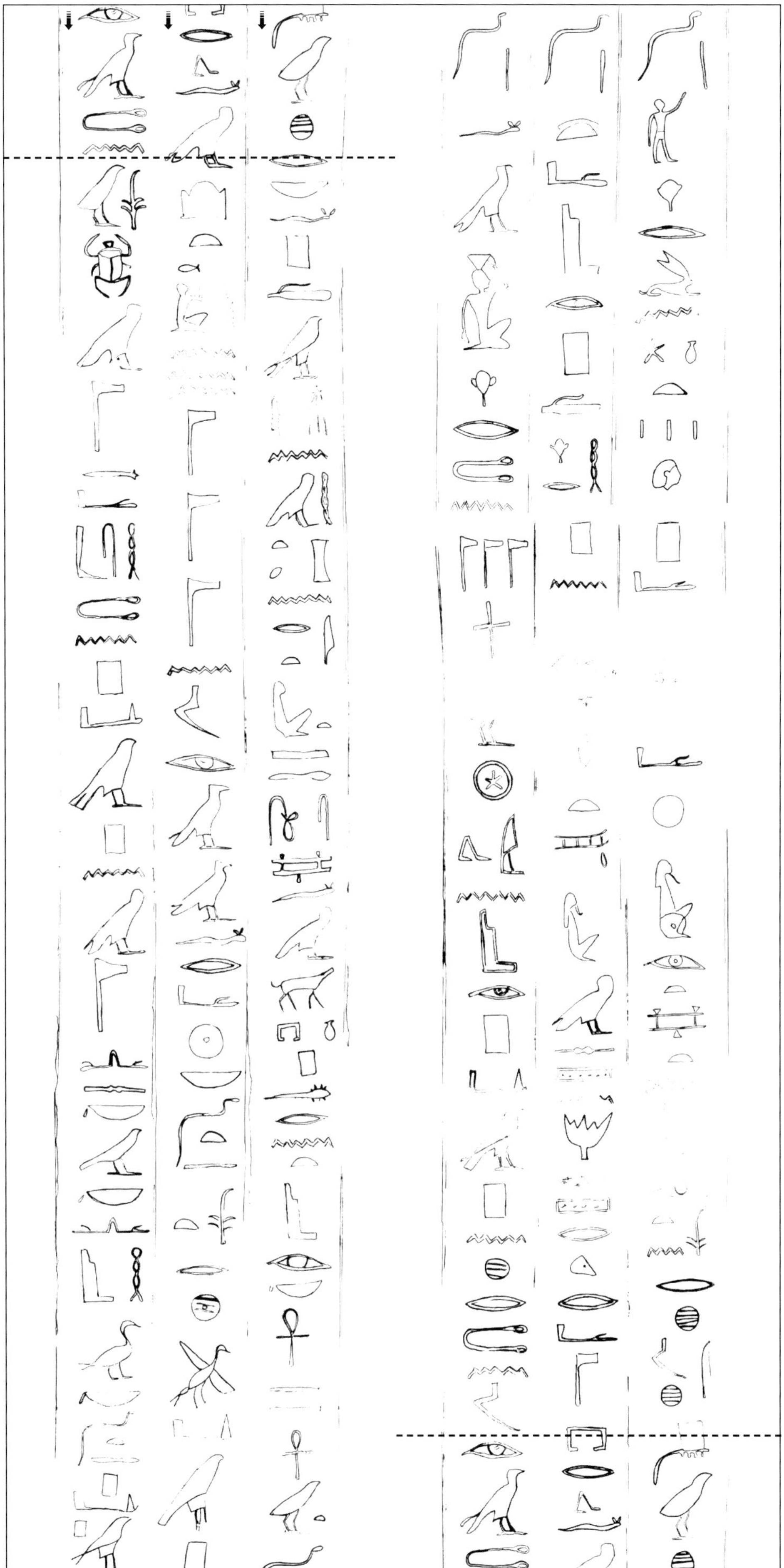

The absence of a monumental sarcophagus in Padihor's burial chamber might have led the editors and composers of the textual programme to place the text (PT 249) onto the ceiling in combination with two other texts from the same general context of the Pyramid Text corpus (PT 251 and 252).

a) PT 251 (§269): (1) *ḏd-mdw i ḥry wnwt tp-ˁ.w Rˁ*[313] *ir wꜣ.t n Wsir rḫ nswt imꜣḫw ḫr nb=f Pꜣ-di-ḥr ms n Ndm-Bꜣst.t-n-ir.t mꜣˁ-ḫrw swꜣ=f m-ḫnw pḫr n.t Wsir nb ˁnḫ-tꜣ.wy ˁnḫ tw ḏ.t*

b) PT 249 (§266): (2) *ḏd-mdw ḫˁ Wsir Pꜣ-di-ḥr pn m Nfrtm m sšn r šrt Rˁ pr=f m ꜣḫ.t wˁb nṯr.w n mꜣꜣ=f rˁ nb ḏ.t*[314] *rḫ nswt Pꜣ-di-ḥr pn*

c) PT 252 (§272): (3) *ḏd-mdw fꜣ hr.w=ṯn nṯr.w imyw dwꜣ.t iy.n Wsir Pꜣ-di-ḥr pn ḫr=ṯn mꜣꜣ=ṯn sw ḫpr m nṯr ˁꜣ ḥbs=ṯn Pꜣ-di-ḥr pn m nṯr*

d) PT 422 (§764): *n sk=k n ḥtm*[315]*=k ḏ.t Pꜣ-di-ḥr pn*

a) PT 251 (§269):[316] (1) Recitation: Oh the one that is on top of the 'hour'-stars[317] that precede the sun, make way for the Osiris, the king's acquaintance,[318] the *imꜣḫw* near his lord, Padihor, born of Nedjem-bastet-en-iret, justified, that he may pass within the circuit of Osiris, lord of Anchtawy, living forever.[319]

b) PT 249 (§266):[320] (2) Recitation: This Osiris Padihor will appear as Nefertem, as/on the lotus at the nose of Ra when he emerges from the horizon, at whose sight the gods will become purified, daily and forever – the king's acquaintance, this Padihor.

c) PT 252 (§272):[321] (3) Recitation: Lift your face, gods who are in the Duat: this Osiris Padihor has come towards you, that you may see him having become the great god. May you clothe this Padihor as a god![322]

d) PT 422 (§764):[323] You shall not perish; you shall not come to an end forever, this Padihor.

The texts on the ceiling represent the last phase in the textual programme engraved on the walls of the burial chamber. The inscriptions – copies of passages of four different Pyramid Texts utterances – all deal with the rejuvenation and resurrection of Padihor, his ascension into heaven and his transformation into a god: the ultimate result of a perfect performance of all rituals and of the textural programme applied to the walls of the burial chamber.[324] The usual location of these texts, in particular the passage from PT utterance 249 (§266), in the centre of the lid of the monumental sarcophagus in other contemporary shaft tombs, was moved to the ceiling in Padihor's burial chamber, which was never meant to house such a monumental sarcophagus.

---

313 The determinative of the god was engraved above a sun disc, traces of which are still visible.

314 *ḏ.t* does not figure in the other known examples of this text. In all other texts this passage ends with *rˁ nb* or 'daily'.

315 See Wb III, 197 for this particular writing.

316 For various previous translations of PT 251, consult Faulkner, *Pyramid Texts*, p. 62, and Allen, *Pyramid Texts*, pp. 42-43.

317 See Willems, *The Coffin of Heqata*, p. 184.

318 On this title see already Chapter 1.2.2 in this volume.

319 The end of the text represents a variation on PT utterance 251 (§269) where the deceased is admitted into the circle of 'Belligerent-Face' or *ˁḥꜣw–ḥr* (an epithet of the sun according to Allen, *Pyramid Texts*, p. 427) instead of Osiris.

320 For various previous translations of PT 249, consult Faulkner, *Pyramid Texts*, pp. 60-61, and Allen, *Pyramid Texts*, p. 42.

321 For various previous translations of PT 252, consult Faulkner, *Pyramid Texts*, p. 62, and Allen, *Pyramid Texts*, p. 43.

322 A variation on the more commonly found passage: *ḏbꜣ N* or 'N is robed'.

323 For various previous translations of PT 422, consult Faulkner, *Pyramid Texts*, pp. 139-140, and Allen, *Pyramid Texts*, pp. 100-101. This passage is usually preceded by *ˁnḫ rn=k tp tꜣ nḥḥ rn=k tp tꜣ* or 'may your name live upon earth, may your name endure upon earth'.

324 On the ascension aspect in the Pyramid Texts, consult Davis, *JNES* 36/3 (1977), pp. 161-179.

The exclusive occurrence of the falcon or Horus-hieroglyph in the writing of the name of Padihor on the ceiling might be related to the contents of these texts: the ascension of the deceased into heaven.[325] Other passages from the Pyramid Texts corpus refer to the king taking on the shape of various birds and using this shape to ascend into heaven. Next to a variety of birds such as herons, swallows or geese[326] it is of course the guise of the falcon, the symbol of kingship and the representation of Horus, which is the most preferred form for the pharaoh to take.[327] The recurring presence of the falcon or Horus-hieroglyph exclusively in the writing of Padihor's name on the ceiling could well be a reference to this ascension-aspect of the texts and suggest that Padihor had successfully reached the afterlife.

1.3.7. Proofreading in the burial chamber of Padihor[328]

One of the most remarkable features of the inscriptions on the walls of Padihor's burial chamber is that a number of signs have been corrected or accentuated in black ink after all the texts had been engraved (Pl. 7a-d). This must have been done after all the walls of the burial chamber had been engraved with texts but still before the actual burial took place.[329] The additions in black ink can be observed on all four walls and fall into two distinct groups: the accentuation of several signs whose engraving had been poorly executed or was completely absent, and the correction of (mostly) wrongly engraved signs (see the overview in Table III).

The following additions and corrections in black ink could be observed on the walls of the burial chamber:

- East wall, column 7: the determinative of the word *sẖn* in the offering list originally written as a piece of meat (a flat F51?) or a rib (F42?) was amended to low and very broad bread (X4?) (Fig. 9, Pl. 7a).

- East wall, column 7: the uniliteral sign *r* (D21) was altered into the sign of the mouth from which corn sprouts forth (D154) for the expression *iʿw-rꜣ*. To the accompanying vertical stroke (Z1) below the signs *sn* (T22) and *ḥr* (D2) were added, while further below another sign resembling the viper *f* (I9) but facing in the opposite direction was written in black ink, apparently to create the expression *fꜣj šns* in the offering list (Fig. 9, Pl. 7a).

- East wall, column 9: the outline of a hand, the uniliteral sign *d* (D46), was added in black ink below the engraved uniliteral signs *s* (S29) and *m* (G17), forming the word *msdmt* in the offering list (Fig. 9).

- North wall, column 22: the biliteral *mr*-sign (U6) was drawn twice in black ink – first with its point to the east, then to the west – over the last *nṯr*-sign (R8) in a group of three *nṯr.w*-signs, while a new *nṯr*-sign was added in black ink immediately to the west of the engraved *nṯr*-sign (Fig. 10, Pl. 7b). The reason behind this correction in PT 269 is unclear since it was unnecessary.

- South wall, column 5: the engraved uniliteral sign *p* (Q3) was changed to the correct sign of the butcher's block (T28) in the word *ẖꜣsw* in CT 151 (Fig. 11).

- West wall, column 3: the sign of the Horus falcon (G5) was changed to the correct sign of the vulture (G1) in the verb *mꜣꜣ* in PT 77 (Fig. 12, Pl. 7c).

- West wall, columns 4 (twice), 5 (twice) and 6: the erroneous combination of the sign of the embracing arms (D32) and the uniliteral sign *s* (S29) was corrected by

[325] See already Chapter 1.2.1 in this volume.

[326] See for instance: PT utterances 467 (§891); 519 (§1216); 521 (§1225); 626 (§1770), and 682 (§2042).

[327] See for instance: PT utterances 467 (§891); 488 (§1048-1049); 626 (§1770), and 682 (§2042).

[328] For a detailed study of various examples of proofreading on the walls of the tombs in the Saite-Persian necropolis at Abusir, see already Bareš, in Régen – Servajean, *Verba Manent*.

[329] Besides possible religious objections to this being done after the burial, there would not have been enough place to do this in Padihor's small burial chamber after the coffin and funerary equipment had been installed. In most cases the amount of time between the finishing of the decoration of the burial chamber and the burial can hardly be estimated. The burial chamber of Iufaa, though unfinished, appears to have been left open for several months according to Bareš – Smoláriková – Strouhal, *ZÄS* 132 (2005), p. 103, n. 42.

Table III.
Overview of the corrections and accentuations of the engraved texts in black ink

Wall	Column	Original engraving	Correction (black ink)
East	7	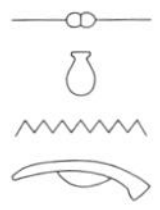	
East	7		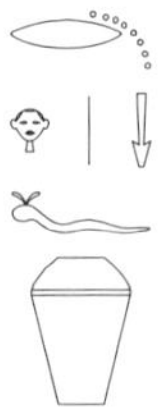 for 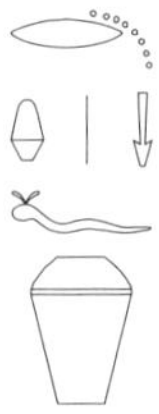
East	9		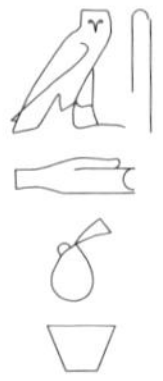
North	22	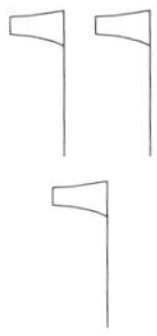	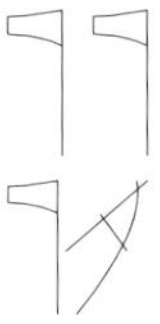 and 
South	5	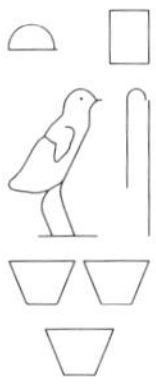	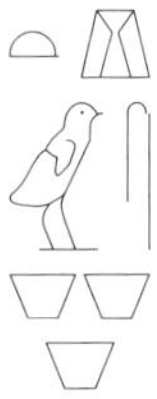
West	3	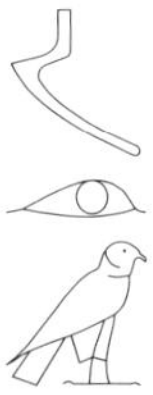	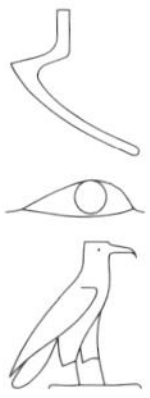
West	4 (twice), 5 (twice), 6	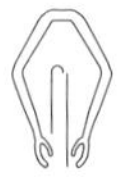	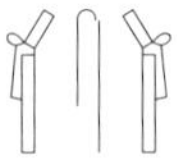
West	6		
West	8	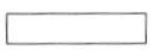	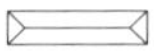
West	8		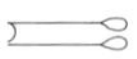

adding twice the sign T13 symmetrically on both sides of the *s*-sign, thus forming the verb *rs* in PT 81 (Fig. 12, Pl. 7c-d).

- West wall, column 6: the poorly engraved hieroglyph of the owl (uniliteral sign *m* or G17) was accentuated in black ink in PT 81 (Fig. 12, Pl. 7d).

- West wall, column 8: a central stroke was added in black ink in the uniliteral *š*-sign (N37 to N38) in PT 81 (Fig. 12).

- West wall, column 8: the poorly engraved hieroglyph of the rope (uniliteral sign *t* or V13) was accentuated in black ink in PT 81 (Fig. 12).

A number of these corrections and additions could have been done in the relief itself since some of the changes could have made use of the already existing hieroglyphs. Covering the incorrect part with fine mortar and cutting new hieroglyphs was another possibility. All observed corrections within the burial chambers of the Saite-Persian cemetery at Abusir appear, however, to have been carried out in black ink. A similar practice has already been observed in the inscriptions in the nearby tombs of Udjahorresnet[330] and Iufaa. According to Ladislav Bareš it seems that these corrections were carried out by one and the same (group of) person(s) who functioned in the same manner as proofreaders in modern times.[331] It is impossible to ascertain whether the individual who designed the textual programme for the walls of the burial chambers and outlined the draft of the inscriptions and the individual who later on made the corrections in black ink were one and the same person.

1.3.8. Conclusion

The textual programme designed for the walls and ceiling of Padihor's burial chamber consists of a compact but at the same time exhaustive set of inscriptions (excerpts from various passages of the Pyramid Texts and Coffin Texts) that provided the deceased with the necessary means to ascend into heaven and secure his rightful place in the afterlife. The limited amount of space available on the walls of the burial chamber – the smallest burial chamber in a large shaft tomb to be excavated to this day (table I) – undoubtedly influenced its designer(s)' decisions about which text passages to include. It resulted for example in the reduction of the offering list on the east wall[332] and the abbreviation of several texts.[333] The entirety of Padihor's textual programme conforms to the standards and schemes found in a number of Twenty-Sixth Dynasty tombs, but at the same time it also shows an amount of originality in the choice of certain texts and their location within the burial chamber.

The choice of texts and their specific location on the walls and ceiling of Padihor's chamber are in many ways similar to the textual programme applied to the walls of the chambers of several large middle to late Twenty-Sixth Dynasty shaft tombs in Saqqara, specifically the burial complexes of Amuntefnakht, Tjannehebu, Padinese, Psamtek 'the physician', and Padineith and to a lesser degree Hekaemsaf (Table IV). All these tombs are located within and around the pyramid complex of Unas. The detailed study of the orthography and grammar of Padihor's inscriptions and comparison with the same texts in other burial chambers[334] clearly indicates that Padihor's texts were not copied from a specific tomb,[335] but rather that these burial complexes shared a preference for a certain type of texts in a certain combination and in a specific location on the walls of the burial chamber. The general pattern, found in the other tombs, is interrupted in Padihor's burial chamber by the inclusion of texts not found in large Late Period shaft tombs (such as PT 268 on the north wall). The relocation of PT 249, originally located in the very centre of the monumental sarcophagus in several burial chambers (table IV), to the ceiling of Padihor's chamber which never housed a monumental sarcophagus, and its combination with the thematically similar PT spells 251 and 252 document the originality of Padihor's textual programme.[336]

---

330 Bareš, *Abusir IV*, pp. 51-61: corrections in black of the inscriptions written in red ink.

331 Bareš, in Régen – Servajean, *Verba Manent*. See also W.J. Tait, 'Exuberance and Accessibility: Notes on Written Demotic and the Egyptian Scribal Tradition', in: T. Gagos – R.S. Bagnall (eds.), *Essays and Texts in Honor of J. David Thomas*, (American Studies in Papyrology 42), 2001, pp. 31-39 on literacy in ancient Egypt.

332 The typical tabular offering list was broken up into 12 text columns, containing less than half the number of offerings found in the lists in other shaft tombs (see Chapter 1.3.2).

333 For instance the final passage of PT utterance 269 (§381-382) was not copied on the north wall of Padihor's burial chamber, while it does feature on the walls of the other, larger burial chambers (see Chapter 1.3.3).

334 The information is contained in the many footnotes in this chapter.

335 Gestermann's study of the various CT spells that occur in Late Period tombs also indicated that no single source could be established for these texts – Gestermann, *Sargtexte in spätzeitlichen Grabanlagen*, pp. 408-447.

336 PT 251 and 252, like PT 268, do not feature on the walls of a single presently known Late Period large shaft tomb (see Chapters 1.3.3 and 1.3.6).

Table IV. Overview of the inscriptions in Padihor's burial chamber and in other Late Period monumental shaft tombs.

Padihor's Burial Chamber			Late Period Shaft Tombs		
Body	**Wall**	**Text**	**Body**	**Wall**	**Tomb**
Head	West	PT 25	Head	West North	Hekaemsaf Padinese
			Right	West South	Padineith, Tjannehebu, Psamtek 'the physician' and Padinese Amuntefnakht
			Left	North	Psamtek 'the treasurer' and Udjahorresnet
		PT 77	Head	West North	Amuntefnakht and Hekaemsaf Padineith, Tjannehebu, Psamtek 'the physician' and Padinese
			Foot Left	East North	Hor Psamtek 'the treasurer'
		PT 78	Head	West North	Amuntefnakht Padineith, Tjannehebu, Psamtek 'the physician' and Padinese
			Foot Left	East North	Hor Psamtek 'the treasurer'
		PT 81	Head	West North	Amuntefnakht and Hekaemsaf Padineith, Tjannehebu, Psamtek 'the physician' and Padinese
			Foot Left	East North	Hor Psamtek 'the treasurer'
Foot	East	Offering list	Foot Right	East East West South	Udjahorresnet Padinese Tjannehebu, Psamtek 'the physician' and Padineith Amuntefnakht, Hor and Hekaemsaf,
Left	North	PT 268	—	—	—
		PT 269	Left	North East	Amuntefnakht Padineith, Tjannehebu and Psamtek 'the physician'
Right	South	CT 151-625	Right Feet Head	North South East West	Amuntefnakht Padinese and Tjannehebu Neferibra-sa-Neith Psamtek 'the treasurer'
		CT 208	Left Feet	South South East	Amuntefnakht Padinese Neferibra-sa-Neith
		CT 716	Right Left Feet	East South South East	Tjannehebu Amuntefnakht Padinese Neferibra-sa-Neith
		CT 352	Feet	South East	Padinese Neferibra-sa-Neith and Psamtek 'the treasurer'
Above	Ceiling	PT 249	Above	Ceiling Sarco-phagus	Hor (on the outside of the burial chamber) Amuntefnakht, Hor, Udjahor, Neferibra-sa-Neith, Tjannehebu, Psamtek 'the physician', Pakap and Nekau (in the centre of the lid)
		PT 251	—	—	—
		PT 252	—	—	—
		PT 422	—	—	—

The various inscriptions engraved on the walls of Padihor's burial chamber bear strong similarities not only to the textual corpus found on the walls of several burial chambers in and around the pyramid complex of Unas in Saqqara, but also to a particular monument found in Abusir: the inner basalt sarcophagus of Iufaa. The presence of PT 25 and 269 on its north exterior side, PT 81 on its bottom (outside), and the CT sequence 151-625-208-716 and CT 352 on its south exterior side seem to suggest as much. Although some of these texts feature also on the walls of Iufaa's burial chamber and monumental rectangular sarcophagus, one has the impression that the typical textual programme, found on the walls of the aforementioned burial chambers in Saqqara and in Padihor's tomb, was engraved mainly on Iufaa's inner sarcophagus, whose detailed study is still a work in progress. By engraving the text on the inner sarcophagus, the priest(s) (possibly even Iufaa himself) who designed the textual and decorative programme managed to free up parts of the walls of the burial chamber for the inclusion of a series of inscriptions not attested in any other large shaft tomb of the Twenty-Sixth and early Twenty-Seventh Dynasty. The textual corpus on the walls of Padihor's burial chamber in general followed well-established patterns, but its designer did not shy away from introducing his own bit of originality, either.

1.4. Finds

1.4.1. The shabtis of Padihor[337]

The only[338] reasonably preserved remains of the burial equipment of Padihor consist of a set of at least a dozen shabtis discovered during the clearance of the area to the north of the north-west corner of the main shaft (excavation nos. 99/R/01 and 131/R/01a, bottom part), in the heap of sand that sloped down from the entrance into the burial chamber, and scattered in the burial chamber itself (excavation nos. 131/R/01a-o). No trace of a shabti container came to light during the excavation of the burial complex. The recovered set consists of five almost completely preserved shabtis, fragments of the legs and feet of seven shabtis and fragments of the head (sometimes with a part of the body) of four shabtis (Pl. 8a). Due to the absence of joints between some of the fragments of the feet and legs on the one hand and the head (and body) on the other, it is impossible to ascertain whether some of the fragments come from one and the same piece.[339] A minimal count suggests that at least a dozen shabtis survived the robbery of the tomb, although the number might have been as high as 16. The total height of the shabtis, based on the five almost completely preserved statuettes, varies between 11.8 and 13.8 cm, while the width ranges from 3.2 to 3.8 cm. All fragments were produced in the so-called 'Egyptian' faience,[340] with the glaze ranging from light blue-green to light green – the typical glaze of most shabtis discovered in the Abusir shaft tomb necropolis.[341]

All fragments and statuettes portray a similar shabti figure: Osirian or mummiform in shape, with a lappet or tripartite wig, long plaited beard, the hands crossed on the chest with the right hand over the left one, and with a hoe in the right hand and a pick in the left hand. A bag, held in the right hand, is slung over the left shoulder. The shabti also had an inscribed dorsal pillar and a pedestal in a trapezoidal shape.[342] A single

[337] On these shabtis consult also Bareš – Dvořák – Smoláriková – Strouhal, *ZÄS* 129 (2002), p. 105; Bareš, in Györy (ed.), *'Le lotus qui sort de la terre'*, pp. 23–28, and Bareš – Smoláriková, *Abusir XVII*, pp. 231 and 234.

[338] On the bottom of a blue-green faience scarab the name *P3-di-Ḥr-(n-)p* is inscribed. It was discovered near the opening of the small access shaft to the east of the enclosure wall of the tomb of Udjahorresnet and it was probably also part of Padihor's burial equipment. The thieves that robbed Padihor's tomb might have lost it when exiting the Abusir necropolis. On this scarab consult Bareš, *Abusir IV*, pp. 68 (excav. no. 97/H/89), 71 (fig. 2 – for the location of the small shaft) and plate 14, fig 50. See already p. 41 in this volume.

[339] Whenever possible the shabtis were joined together again. This work was carried out by Martin Dvořák, restorer of the Czech archaeological mission at Abusir.

[340] In general: P.T. Nicholson – E. Peltenburg, 'Egyptian Faience', in P.T. Nicholson – I. Shaw (eds.), *Ancient Egyptian Materials and Technology*, Cambridge 2000, pp. 177-194 and P.T. Nicholson, 'Faience Technology', in W. Wendrich (ed.), *UCLA Encyclopedia of Egyptology*, Los Angeles 2009 [= http://escholarship.org/uc/item/9cs9x41z].

[341] According to Bareš, in H. Györy (ed.), *'Le lotus qui sort de la terre'*, p. 27.

[342] Similar to types XIA1 ('Saite mummy with dorsal pillar and plain wig') and XIA5 ('mummy with back pillar and wig separated' or the 'late mummy' type) according to H.D. Schneider, *Shabtis. An Introduction to the History of Ancient Egyptian Funerary Statuettes with a Catalogue of the Collection of Shabtis in the National Museum of Antiquities at Leiden* I, (Collections of the National Museum of Antiquities at Leiden 2), Leiden 1977, pp. 225-231.

column of text, in rough hieroglyphic signs, was incised under the glaze on the dorsal pillar, and at times also partly at the rear and the sides of the head (i.e. on the wig). The text always consisted of an abbreviated version of the common shabti spell, often with several of the words corrupted.[343] The basic text found (in fragments) on all Padihor's shabtis reads as follows: *Ꞽr ꞽp tw Wsꞽr Pꜣ-dꞽ-ḥr r ꞽr kꜣwt nbt m ẖrt-nṯr mk wꞽ kꜣ=k* or 'If one counts off the Osiris[344] Padihor to do every work in the 'God's land'; 'here I am' you shall say'.

The main characteristics of the individual shabtis and shabti fragments can be described as follows:

a. Excav. no. 99/R/01 (Fig. 14a, Pl. 8b-a)
Faience, light green-blue glaze
a) fragment of the head: height: 3.5 cm, max. width: 2.6 cm; b) fragment of the body: height: 6.8 cm, max. width: 3.2 cm.

Shabti in Osirian or mummiform shape, with a lappet or tripartite wig, long plaited beard, and remains of a pick at the right shoulder. The two fragments most likely come from a single shabti, which however could not be joined together. They were discovered to the north of the northwest corner of the main shaft of the tomb. A single column of text, in rough hieroglyphic signs, was incised under the glaze on the dorsal pillar. The text starts to the right of the face of the shabti and reads: *ꞽr ꞽp tw Wsꞽr ... kꜣwt nb.t(?) m ẖrt-nṯr mk <wꞽ> kꜣ[=k]* or 'If one counts off the Osiris ... every? work in the 'Gods land'; 'here <I am>' [you] shall say'.

b. Excav. no. 131/R/01a (Fig. 14b, Pl. 8b-b)
Faience, light green-blue glaze
Height: 13.8 cm, max. width: 3.8 cm.

Shabti in Osirian or mummiform shape with a lappet or tripartite wig, long plaited beard, hands crossed on the chest with the right hand over the left one, with traces of a hoe in the right hand, a pick in the left hand and a bag over the left shoulder, with an inscribed dorsal pillar and a pedestal in a trapezoidal shape. The shabti was found in three pieces that could be joined together again. The top two fragments come from the east part of the burial chamber, while the bottom fragment was discovered on the surface near the opening of the main shaft together with the previously discovered shabti. The remarkable difference in the colour of the faience glaze of these fragments is undoubtedly the result of the different conditions in which they were preserved. A single column of a very corrupt text in rough hieroglyphic signs was incised under the glaze on the dorsal pillar. The texts reads: *Wsꞽr Pꜣ-dꞽ-ḥr Wsꞽr Pꜣ-dꞽ-ḥr r ꞽr kꜣwt nbt m ẖrt-nṯr mk <wꞽ> kꜣ=k* or 'Osiris Padihor, (if one counts off) Osiris Padihor to do every work in the 'God's land'; 'here <I am>', you shall say'.

c. Excav. no. 131/R/01b (Fig. 14c, Pl. 8b-c)
Faience, light green-blue glaze
Height: 11.8 cm, max. width: 3.3 cm.

Shabti in Osirian or mummiform shape with a lappet or tripartite wig, long plaited beard, hands crossed on the chest with the right hand over the left one, with a hoe in the right hand, a pick in the left hand and a bag over the left shoulder, with an inscribed dorsal pillar and a pedestal in a trapezoidal shape. The shabti was found broken into two pieces that could be joined together again. A single column of a very corrupt text, in rough hieroglyphic signs, was incised under the glaze on the dorsal pillar. The text reads: *Wsꞽr Pꜣ-dꞽ-ḥr Wsꞽr Pꜣ-dꞽ-ḥr <r> ꞽr kꜣwt nbt*[345] *m <ẖrt-nṯr> mk <wꞽ> kꜣ=k* or 'Osiris Padihor, (if one counts off) Osiris Padihor <to> do every work in <the 'God's land'>; 'here <I am>', you shall say'.

---

343 Shabti spell, version VIIA. See Schneider, *Shabtis* I, pp. 45-61, and 78-158 (development of the spell), and 118-126 (on version VIIA).

344 On the Osiris-title, see Schneider, *Shabtis* I, pp. 134-135.

345 The *nb*-sign (Gardiner V30) is written as *k* (V31).

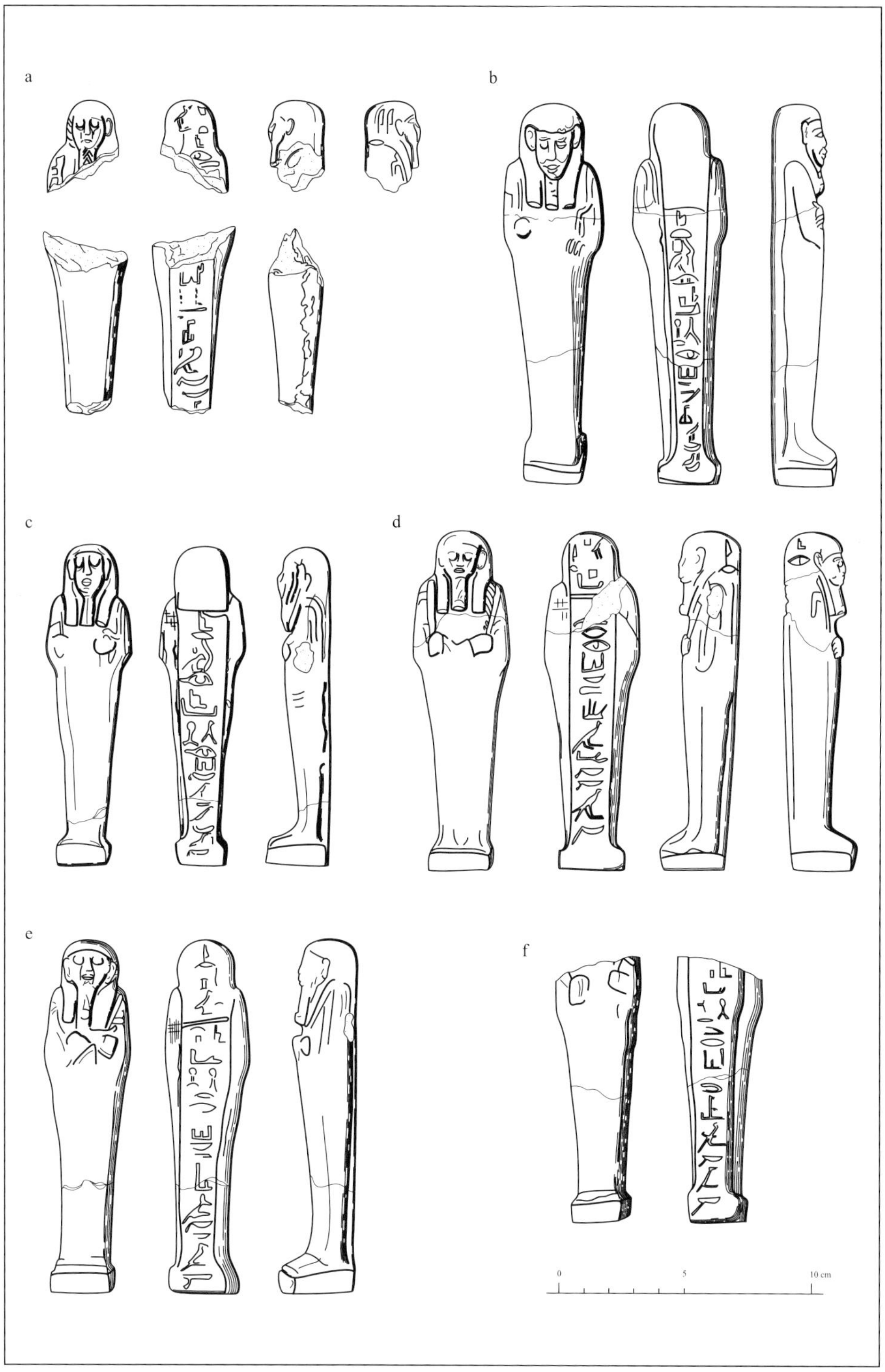

Fig. 14
The shabtis of Padihor

d. Excav. no. 131/R/01c (Fig. 14d, Pl. 8b-d)
Faience, light green-blue glaze
Height: 12.1 cm, max. width: 3.6 cm.

Shabti in Osirian or mummiform shape with a lappet or tripartite wig, long plaited beard, hands crossed on the chest with the right hand over the left one, with a hoe in the right hand, a pick in the left hand and a bag over the left shoulder, with an inscribed dorsal pillar and a pedestal in a trapezoidal shape. The shabti was found broken into three pieces that could be joined together again. A single column of text, in rough hieroglyphic signs, was incised under the glaze on the side of the head and on the dorsal pillar. The text reads: *Ỉr ip tw Wsir Pꜣ-di(-ḥr) r ir kꜣwt nbt m ḫrt-nṯr mk* <*wi*> *kꜣ=k* or 'If one counts off the Osiris Padi(hor) to do every work in the 'God's land'; 'here <I am>', you shall say'.

e. Excav. no. 131/R/01d (Fig. 14e, Pl. 9-a)
Faience, light green-blue glaze
Height: 12.5 cm, max. width: 3.1 cm.

Shabti in Osirian or mummiform shape with a lappet or tripartite wig, long plaited beard, hands crossed on the chest with the right hand over the left one, with a hoe in the right hand, a pick in the left hand and a bag over the left shoulder, with an inscribed dorsal pillar and a pedestal in a trapezoidal shape. The ushabti was found broken into two pieces that could be joined together again. A single column of text, in rough hieroglyphic signs, was incised under the glaze on the dorsal pillar. The text reads: *Ỉr ip tw Wsir Pꜣ-di-ḥr r ir kꜣwt nbt m ẖrt-nṯr mk <wi> kꜣ=k* or 'If one counts off the Osiris Padihor to do every work in the 'God's land'; 'here <I am>', you shall say'.

f. Excav. no. 131/R/01e (Fig. 14f, Pl. 9-b)
Faience, light green-blue glaze
Height of the preserved part: 9.8 cm, max. width: 3.1 cm.

Fragment of a shabti in Osirian or mummiform shape with the head missing. The remaining piece still shows the hands crossed on the chest with the right hand over the left one, with the remains of a hoe in the right hand and the remains of a pick in the left hand, with an inscribed dorsal pillar and a pedestal in a trapezoidal shape. On the dorsal pillar remnants of one column of text in rough hieroglyphic signs was incised under the glaze. The remaining text reads: ... *Wsir Pꜣ-di-ḥr r ir kꜣwt <nbt> m ẖrt-nṯr mk <wi> kꜣ=k* or '(If one counts off) the Osiris Padihor to do <every> work in the 'God's land'; 'here <I am>', you shall say'.

g. Excav. no. 131/R/01f (Fig. 15g, Pl. 9-c)
Faience, light green glaze with a different shade on the respective fragments.
Height of the preserved part: 8.2 cm, max. width: 3.5 cm.

Fragment of the lower half of a shabti in Osirian or mummiform shape with the head and shoulders missing. The remaining piece still shows the hands crossed on the chest, part of the dorsal pillar and the pedestal in a trapezoidal shape. The piece was found broken into two parts that could be joined together again. On the dorsal pillar one column of text in rough hieroglyphic signs was incised under the glaze. The remaining text still reads: ... *mk <wi> kꜣ=k* or '... 'here <I am>', you shall say'.

h. Excav. no. 131/R/01g (Fig. 15h, Pl. 9-d)
Faience, light green glaze.
Height of the preserved part: 5.7 cm, max. width: 2.9 cm.

Fragment of the body of a shabti in Osirian or mummiform shape, with the feet, head and shoulders missing. On the dorsal pillar one column of text in rough hieroglyphic signs was incised under the glaze. The remaining text reads: ... *m ẖrt-nṯr mk <wi> kꜣ<=k>* or '... in the 'God's land'; 'here <I am>', <you> shall say'.

i. Excav. no. 131/R/01h (Fig. 15i)
Faience, light blue-green glaze.
Height of the preserved part: 4.1 cm, max. width: 2.1 cm.

The lower part of the legs of a shabti, presumably in Osirian or mummiform shape, with an inscribed dorsal pillar and a pedestal in a trapezoidal shape. On the dorsal pillar one column of text in rough hieroglyphic signs was incised under the glaze. The remaining text reads: ... *mk <wi> kꜣ=k* or '... 'here <I am>', you shall say'.

j. Excav. no. 131/R/01i (Fig. 15j)
Faience, light blue-green glaze.
Height of the preserved part: 3.2 cm, max. width: 2.0 cm.

The feet of a shabti, presumably in Osirian or mummiform shape, with an inscribed dorsal pillar and a pedestal in a trapezoidal shape. On the dorsal pillar one column of text in rough hieroglyphic signs was incised under the glaze. The remaining text reads: ... *ẖrt-nṯr mk <wi> kꜣ=k* or '... the 'God's land'; 'here <I am>', you shall say'.

Fig. 15
The shabtis of Padihor

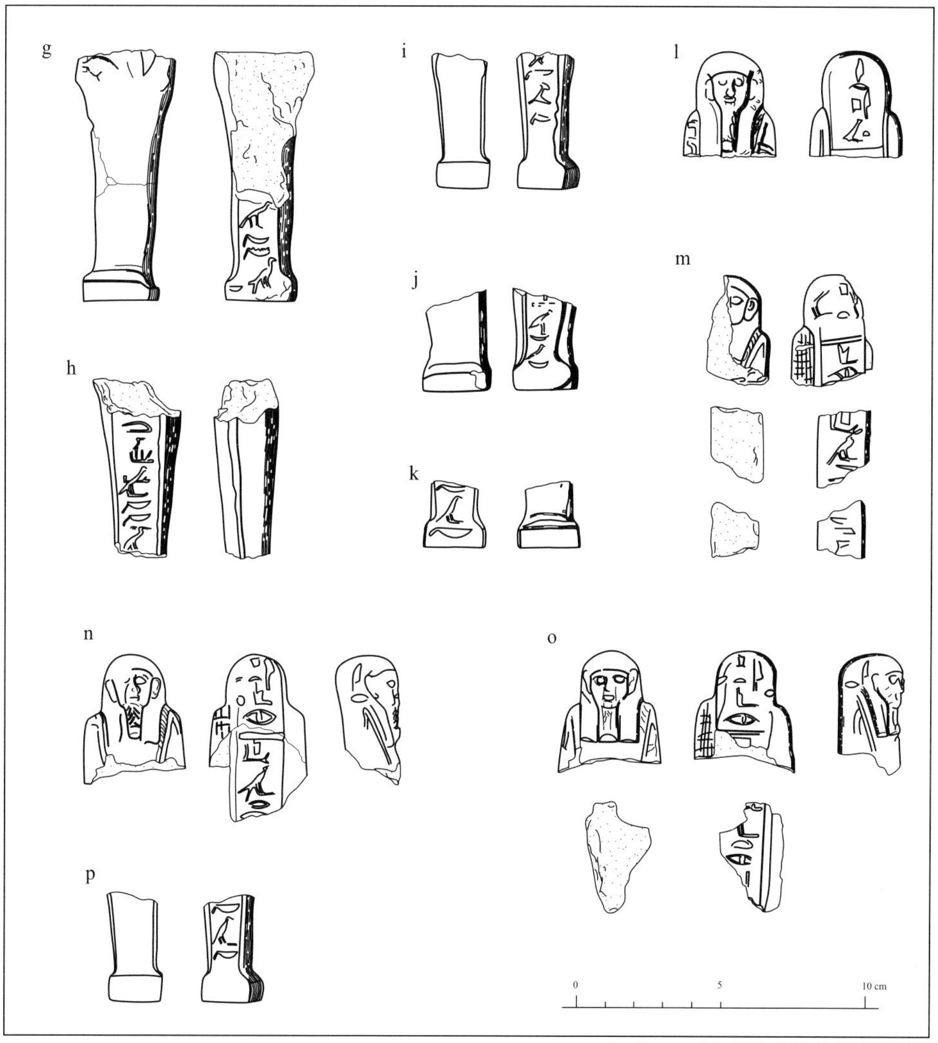

k. Excav. no. 131/R/01j (Fig. 15k)
Faience, light blue-green glaze.
Height of the preserved part: 2.2 cm, max. width: 1.8 cm.

The feet of a shabti, presumably in Osirian or mummiform shape, with an inscribed dorsal pillar and a pedestal in a trapezoidal shape. On the dorsal pillar one column of text in rough hieroglyphic signs was incised under the glaze. The remaining text reads: … *k3=k* or '… you shall say'.

l. Excav. no. 131/R/01k (Fig. 15l, Pl. 9-e)
Faience, light blue-green glaze.
Height of the preserved part: 3.5 cm, max. width: 3.2 cm.

Head of a shabti in Osirian or mummiform shape, with a lappet or tripartite wig, long plaited beard, hands most likely crossed on the chest with the right hand over the left one, with a hoe in the right hand, a pick in the left hand and a bag over the left shoulder. On the rear side of the head a single column of text in rough hieroglyphic signs was incised under the glaze. The remaining text reads: *ir ip tw* … or 'If one counts off…'.

m. Excav. no. 131/R/01l (Fig. 15m, Pl. 9-f)
Faience, light blue-green glaze.
Height of the preserved part: 9.0 cm, max. width: 2.5 cm.

Three fragments of a shabti in Osirian or mummiform shape, with the feet missing. The statuette is dressed with a lappet or tripartite wig and long plaited beard. Its hands are crossed on the chest, it holds a hoe in the right hand and has a bag slung over the left shoulder. A single column of text, in rough hieroglyphic signs, was incised under the glaze on the rear side of the head and on the dorsal pillar. The remaining text reads: (*Ỉr*) *ip tw Wsir Pꜣ-di-ḥr r ir* <*kꜣwt*> *nbt m ḫrt-nṯr* ... or '(If) one counts off the Osiris Padihor to do every <work> in the 'God's land'...'.

n. Excav. no. 131/R/01m (Fig. 15n, Pl. 9-g)
Faience, light green glaze.
Height of the preserved head: 3.7 cm, max. width: 3.2 cm.

The head and part of the body of a shabti in Osirian or mummiform shape, with a lappet or tripartite wig, long plaited beard, hands most likely crossed on the chest with the right hand over the left one, with a hoe in the right hand, a pick in the left hand and a bag over the left shoulder, and an inscribed dorsal pillar. The piece was found broken into two parts that could be joined together again. A single column of text, in rough hieroglyphic signs, was incised under the glaze on the side of the head and on the dorsal pillar. The remaining text reads: *Ỉr ip tw Wsir Pꜣ-di-ḥr r ir* ... or 'If one counts off the Osiris Padihor to do ...'.

o. Excav. no. 131/R/01n (Fig. 15o, Pl. 9-h)
Faience, light blue-green glaze.
Height of the preserved part: 9.8 cm, max. width: 3.1 cm.

The head and body of a shabti in Osirian or mummiform shape, with a lappet or tripartite wig, long plaited beard, hands crossed on the chest, with a hoe in the right hand, a pick in the left hand and a bag slung over the left shoulder, and an inscribed dorsal pillar. The legs of the statuette are missing. The piece was found broken into several pieces that could be partly joined together again. A single column of text, in rough hieroglyphic signs, was incised under the glaze on the side of the head and on the dorsal pillar. The remaining text reads: *Ỉr ip tw Wsir Pꜣ-di-ḥr r ir kꜣwt*... or 'If one counts off the Osiris Padihor to do (every) work...'.

p. Excav. no. 131/R/01o (Fig. 15p)
Faience, light blue-green glaze.
Height of the preserved part: 3.0 cm, max. width: 2.1 cm.

Fragment of the feet of a shabti, most likely in Osirian or mummiform shape, with an inscribed dorsal pillar and a pedestal in a trapezoidal shape. On the dorsal pillar a column of text in rough hieroglyphic signs was incised under the glaze. The remaining text reads: ... *kꜣ=k* or '... you shall say'.

Numerous other shabtis were discovered during the clearance of other Late Period shaft tombs and their subsidiary burials in the Saite-Persian necropolis at Abusir.[346] In order to better place the shabtis discovered in Padihor's burial complex within the

[346] The find circumstances and further information on the shabtis discovered in other Late Period shaft tombs, outside the Saite-Persian necropolis at Abusir, can for instance be consulted in Barsanti, *ASAE* 1 (1900), p. 162 (Psamtik); Barsanti, *ASAE* 1 (1900), p. 233 (Padinese); Barsanti, *ASAE* 1 (1900), p. 263; Bresciani – Pernigotti – Giangeri-Silvis, *Ciennehebu*, pp. 52-55 (with numerous references to the current locations of the shabtis), pls. xx-xxiii, and xli-xlii, and H.A. Schlögl – C Meves-Schlögl, *Ushebti. Arbeiter im ägyptischen Totenreich*, Wiesbaden 1993, pp. 46-49 (Tjannehebu); Barsanti, *ASAE* 2 (1901), p. 99 (Padineith); Barsanti, *ASAE* 3 (1902), p. 209 (Udjahor); Daressy, *ASAE* 4 (1903), p. 78 (Hor-khebit); Barsanti, *ASAE* 5 (1904), pp. 71-72; J.-C. Goyon, 'La statuette funéraire I.E. 84 de Lyon et le titre saïte 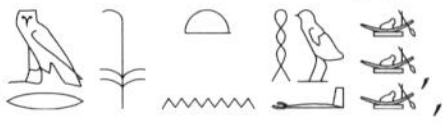', *BIFAO* 67 (1967), pp. 159-171, and G. Björkman, 'A Funerary Statuette of Hekaemsaf, Chief of the Royal Ships in the Saitic Period', *From the Gustavianum Collections in Uppsala, 1974*, (BOREAS. Uppsala Studies in Ancient Mediterranean and Near Eastern Civilizations 6), Uppsala 1974, pp. 76-78 (Hekaemsaf); S. Pernigotti, 'Saitica I', *EVO* 7 (1984), pp. 23-26 (Neferibra-sa-Neith); Firth, *ASAE* 29 (1929), pp. 69-70, and Drioton – Lauer, *ASAE* 51 (1951), pp. 476-477, 480 and pls. viii and xi (Neferibra-sa-Neith and Wahibremen). See also J.-F. Aubert – L. Aubert, *Statuettes égyptiennes. Chaouabtis, ouchebtis*, Paris 1974, pp. 233-237.

Owner	Shabti length (cm)	Shabti width (cm)	Schneider Type	Inscription	Location
Padihor	11.8 – 13.8	3.2 – 3.8	XIA1 – XIA5	Abbreviated shabti spell	dorsal pillar
Udjahorresnet	12.7 – 13.9	3.3 – 3.9	XIA5	Osiris + T + N +M	front and back side
Menekhibnekau	17.9 – 19.0	4.8 – 5.5	XIA1 – XIA5	Abbreviated shabti spell (+ M)	dorsal pillar
Iufaa	13.1 – 16.0	3.5 – 5.4	XIA5	T + N + M	front side
Imachetcheretresnet	4.7 – 7.2 (on average 6.0)	1.5 – 2.3 (on average 1.8)	XIA5	—	—
Nekau	5.8 – 7.8 (mostly 6.3 – 6.5)	1.8 – 2.1	XIA1	*sḥḏ*-formula + T + N	back side
Gemenefhorbak	7.3 – 10.6	1.9 – 2.8	XIA5	Osiris + T + N	front side

Table V.
Shabtis from the Saite-Persian cemetery at Abusir (T = title(s), N = name and M = mother's name).

local historical and stylistic context a brief overview of the other shabtis discovered in the Abusir shaft tombs is presented in the following paragraphs and in table V.

a) Udjahorresnet: only five shabtis of the tomb owner came to light in his burial complex: two in the sand filling of the main shaft above the burial chamber and three in the corridor connecting the burial chamber with the east subsidiary shaft.[347] The shabtis were made of light blue-green faience and are similar in shape – a rather crudely executed standing mummiform figure with a tripartite wig and straight beard, holding a hoe in each hand; the hands are crossed on the chest with the right hand placed over the left one. The right hand holds a bag that is slung over the left shoulder.[348] The shabtis are inscribed with two single columns of text, on the front and back side respectively, and identify the tomb owner: (1) *Wsir wr-synw Wḏ3-ḥr-Rsnt* (2) *ms n Ἰtm-ir-di.s* or 'The Osiris, Chief Physician, Udjahorresnet, born of Atemirdis'.[349]

b) Menekhibnekau: only four faience shabtis of the tomb owner have been discovered in the burial complex: one intact piece at the south end of the corridor leading from the south subsidiary shaft to the burial chamber, a broken shabti in the sand above the south-west corner of the chamber (ca. 30 cm above its roof), and the broken foot-ends of two shabtis in the sand in the north-west corner of the burial chamber.[350] The shabtis represent an Osirian figure with a striated tripartite wig, long plaited beard and hands crossed on the chest with the right hand placed over the left one. The figures hold a hoe in the right hand, a pick in the left hand and have a bag slung over the left shoulder. The shabtis have a dorsal pillar and are positioned upon a pedestal in a trapezoidal shape.[351] An inscription consisting of a single column of text is located on the dorsal pillar. The text is, similar to the inscription on the shabtis of Padihor, a shortened version of the common shabti spell.[352] Next to the name of the tomb owner the text on one occasion contains also his mother's name: Sat-Hapi.

c) Iufaa: a total of 408, mainly light blue glazed, faience shabtis were discovered in Iufaa's tomb. The shabtis were found in two wooden shabti containers located in the small corridor to the north (203 pieces) and south (205 pieces) of the outer sarcophagus.[353] The shabtis are almost identical in shape and represent an Osirian figure with a striated tripartite wig, long plaited beard and hands crossed on the chest with the right hand placed over the left one. The figures hold a hoe in the right hand, a pick in the left hand and have a bag slung over

[347] Bareš, *Abusir IV*, p. 67 and figs. 46-47 and 52-53, and Bareš, in H. Győry (ed.), *'Le lotus qui sort de la terre'*, pp. 23-24. Excavation nos. 70/H/89 and 115/H/89. The central shaft still contained the lower half of a sixth shabti – an intrusive one as the inscription suggests: Bareš, *Abusir IV*, p. 69.

[348] Type XIA5 according to Schneider, *Shabtis* I, p. 225-231 (and fig. 32 in volume III). See also Aubert – Aubert, *Statuettes égyptiennes*, pp. 233-237 and fig. 59 for parallels.

[349] Schneider, *Shabtis* I, p. 134.

[350] Bareš – Smoláriková – Strouhal, *ZÄS* 132 (2005), pp. 97-98, and Bareš – Janák – Landgráfová – Smoláriková, *ZÄS* 135 (2008), pp. 107-108. Excavation nos. 614/S/03, 680/S/07 and 697/S/07a-b.

[351] The shabtis resemble mostly Schneider, *Shabtis* III, figs. 30-31 = types XIA1 ('Saite mummy'-type) and XIA5 (the 'Late mummy'-type).

[352] Schneider, *Shabtis* I, Version VIIA.

[353] Bareš – Smoláriková, *Abusir XVII*, pp. 63, and 224-225, and Bareš, in H. Győry (ed.), *'Le lotus qui sort de la terre'*, pp. 24-26. Excavation nos. 65/R/96 (north) and 69/R/96 (south).

the left shoulder.[354] The shabtis have a dorsal pillar and are positioned upon a pedestal in a trapezoidal shape. The inscription, consisting of a single column of text, is located on the front side and contains the title and name of Iufaa and the name of his mother: *ẖrp ḥwwt Ỉwf-ꜥꜣ ỉr n ꜥnẖ(ty).s(y)* or 'The Administrator of the Palaces, Iufaa, born of Anchtes'.

d) Heavily eroded fragments of the lower half of two or three shabtis were discovered at the bottom of the main shaft of the anonymous tomb R3. The fragments were not inscribed and are too weathered to provide any information on their outlook.[355]

Next to the recovered shabtis of the owners of the Saite-Persian shaft tombs in the Abusir cemetery, sets of shabtis were also discovered among the burial equipment from the subsidiary burials of Imachetcheretresnet, Nekau and Gemenefhorbak within the burial complex of Iufaa:

e) Imachetcheretresnet, most likely a sister of Iufaa, was buried in a southern lateral corridor that adjoined Iufaa's burial complex.[356] A total of 405 shabtis were found at the foot end of her coffin and in the sand around it.[357] The faience shabtis, in varying shades of light blue-green, are generally small and roughly executed and each shabti stands on a small rectangular plinth. The shabtis are Osirian in shape, wear a tripartite wig and have their hands crossed on the chest. The figures hold a hoe in the right hand and a pick in the left hand.[358] Only four pieces were inscribed under the glaze on the back side: two fragments bore the title and name of the owner: *sḥḏ ỉt-nṯr Nkꜣw* or 'The Illuminated One,[359] the God's Father Nekau'. These two shabtis most likely belong to the burial equipment of Nekau, buried nearby in the west wall of the west subsidiary shaft of Iufaa's burial complex.[360] The text on the other two inscribed shabtis was mostly illegible.[361]

f) Nekau was buried in the west wall of the western subsidiary shaft of Iufaa's burial complex.[362] A total of 403 shabti figures were found inside and under a small and badly decomposed wooden chest immediately behind the walled up entrance to his burial.[363] The rather flat shabtis were coarsely produced in light blue glazed faience. The statuettes are Osirian in shape, with a tripartite wig and long straight beard.[364] With the exception of a few shabtis, most were inscribed on the back side with the *sḥḏ*-formula and the name and title of their owner: *sḥḏ ỉt-nṯr Nkꜣw* or 'The Illuminated One, the God's Father, Nekau'.

g) Gemenefhorbak was also buried in the western subsidiary shaft (north wall) of Iufaa's burial complex.[365] A total of 246 complete and circa 117 broken shabtis were recovered from an open wooden box positioned in a recess in the east wall.[366] The shabtis are produced in various shades of Egyptian faience, ranging from light to dark blue or green. The figurines are Osirian or mummiform in shape, with a tripartite wig and a long straight beard. The hands are crossed on the chest, the right one holds a hoe and the left one holds a pick; a bag is slung over the left shoulder. The statuettes are equipped with a plinth and a dorsal pillar.[367] Not all Gemenefhorbak's shabtis have

---

[354] The shabtis resemble mostly Schneider, *Shabtis* III, fig. 31 (= type XIA5).

[355] See also Chapter 2.1 in this volume.

[356] On the burial of Imachetcheretresnet consult Bareš – Smoláriková, *Abusir XVII*, pp. 97-115.

[357] Bareš – Smoláriková, *Abusir XVII*, pp. 105, 109, fig. 32/9 and pl. 53i-j, and Bareš, in H. Győry (ed.), *'Le lotus qui sort de la terre'*, pp. 26-27. Excavation no. 142/R/01.

[358] Schneider, *Shabtis* III, fig. 31 (= type XIA5).

[359] Schneider, *Shabtis* I, pp. 131-133 on this formula.

[360] A number of shabtis with the same inscriptions were discovered with his burial equipment – see further.

[361] The text *Wsir (?)ps … it nṯr ms n di …(?)* or "Osiris, (?)...God's father, born to...(?)" could be read on one of the shabtis – Bareš – Smoláriková, *Abusir XVII*, p. 109.

[362] On the burial of Nekau consult Bareš – Smoláriková, *Abusir XVII*, pp. 116-155.

[363] Bareš – Smoláriková, *Abusir XVII*, pp. 128, 132, fig. 42/2 and pl. 63a-b. Excavation no. 174/R/03.

[364] The type is in general similar to Schneider, *Shabtis* III, fig. 30 (= type XIA1).

[365] On the burial of Gemenefhorbak consult Bareš – Smoláriková, *Abusir XVII*, pp. 156-162.

[366] Bareš – Smoláriková, *Abusir XVII*, pp. 156, 159, fig. 47/4 and pl. 68a. Excavation no. 194/R/04.

[367] The shape of the shabtis is similar, but not identical, to Schneider, *Shabtis* III, fig. 31 (= type XIA5).

been inscribed. The most common and always frontally incised inscription reads *Wsir ḥrp ḥwwt Gm.n.f-ḥr-b3k* (*mꜥ3-ḫrw*) or 'The Osiris, the Administrator of Palaces, Gemenefhorbak (justified)'. A variant (three occurrences) reads *Wsir it nṯr ḥrp ḥwwt Gm.n.f-ḥr-b3k* or 'The Osiris, the God's Father, the Administrator of Palaces, Gemenefhorbak'.

The brief overview of the numerous shabtis recovered during the excavation of the Saite-Persian shaft tomb cemetery at Abusir indicates that a general preference existed for a single shabti-shape: the mummy type with a dorsal pillar (type XIA), and two specific sub-types: XIA1 ('the Saite mummy type') and XIA5 ('the late mummy type').[368] The main differences among the various sets of shabtis relate to their size and the type and location of the inscription. The owners of the large shaft tombs (Udjahorresnet, Iufaa and Menekhibnekau) have larger size shabtis (12.7 to 19.0 cm in height and 3.2 to 5.5 cm in width), while the individuals buried in subsidiary tombs within the burial complex of Iufaa possess smaller-sized statuettes (4.7 to 10.6 cm in height, but 6.0-7.0 cm on average, and 1.5-2.8 cm in width). Size-wise, the shabtis of Padihor, the owner of the smallest Late Period shaft tomb so far excavated, figure exactly in the middle between these groups: they are the smallest among the tomb owners' shabtis, but larger than those of the owners of subsidiary tombs.

Padihor's shabtis differ extensively from most other sets in the type of inscription that was engraved on the dorsal pillar: an abbreviated version of the shabti spell. Only the few recovered shabtis of Menekhibnekau appear to have had style and text similar to Padihor's – although their execution is generally of much higher quality. With the exception of Imachetcherestresnet's shabtis which were uninscribed, the inscription on the shabtis – whether on the front, back or on both sides – of the other individuals buried in the Saite-Persian cemetery at Abusir opens with the Osiris (Udjahorresnet and Gemenefhorbak) or *sḥḏ*-formula (Nekau) and usually contains the title(s) and the name of their owner (Nekau and Gemenefhorbak) and sometimes also the name of the owner's mother (Udjahorresnet and Iufaa).

1.4.2. Other finds

a. Remnants of a wooden coffin

Remnants of a wooden coffin, perhaps anthropoid in shape,[369] with small remains of black paint were discovered in the small space between the burial chamber and the wall of the burial shaft and in the sand filling of the subsidiary shaft. The wooden fragments were partly decomposed and rotten and their state made it impossible to conserve them.

b. A fragment of a thin gold leaf (2.6×1.0 cm, Pl. 9-i)[370] was found at the bottom of the main shaft of Padihor's tomb in the sand in front of the burial chamber. It might have come from the decoration of the completely destroyed coffin, but it was more likely a fragment of a sheath or foil intended to cover the fingertips or toe tips of the deceased. All finger- and toe tips of Iufaa were also covered by a thin sheath of pure gold,[371] and similar golden sheaths were also recovered in other Late Period shaft

368 Schneider, *Shabtis* I, pp. 225-231, and figs. 30-31 (volume III).

369 In several Late Period shaft tombs an (anthropoid) wooden coffin was found inside a stone anthropoid sarcophagus located inside a monumental rectangular stone sarcophagus. See for instance Barsanti, *ASAE* 3 (1902), p. 210 (Udjahor); Barsanti, *ASAE* 5 (1904), p. 75 (Hekaemsaf); Firth, *ASAE* 29 (1929), p. 70, and Drioton – Lauer, *ASAE* 51 (1951), pp. 474, and 481-482 (Neferibra-sa-Neith and Wahibremen); Bareš – Smoláriková, *Abusir XVII*, pp. 58-59 (Iufaa) or S. Ikram – A. Dodson, *The Mummy in Ancient Egypt. Equipping the Dead for Eternity*, Cairo 1998, pp. 269-270. Padihor's burial chamber was, given its reduced size, never designed to receive a monumental stone sarcophagus, and the tomb owner was probably buried only inside a wooden coffin. See already pp. 35 and 68.

370 Excavation no. 133/R/01. Bareš – Smoláriková, *Abusir XVII*, p. 234.

371 Bareš – Smoláriková, *Abusir XVII*, pp. 60, 229 and pl. 41a-d. The size of the gold sheaths in Iufaa's tomb is as follows: max. 2.1 cm for the fingertips and 2.8 cm for the toe tips.

tombs from the mummies of Padineith, Hekaemsaf, Tjannehebu, Udjahor and Wahibremen.[372]

c. Several fragments of a dish,[373] glazed in yellow and brown with remains of a green decoration, were found in the corridor connecting the entrance shaft with the burial chamber. (Pl. 9-j) The fragments most likely date to the 18th or 19th century.[374] The occurrence of the fragments in the substructure of the tomb is possibly related to the presence of an Arabic inscription engraved on the south wall of the same corridor, near the entrance to the burial chamber.[375]

1.5 An Arabic inscription in Padihor's shaft tomb

František Ondráš

In the corridor leading from the subsidiary shaft to Padihor's burial chamber an Arabic inscription was engraved into the south lateral wall. The inscription reads as follows (Pl. 10a-b):

الله ربي وربكم واحد
هذا فضل الباري
حفيدي عبد الله or حفيد ابن عبد الله

Transcription:
Allāh rabbī wa rabbukum wāhid
hādhā fadl al-bārī
hafīdī Abdallāh or *hafīd ibn Abdallāh*

Translation:
Alláh is my and your god / Lord
This is the merit of the Creator
My grandson Abdallāh or *grandson of son Abdallāh*

The Arabic inscription has three lines. The rhetoric meaning of the first line is reminiscent of a proclamation of faith, to which the expression *wāhid*, i.e. one, is central, leading to another possible translation for the line: *I and you have a common God*, or *I and you have one common God*, alternatively. The emphasis is on the meaning of the term *one*, which implies that the author of the text referred to the fact that the Muslim population of Egypt worships the same God as their ancestors – the ancient Egyptians.

The semantic content of the second line contains information concerning God's greatness, generosity and love of man. God enabled man to create a monument whose spectacular beauty still fascinates visitors to the site centuries after it was created. Muslims and Christians alike use the expression *this is the merit of the Creator* to express gratitude to the Maker and their respect and admiration for his creative powers.

The third line discloses the author's identity and can be interpreted in two ways. The first option, based on the anticipated expression *my grandson Abdallāh*, refers to the author's attempt to leave a record of his and his grandson *Abdallāh*'s visit to the site. The second option develops the formulated hypothesis by means of a probable identification of the text's author, i.e. by means of stating the name *grandson of son Abdallāh*.

---

[372] See Barsanti, *ASAE* 1 (1900), p. 269; Barsanti, *ASAE* 2 (1901), p. 103; Barsanti, *ASAE* 3 (1902), p. 211; Barsanti, *ASAE* 5 (1904), p. 77, and Firth, *ASAE* 29 (1929), p. 70. On this practice in general, consult for instance Ikram – Dodson, *The Mummy in Ancient Egypt*, pp. 146-147.

[373] Excavation no. 129/R/01. See also Bareš – Smoláriková, *Abusir XVII*, p. 234.

[374] Personal communication with Dr. Vlastimil Novák (Náprstek Museum of Asian, African and American Cultures, Prague) during his visit to the site (01. 04. 2001).

[375] On this inscription, consult the contribution by František Ondráš in Chapter 1.5.

The scientific identification of the author within the cultural, historical and social context is hindered because it was not possible to carry out highly sophisticated analyses of the natural material, i.e. of the rock on which the inscription had been written, or rather, engraved. The author was without doubt an educated man and skilful scribe. The inscription's technical execution is of high quality despite the fact that its location is accessible with a degree of difficulty. It is hardly possible to date the inscription because the employed ductus was a common occurrence during several historical periods. An objective evaluation of the historical circumstances surrounding the author's visit to the given archaeological location also remains a hypothesis.

1.6 Conclusion

The 'King's Acquaintance' Padihor found his final resting place in the Saite-Persian cemetery at Abusir at the relatively young age of 28-32 years. His tomb is located between two groups of tombs: to the east of Padihor's tomb we find a series of monumental burial complexes (Udjahorresnet, Iufaa, Menekhibnekau and others); to the west we see a group of several middle-sized and small shaft tombs, including the anonymous tomb R3, which appear to form a second row of funerary complexes.

Padihor's burial complex contains all typical architectural components of a Late Period shaft tomb (a large main shaft with a constructed burial chamber at its bottom, a subsidiary shaft and a connecting corridor), but on a much smaller scale than the complexes of his predecessors in Saqqara and Giza and of his contemporaries in Abusir (table I). The changing and unstable political situation in Egypt at the turn of the Twenty-Sixth to the Twenty-Seventh Dynasty or his (lower?) social position might have led Padihor to commission a burial complex that contained all the essential elements of a standard shaft tomb, but on a much reduced scale.

The textual programme designed for the walls and ceiling of Padihor's burial chamber consists of a compact set of inscriptions (excerpts from various passages of the Pyramid Texts and Coffin Texts) that provided the deceased with the necessary means to ascend into heaven and attain his rightful place in the afterlife. The choice of texts and their specific location on the walls and ceiling of Padihor's chamber bears many similarities not only to the textual programme applied to the walls of the burial chambers of several large middle to late Twenty-Sixth Dynasty shaft tombs located especially around the pyramid complex of Unas in Saqqara (table IV), but also to a particular monument which can be found in Abusir, namely the inner basalt sarcophagus of Iufaa.

The study of the orthography, content and grammar of Padihor's inscriptions and its comparison with the same texts in the other burial chambers indicates that Padihor's texts were not copied from a specific tomb, but rather that these burial complexes shared a preference for a number of Pyramid Texts and Coffin Texts in a recurring combination and in a specific location on the walls of the burial chamber. The general pattern as found in the other tombs is interrupted in Padihor's burial chamber by the inclusion of texts not found in any large Late Period shaft tombs (such as PT 268). A number of hieroglyphs in the inscriptions on the walls of the burial chamber were corrected in black ink after all the texts had been engraved. The additions in black ink can be observed on all four walls and fall into two distinct groups: the accentuation of several signs whose engraving had been poorly executed or was completely absent, and the correction of (mostly) wrongly engraved signs (table III).

The tomb was completely robbed and the only reasonably preserved remains of the burial equipment of Padihor consist of a set of about a dozen shabtis carrying his name, and fragments of a wooden coffin. The name Padihor itself (table II) was common throughout the Late Period. None of the presently known bearers of the name from the Twenty-Sixth or early Twenty-Seventh Dynasty can however be identified with the owner of this shaft tomb with any degree of certainty. The almost complete absence of biographical information in the inscriptions from Padihor's burial chamber, with the exception of the mother's name (Nedjem-bastet-en-iret) and a single honorific title ('king's acquaintance' or *rḫ nswt*), means that little can be said about the owner of this burial complex beyond the information obtained by the anthropological and palaeo-pathological analysis of the few remains of his body.

The ongoing excavation of other small and middle-sized shaft tombs located along a north-west – south-east line running immediately to the east of Padihor's tomb may provide further information on the development of the Saite-Persian cemetery at Abusir and Padihor's place within the necropolis.

Chapter 2
The Anonymous Tomb R3

Květa Smoláriková

2.1. Archaeology and architecture of the tomb complex

To the north-east of the huge shaft tomb of Iufaa,[376] at a distance of about 60 m from the north-east corner of its enclosure wall, a mud-brick structure was detected and examined during the spring season of 2002 (Fig. 1, Pl. 1).[377] Its contours were clearly visible on the almost flat desert surface and this had most likely aroused attention of the local tomb robbers.[378] After one short season of archaeological excavation, this structure turned out to be another shaft tomb, medium in size and unique in its architectural layout (Fig. 16, Pls. 11a, 14a, and 16a). The identity of the tomb owner was not revealed during the excavations and the tomb has kept its archaeological designation 'R3'.[379]

The tomb superstructure, preserved only to the height of three to five courses of mud bricks, is square in plan, with each side measuring about 11.50 m. The masonry consists of a large mass of sun-dried mud bricks, measuring about 40-42×19-20×10-12 cm,[380] with the projection of one brick at the surviving corners. The masonry is in some places heavily disturbed by the removal of great portions of mud bricks. This is for the most part the result of the tomb robbers' attempts to find the entrance to the tomb. Some other pits and intrusions into the masonry are most likely the result of several poor secondary burials interred on this spot (Pls. 14c, 15a, and 17a). Badly decayed remains of three individuals were found on the east side of the superstructure: a 30-40 year old male, a 20-25 year old male and a 20-25 year old female.[381] Secondary burials such as these three occur only occasionally in the Saite-Persian cemetery at Abusir, especially in comparison with the north part of the nearby Abusir royal cemetery.[382] These secondary burials were, however, certainly not exceptional and can be connected in part with the cult of Udjahorresnet that flourished 170 years after his death in Mem-

---

376 Bareš – Smoláriková, *Abusir XVII.*

377 The preliminary excavation report of this tomb can be consulted in Bareš – Bárta – Smoláriková – Strouhal, *ZÄS* 130 (2003), pp. 147-155. Information on the tomb can also be found in Bareš, in *Abusir. Secrets of the Desert and the Pyramids*, p. 173; Smoláriková, in Bárta – Coppens – Krejčí (eds.), *Abusir and Saqqara in the Year 2005*, pp. 45-47, and Stammers, *Elite Late Period Egyptian Tombs*, esp. pp. 114-115.

378 The masonry of the tomb, badly destroyed by wind erosion, was covered with only a few centimetres of sand; occasionally, fragments of eroded fine stones (basalt and diorite) and pebbles of various sizes were also present. Of the artefacts obtained during the exploration of the surface, fragments of pottery and a shard of the body of a small faience cup (light blue-green in colour) should be mentioned. From time to time, especially during the winter season with its strong winds, large portions of the masonry were completely exposed. The exact position of this structure can be seen on the archaeological maps of the Abusir necropolis published to date, e.g., by Bárta, in Bárta – Krejčí (eds.), *Abusir and Saqqara in the Year 2000*, p. 345, (designated U-S-9). This map also clearly shows the very interesting location of the shaft tombs in the widely open desert at Abusir: huge complexes belonging to Udjahorresnet, Iufaa, Menekhibnekau and others, closed the cemetery from the west, while beyond them, i.e. towards the core of the cemetery area, all the lesser tombs are situated, including R3 and Padihor's tomb. In Saqqara and Giza the shaft tombs are spread all around the earlier – mostly Old Kingdom – structures. See Smith, in Helck – Otto (eds.), *Lexikon der Ägyptologie* V, p. 415, and el-Sadeek, *Twenty-Sixth Dynasty Necropolis at Gizeh*, p. 7, and plan I.

379 The nearby tomb of Padihor was originally designated 'R1' and the burial complex of Iufaa 'R'.

380 Spencer, *Brick Architecture*, p. 76.

381 Excavation nos. 146-148/R/02. See Bareš – Bárta – Smoláriková – Strouhal, *ZÄS* 130 (2003), p. 154. See also the contribution by E. Strouhal in Chapter 3.

382 E. Strouhal – L. Bareš, *Secondary Cemetery in the Mastaba of Ptahshepses at Abusir*, Prague 1993; Bareš, in Daoud – Bedier – Abdel Fattah (eds.), *Studies in Honor of Ali Radwan*, pp. 177-182, and Krejčí, J. – Verner, M. – Callender, V.G., *Abusir XII. Minor Tombs in the Royal Necropolis I (The Mastabas of Nebtyemneferes and Nakhtsare, Pyramid Complex Lepsius no. 24 and Tomb complex Lepsius no. 25)*, Prague 2008, pp. 48-51, 159-161.

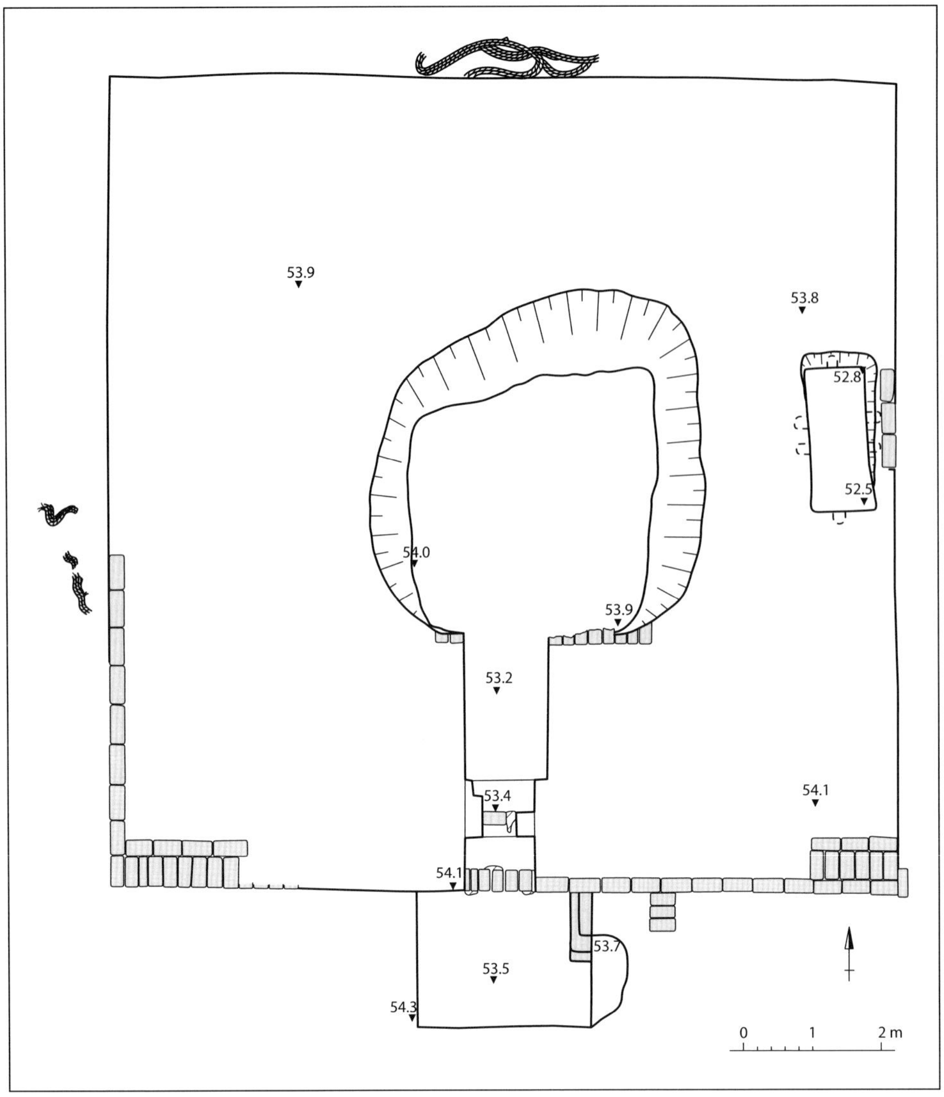

Fig. 16
The superstructure of the anonymous tomb R3

phis. People had themselves buried on this spot intentionally in order to partake in the spiritual power of this honoured man.[383]

The entrance to the tomb is located in a small rectangular courtyard (1.90 by 2.50 m) in the centre of the south wall of the burial complex (Fig. 16). The courtyard is situated about 0.40 m below ground level, which is indicated by the courses of mud bricks. Three steps made of mud brick directly adjoin the east part of the south façade of the tomb and provide access to the courtyard from the upper level. In front of these steps a rather small (protective?) base of an originally higher mudbrick wall, which adjoined the façade, was revealed (Fig. 16, Pls. 11a, and 12b). With the exception of the area surrounding the steps, the outer façade of the mud brick superstructure was not plastered.[384] The preserved part of the masonry was most probably originally situated

[383] R. Anthes, *Mit Rahineh 1956*, Philadelphia 1965, pp. 98-100 (n. 38); T. Holm-Rasmussen, 'Collaboration in Early Achaemenid Egypt. A New Approach', in E. Christiansen – A. Damsgaard-Madsen – E. Hallager (eds.), *Studies in Ancient History and Numismatics, presented to Rudi Thomsen*, Aarhus 1988, pp. 29-38, and Bareš, *Abusir IV*, 1999, pp. 41-43, with further references. In light of these facts the strictly negative approach of some Egyptologists to Udjahorresnet's policy after the Persian occupation of Egypt seems to be ungrounded; most recently on this topic see K. Smoláriková, *Saite Forts in Egypt. Political-Military History of the Saite Dynasty*, Prague 2008, pp. 44-45.

[384] One may compare it with a similar situation at the east façade of Iufaa's enclosure wall: the Nile mud plaster suddenly ends on an almost exactly horizontal line about 0.5 m above the lowermost course of masonry. This line most likely shows the original ground level. See Bareš – Smoláriková, *Abusir XVII*, p. 35.

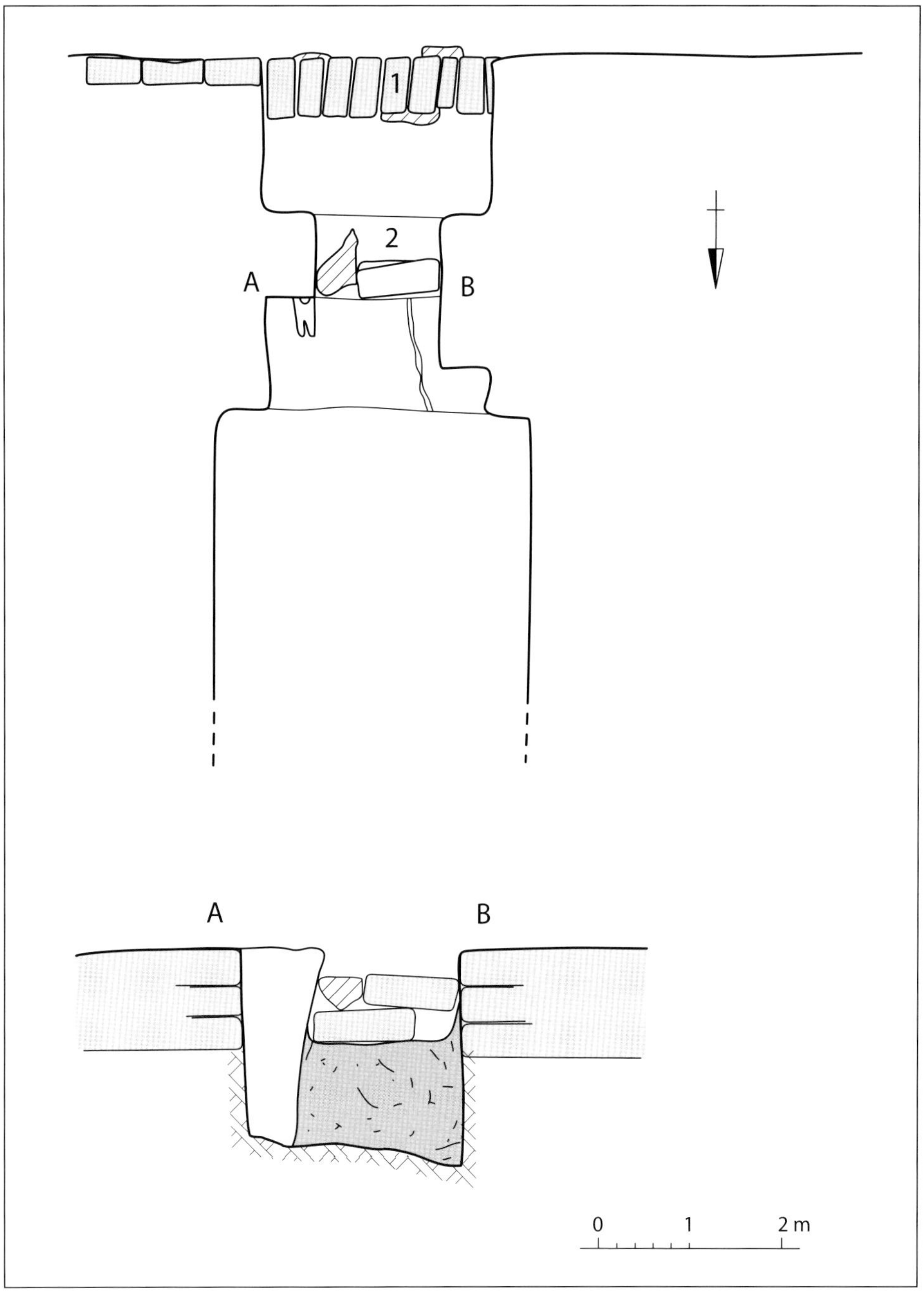

Fig. 17
The walled entrances (1-2) to the main shaft and a section of the inner one (2)

below ground level. The presence of the sunken courtyard seems to corroborate this conjecture, since its outer walls must have been considerably higher than the presently preserved 0.40 m.

A narrow corridor, with its bottom partly dug into the shale bedrock and plastered with Nile mud, leads from the middle of the southern façade and the courtyard directly to the centrally situated shaft (Fig. 16). The entrance to this corridor was originally walled shut with two mud brick walls which were plastered on the outside with Nile mud (Fig. 17, Pls. 12a, 13c, and 16b). The outer entrance (about a metre wide) was blocked with a rather carefully built mud brick wall of about 40-42 cm in thickness, i.e. the entire length of a single brick (Fig. 18). The inner entrance had the same thickness but was only 45 cm wide. Its threshold consisted of two heavily plastered courses of mud bricks above the level of the floor. The entrance itself was blocked with mud bricks, scattered in a haphazard manner, and fragments of stones (Pl. 17b). Originally a single-leaf door (about 0.80 cm wide) was installed behind this narrow entrance and its wooden door pivot is still preserved on the east side. Past this entrance the corridor, 1.20 m wide at this spot, continues in the direction of the shaft (Pl. 16b). It seems that

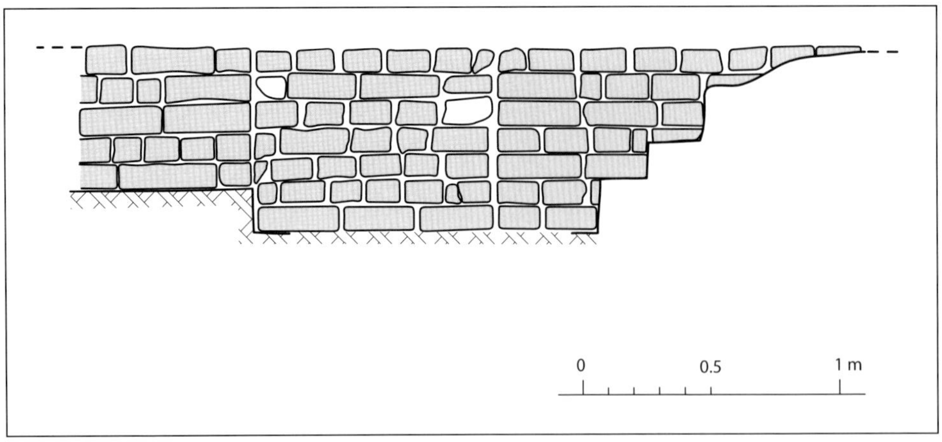

Fig. 18
The walled outer entrance (1)

the natural *tafla* bedrock was used as its floor because only a small part of the passage right behind the door was covered with a thick layer of plaster. Using the width of the door it is possible to theoretically postulate its height. If the width to height ratio of the door in general varied from 1:2 to 1:3,[385] depending on the proportions of the building, the height of the door in the corridor might have been between 1.60 and 2.40 m. In light of the general dimensions of the tomb, the former height seems to be more plausible. At a later point in time the door might have been dismantled and reused elsewhere because no traces of wood were retrieved from the shaft or from anywhere else in the vicinity of the burial complex. It is at present impossible to explain why the entrance to the tomb was blocked twice while the inner wall on its own was enough to close off the tomb's interior. A stela might have been located on the spot, but no traces were recovered.[386]

In the middle of the mud-brick structure the entrance corridor ends in a wide crater with the walls dug into a rather irregular round shape. At the upper edge of the *tafla* bedrock a deep shaft was excavated in the very centre of the crater. The shaft was most likely originally covered by one or more layer(s) of mud brick masonry.[387] A number of these large mud bricks, projecting over the edge of the shaft in the *tafla* bedrock, are well preserved in the north-east corner of the entrance corridor leading to the main shaft.

The shape of the mud-brick superstructure of tomb R3, with a corridor leading directly to a deep central shaft, has for the time being no parallel among the tombs of this type – the huge Late Period shaft tombs discovered in Abusir, Saqqara and Giza.[388] The general arrangement and layout of the burial complex is reminiscent of the situation underneath the Step Pyramid of Djoser at nearby Saqqara, where a new corridor was dug in the same place during the Saite Period.[389] Keeping in mind the vicinity of this monumental building, situated within view of tomb R3, the incorporation of this corridor into this new type of tomb may represent yet another example of the intentional imitation of (parts of) monuments of the past and the borrowing of an archaising feature. The panelled outer façade of the enclosure wall surrounding the tomb of Iufaa,[390] together with various other building elements identified in the layout of the shaft tombs, testify to this general trend.[391]

[385] Arnold, *The Encyclopedia of Ancient Egyptian Architecture*, pp. 74-75.
[386] See for instance Bareš – Smoláriková, *Abusir XVII*, pp. 35, and 38-39.
[387] This situation can be compared with the mass of blocks lying above the huge shaft in the superstructure of Djoser's burial complex, see J.-Ph. Lauer, *La pyramide à degrés. II L'Architecture*, Cairo 1936, pl. xix.
[388] There is no limestone enclosure wall that surrounded the main shaft or a small secondary shaft to the west of the burial complex, as mistakenly stated in Stammers, *Elite Late Period Egyptian Tombs*, p. 114.
[389] Firth – Quibell, *The Step Pyramid*, Vol. I – text, pp. 90-91, Vol. II – plates 12 and 22.
[390] Smoláriková, in Bárta – Coppens – Krejčí (eds.), *Abusir and Saqqara in the Year 2005*, pp. 42-48.
[391] This topic will be dealt with in greater detail in Chapter 2.2.

Fig. 19
The north-south section of the anonymous tomb R3

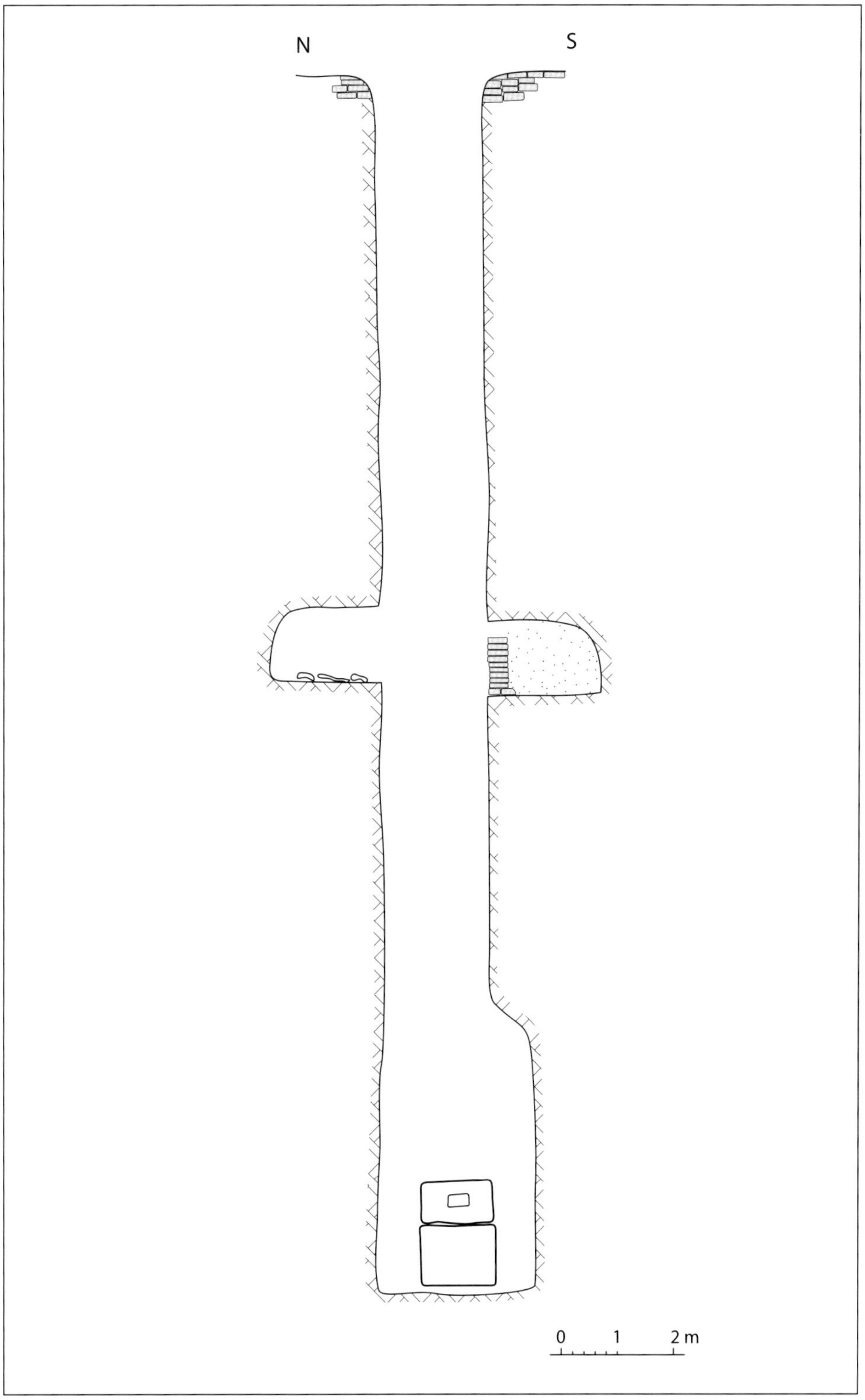

The shaft is orientated north-south and has rather small dimensions – 2.10 by 1.80 m – but in spite of its relatively small size, it is no less than 22 m deep (Fig. 19, Pls. 15a, and 16b). At a depth of about 11 m two niches, each about 1.40 m wide, 1.40 m high and 2.00 m deep, feature in the north and south walls of the shaft. The north niche contained fragments of human bones and remnants of decomposed wood, most likely the remains of a burial in a wooden anthropoid coffin that might have been destroyed by the tomb robbers in antiquity. On a single piece of wood which was covered with a thick layer of black varnish on both sides, remains of hieroglyphs were partly preserved. The signs were written in yellow ochre and it was still possible to identify *ḳr*… This is very probably a fragment of the word *ḳrst* of the invocation formula. No re-

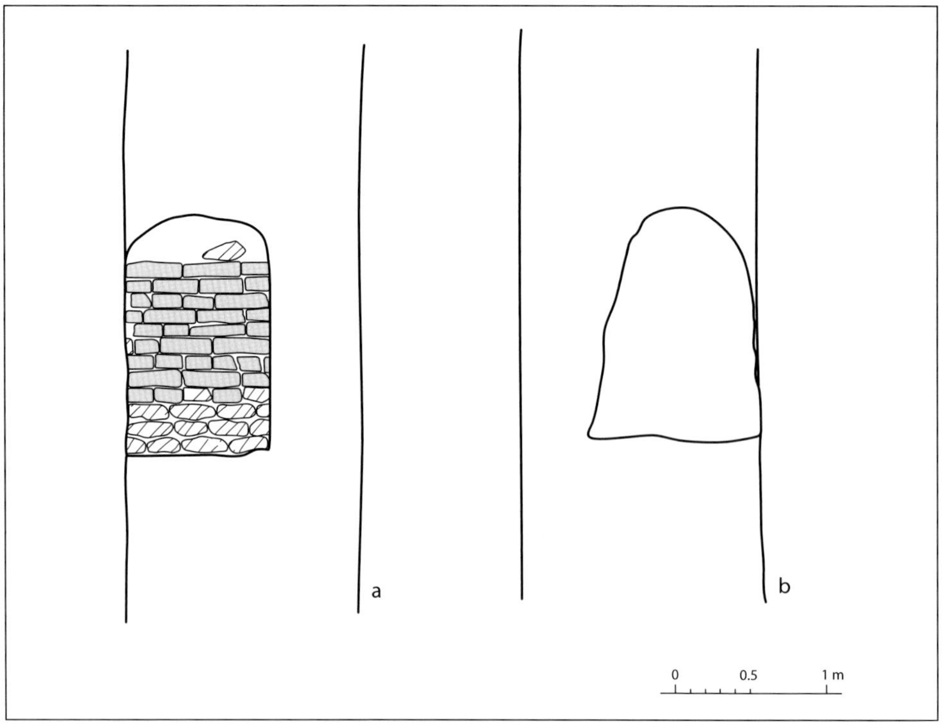

Fig. 20
The niches in the south (a) and north (b) walls of the main shaft

mains of the funerary equipment were discovered in the niche. The opening of the south niche was blocked by an intact wall built of mud bricks of the so-called 'larger size' (40×20×10 cm) and large pieces of *tafla* bedrock,[392] but the niche itself was surprisingly only filled with sand. If the niche was intended to function as a burial site, then it was never used (Fig. 20a, Pl. 13b).

The central shaft, after it had been cleared and left open by the tomb robbers, was completely filled with pure windblown yellow sand.[393] As a consequence the mud brick masonry and *tafla* bedrock surrounding the mouth of the shaft were partly weathered into the shape of a shallow depression. Significant finds from the shaft's filling were rather rare and consisted mainly of heavily eroded shards of Late Roman (Coptic) date. Three (?) heavily eroded fragments of the lower parts of shabtis, all without inscriptions, were discovered in the lowest layers of the filling. The shabtis most likely belong to the original burial equipment of the tomb's occupant(s),[394] but provide no information on the name and the social status of its owner(s). Tomb R3 is thus unique not only owing to the layout of its superstructure – it is also the first unattributed tomb among those so far unearthed in the Saite-Persian cemetery at Abusir.

The shaft grows larger at its bottom into a cavity about 3.20 by 3.20 m and 5.00 m deep. A rather large rectangular sarcophagus was found positioned on a layer of sand, about 30 cm thick, at the bottom of the shaft. The sarcophagus is placed approximately in the centre of the shaft. No traces of a surrounding burial chamber were discovered.[395] The sarcophagus is made of white limestone; it is 2.50 m long and 1.40 m wide, its

[392] This wall, sloping to the south, is too well built to be interpreted as a mere retaining wall made by the tomb robbers to prevent the sand from pouring down from the niche into the shaft. Numerous remains of bird droppings were clearly visible on the outside of the wall. This indicates that the shaft was left open at least to the depth of the niche (11 m) for a period of time.

[393] The occasional occurrence of crumbled mud bricks and crushed *tafla* in the filling most likely came from the heavily destroyed superstructure and the gradually weathered walls of the deep shaft.

[394] It seems that the tomb accommodated at least two burials. Of course, this number does not include the poor secondary burials unearthed in its superstructure.

[395] The position of the sarcophagus directly at the bottom of the shaft and the absence of a burial chamber has a close parallel in the tomb of Udjahor in Saqqara – Barsanti, *ASAE* 3 (1902), pp. 209-212, and PM III, p. 503. For the religious significance of the mound of sand as a primordial mound or 'Osiris Tomb', consult Hornung, *The Ancient Egyptian Book of the Afterlife*, p. 38.

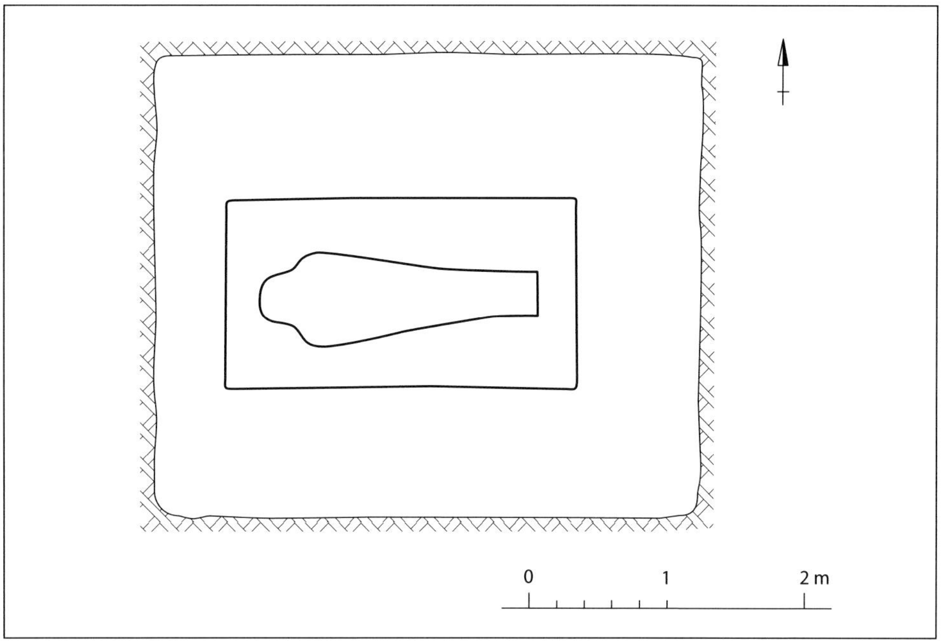

Fig. 21
The main shaft with the limestone sarcophagus at the bottom

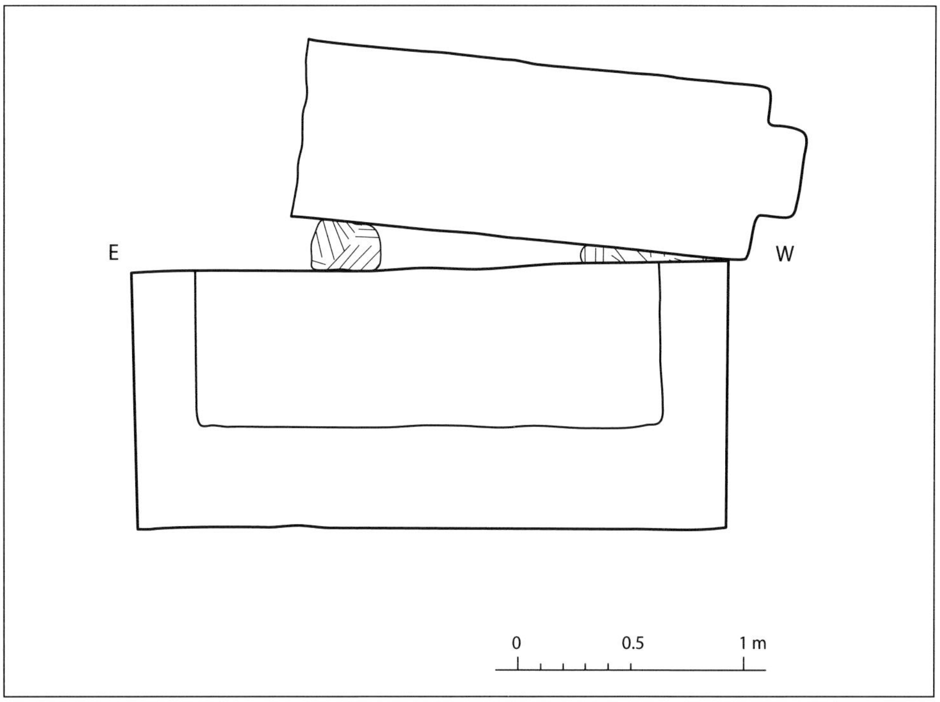

Fig. 22
The east-west section of the limestone sarcophagus with a partly broken lid

chest is 1.06 m high and its lid 0.75 m thick. Inside the chest, a cavity was cut in a roughly anthropoid shape (Fig. 21, Pl. 23a-b). The cavity is about 2 m long, 0.50 m deep and about 0.60 m wide at its broadest point - at the shoulders.[396] The surface of the sarcophagus remained unsmoothed and was decorated only with a rather large – about 0.70 m high – *udjat* eye. The eye was roughly painted in black ink on the east side of the chest. The sarcophagus was found robbed and empty. The inner wooden anthropoid coffin, if it ever existed, has either been lost or destroyed. The east edge of the lid was broken off by the robbers and pieces of the broken lid were found around the sarcophagus (Fig. 22, Pl. 21a-b). Two smaller pieces were placed between the chest and the lid to keep the lid open (Pl. 22c). The only remains found in the cavity at the

[396] The cavity is just large enough to hold a wooden coffin, similar to the aforementioned tomb of Udjahor.

bottom of the shaft consist of various fragments of human bones that might have been part of the original burial. An anthropological analysis indicated that the bones were very badly preserved and belonged to a 35-45 year old male.[397]

The sarcophagus is orientated east-west, with the head of the inner cavity pointing towards the west. Given the somewhat miniature dimensions of the shaft and the size of both parts of the sarcophagus, it must have been lowered into its resting place in a vertical position, most probably suspended from very strong ropes. A rectangular trench – similar to those found to the west of the west subsidiary shafts of Iufaa and Menekhibnekau[398] – was unearthed to the east of the shaft, but still within the superstructure of the tomb (Figs. 16, 23, Pl. 18). The trench is about 2.10 m long, 1.00 m wide and 1.20 m deep. Although no remains of wooden beams or ropes were found inside the trench, the holes (15×15 cm) that are roughly cut into the bedrock on its sides just above its bottom leave no doubt about its purpose. Two holes were situated opposite each other in the longer sides of the trench, and one was excavated in the centre of each of its shorter sides (Pl. 18b-d). In addition to that, ample length of huge ropes was found abutting the west and north sides of the superstructure (Fig. 11).[399] On the north side, the rope was actually found coiled up and tied together with another cord made of twisted plant stalks.[400] It seems that these ropes were simply left beside the walls after they had been used to lower the sarcophagus and its lid to the bottom of the shaft (Pls. 19b-d and 20a-c). This unusually large amount of ropes was discovered in an extraordinary state of preservation due to the particularly favourable conditions brought on by the dry desert sand.

The almost complete lack of original burial equipment means that the tomb can only be dated using indirect evidence. On the basis of its location within the cemetery, one can date the tomb approximately to the same time or only slightly later than the construction of Udjahorresnet's funerary complex. This implies that its construction started at the very end of the Twenty-Sixth Dynasty or at the beginning of the First Persian occupation (early Twenty-Seventh Dynasty).[401] The tomb did not show any

---

[397] Excavation no. 186/R/02. Bareš – Bárta – Smoláriková – Strouhal, *ZÄS* 130 (2003), p. 154. See also the contribution by E. Strouhal in Chapter 3.

[398] Bareš – Smoláriková, *Abusir XVII*, pp. 40-41. See also Rostem, *ASAE* 43, pp. 351-356.

[399] The rope was of the same thickness as that found to the west of the west subsidiary shaft of Iufaa, i.e. about 7-8 cm. A piece of rope, similar in size, was previously also found in the vicinity of Udjahorresnet's tomb, see Bareš, *Abusir* IV, p. 68 (n. 345). A fairly significant assemblage of ropes was recovered from the Saite-Persian cemetery at Abusir. Its more detailed study might significantly clarify and enlarge our knowledge of the cordage industry which flourished in this region during the Late Period.

[400] Several samples, mostly from Deir el-Bahari, were discussed by Donald P. Ryan and David H. Hansen in their study, but not a single sample was derived from the Memphite necropolis – D.P. Ryan – D.H. Hansen, *A Study of Ancient Egyptian Cordage in the British Museum*, (British Museum Occasional Paper 62), London 1987. Another extremely promising site is Tell el-Amarna. A quite comprehensive study of this otherwise neglected material was published as W. Wendrich, 'Preliminary Report on the Amarna Basketry and Cordage', in B.J. Kemp (ed.), *Amarna Report V*, (Occasional Publications 6), London 1989, pp. 169-201. For general information on cordage production, consult E. Teeter, 'Techniques and Terminology of Rope-Making in Ancient Egypt', *JEA* 73 (1987), pp. 71-77 and A.J. Veldmeijer, 'Cordage Production', in W. Wendrich (ed.), *UCLA Encyclopedia of Egyptology*, Los Angeles 2009. [=http://escholarship.org/uc/item/1w90v76c].

[401] It is impossible to establish an exact date for the construction of tomb R3, but it can be tentatively placed in the first half of the long reign of Darius I (522-486 BC) in Egypt, cf. Stammers, *Elite Late Period Egyptian Tombs*, p. 114. The strongest argument for dating the tomb to the reign of Darius I, as Stammers proposes, is – besides its layout – the presence of ample imports coming from the Eastern Mediterranean area (see Chapter 2.3). Due to the short reign of Cambyses (525-522 BC) and in the absence of any written finds bearing the name of this king, not one tomb can be dated to his reign. It is also interesting to note that, similar to the situation in Udjahorresnet's burial chamber, the burial complex of tomb R3 was left unfinished despite the fact that there should have been ample time for its completion. Can we see behind this a shortage of artists, the absence of the owner in the course of the preparation of the tomb decoration, a social degradation of the owner or still something else? On the topic of unfinished burial chambers in the Saite-Persian cemetery at Abusir, see also Bareš – Smoláriková, *Abusir XVII*, p. 54 (n. 121).

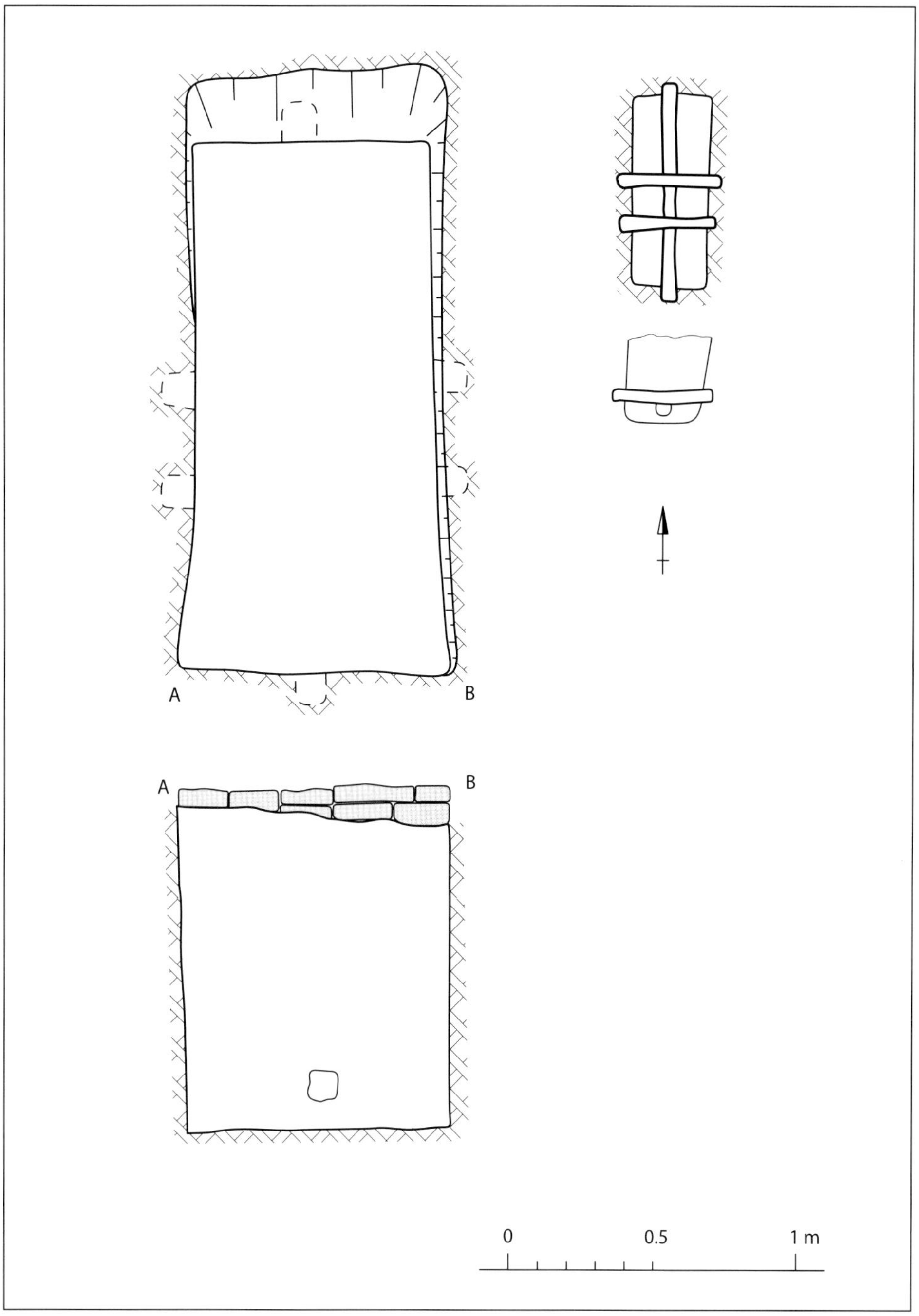

Fig. 23
Plan, section and reconstruction of the device dug into the *tafla* bedrock

evidence of being reused later on – with the exception of the insertion of a few secondary burials.

One can only speculate about the final outlook of its exterior, mainly because the masonry that survived to the present day was situated below ground level. Although the layout of the tomb is unique, its superstructure could have had the shape of a mud brick mastaba about 2 m high and covered with (white) plaster. In general its design may at first glance look similar (except for its size) to the superstructure of the nearby shaft tomb of Padihor (or other lesser tombs that have yet to be excavated) given that the superstructures of these burial complexes were also constructed of mud brick.

The presence of the remains of two (?) burials found in the tomb's substructure suggests that its superstructure, namely the corridor leading to the shaft, remained open for a period of time.[402] It could not be established whether this was connected with the mortuary cult of the tomb owner buried inside the limestone sarcophagus. No traces of any installation for the mortuary cult were found inside or around the tomb's superstructure, but it is possible that the small open courtyard on the south side might have been used for such a purpose (Fig. 16). No mortuary cult installation could be detected in front of the east wall of the huge shaft tomb of Menekhibnekau, either.[403] It cannot be excluded that the remarkably extensive cult installation (16 rooms dug into the *tafla*, once covered with mud brick vaults, and one large open courtyard, Pl. 2a)[404] located about 5-6 m to the east of Iufaa's enclosure wall could have been used not only for Iufaa and the members of his family but for all the owners of the shaft tombs built at that time in the Saite-Persian cemetery at Abusir.[405]

2.2. The architectural development of the 'last' shaft tomb and its model

The anonymous tomb R3 clearly belongs to the relatively large group of the Saite-Persian shaft tombs unearthed in the vast Memphite necropolis, but its layout and building disposition has no vaguely similar, let alone exact parallel in the private funerary architecture of the Late Period.[406] In this chapter I would like to take a closer look at the architectural development of the Late Period shaft tombs, the role of the nearby Step Pyramid as a plausible model, and the place of tomb R3 in this development.

Towards the end of the Twenty-Sixth or Saite Dynasty, the architects and designers decided, for reasons presently unknown, to change the current typical layout of the shaft tomb.[407] Tomb R3 consists of an almost square mud brick superstructure with a deep shaft excavated in its very centre in the *tafla* bedrock. Unlike other shaft tombs, the burial complex does not contain a single small subsidiary shaft (whether to the west, east or south), as was common, but an entrance corridor in the superstructure which leads from the south façade to the shaft in the centre. This innovation does not seem to have been followed by any of the tomb owner's contemporaries, although further excavations in the Saite-Persian cemetery at Abusir might change this picture. At present the tomb is absolutely unique in the long chain of tombs developed in this territory and can be tentatively identified as the 'last' shaft tomb.[408]

In the nearby Step Pyramid of Djoser at Saqqara a similar general design is found, consisting of a horizontal entrance corridor leading to the main shaft with a sarcophagus at its bottom. It is the so-called Saite gallery that was excavated in the south part of the pyramid substructure and provided access to the burial shaft. The building disposition of Djoser's tomb consists of the following architectural elements: an extremely deep shaft housed a massive stone sarcophagus and is surrounded aboveground by a richly panelled enclosure wall which served as a visible boundary and protected the subterranean sections including the subsidiary family tombs. The disposition and layout of this monumental burial complex clearly inspired Djoser's successors.[409] The Saite explorations of the substructure of the Step Pyramid, during which the huge main

---

[402] The presence of a small open courtyard situated in front of the tomb's south façade appears to suggest this as well. One has to bear in mind that the superstructure – while not as impressive as the substructure – must have once been much higher than its presently preserved 30-50 cm. The corridor leading to the centre of the superstructure was undoubtedly covered on its sides and, most probably, also from above. A stela or offering table might have been situated in the now heavily destroyed central part of the superstructure.

[403] Bareš – Janák – Landgráfová – Smoláriková, *ZÄS* 137 (2010 – forthcoming); one can only speculate on the function of an 'altar' in front of the north enclosure wall of the tomb (see Fig. 1).

[404] Bareš, *BACE* 13 (2002), pp. 17-27.

[405] For more information see Bareš – Smoláriková, *Abusir XVII*, pp. 73-80.

[406] See A. Dodson – S. Ikram, *The Tomb in Ancient Egypt. Royal and Private Sepulchres from the Early Dynastic Period to the Romans*, London 2008, pp. 275-287.

[407] On the typical layout of a shaft tomb, see already footnote 51.

[408] Stammers, *Elite Late Period Egyptian Tombs*, p. 33 (n. 508). Stammer's hypothesis that the second subsidiary shaft was a defining feature of the Saite-Persian shaft tombs from the time of Pakap onwards does not stand up to the evidence: the anonymous tomb R3 and the small burial complex of Padihor, which both date from the turn of the Twenty-Sixth to the Twenty-Seventh Dynasty, have no secondary shaft.

[409] R. Stadelmann, *Die ägyptische Pyramiden. Vom Ziegelbau zum Weltwunder*, Mainz 1991, pp. 72-77 mentions the funerary complexes of Sekhemkhet and Khaba.

shaft (28 m deep) was cleared, have been archaeologically documented and verified. The aforementioned long horizontal southern gallery allowed the ancient architects to enter the substructure and gain particular detailed knowledge of its layout. This activity demonstrates their strong interest and desire to study the structure of the monument, and included the careful copying of the stelae of the blue-tiled rooms.[410] To the Saites it appears to have been a way in which to keep hold of their traditions in a changing world.[411] According to Jean-Philippe Lauer, the layout of the huge shaft tombs, as a specific type of the Late Period mortuary architecture, reflects the experience and knowledge gained by the Saite architects in the substructure of the Step Pyramid. The recent archaeological excavations in the Saite-Persian cemetery at Abusir clearly indicate that during the last phase of their development, the shaft tombs became funerary complexes with numerous related structures, not unlike Djoser's burial complex.[412]

The inspiration is evident for instance in the panelled wall surrounding Djoser's mortuary complex. The panelling had been widely used for a long time, particularly in mud brick mastabas, but the Saites only became familiar with the later stone modification of this architectural element.[413] The remains of the outer façade of the enclosure wall in the burial complex of Iufaa are panelled in much the same way as the enclosure wall of the Step Pyramid complex, but Iufaa's outer wall was built of mud brick and the size of its panelling was reduced.[414] The concept of 'adequate reduction' should be kept in mind for most architectural elements of the Saite private mortuary complexes. It could be that speed and economical considerations forced the builders to make use of bricks rather than limestone. The burial complex of Iufaa is the only one in the cemetery at Abusir that has a huge mud brick enclosure wall surrounding a shaft tomb. The mud brick superstructure of R3 is a very specific example in the development of the shaft tombs as it completely misses all trace of an enclosure wall, perhaps with the exception of the small area surrounding the courtyard. A panelled façade might also have been applied to the originally modest superstructure of the nearby tomb belonging to Padihor. His mud brick enclosure wall was preserved in extremely poor condition. It consisted of a double mud brick wall, with the narrow space between both walls filled with debris and sand.

A small sub-group of huge shaft tombs respect the typical layout of this type of mortuary architecture, but still contain one extra feature that might have had a deeper religious significance which is at present difficult to explain satisfactorily. Two shaft tombs – the tomb of Pakap (the so-called 'Campbell's tomb') in Giza[415] and the tomb of Udjahorresnet in Abusir[416] – contain deep narrow trenches that surrounded the main shaft with the burial chamber. Various reasons have been suggested for this unusual modification of an otherwise widely respected layout. The suggestion that this feature provided increased protection against the omnipresent robbers can be excluded: both tombs have been entered several times, while curiously enough several others that did not have this architectural element were found undisturbed, including the nearby located shaft tomb of Iufaa. The layout of the Step Pyramid, and specifically the 'Great Dry Moat', might have been a source of inspiration for this particular architectural fea-

---

[410] J.-Ph. Lauer, *Les Pyramides de Sakkarah,* Cairo 1972, pp. 12-13.

[411] S. Neureiter, 'Eine neue Interpretation des Archaismus', *SAK* 21 (1994), pp. 219-254. See also Stammers, *Elite Late Period Egyptian Tombs*, pp. 83-88 with references.

[412] In this chapter I would like to concentrate mainly on the huge shaft tombs discovered at Abusir because the comprehensive analysis of this type of tombs by M. Stammers contains some inaccurate information – Stammers, *Elite Late Period Egyptian Tombs*, pp. 33 and 114.

[413] Spencer, *Brick Architecture*, p. 117.

[414] L. Bareš, 'Saite-Persian Cemetery at Abusir (Situation Report for January–April 1995)', *GM* 151 (1996), pp. 7-17; L. Bareš – K. Smoláriková, 'The Shaft Tomb of Iufaa at Abusir (Preliminary Report for 1995/1996)', *GM* 156 (1997), pp. 9-26, and most recently Bareš – Smoláriková, *Abusir XVII*, pp. 34-43.

[415] el-Sadeek, *Twenty-Sixth Dynasty Necropolis at Gizeh*, pp. 126-132. See also footnote 73.

[416] Bareš, *Abusir IV*, pp. 45-69.

ture.[417] The 'Great Dry Moat' runs single on three sides of the pyramid complex, and double on the south side.[418] In the case of Udjahorresnet's burial complex its eastern wing was doubled. The width of the trench was reduced to 2 metres and interrupted by several struts or bridges very probably intended to enhance the stability of the walls.[419] The fact that the majority of the Saite shaft tombs at Saqqara are concentrated both inside (the tombs in the mortuary temple of Userkaf)[420] and outside the 'Great Dry Moat' (the tombs around the pyramid of Unas)[421] might indicate that the Saites were very well aware of a significant part of the original extension of this enormous trench. It does not quite prove that they knew as much of the nature of this structure as we do[422] or that they were looking for some details that would help them understand the *raison d'être* of this trench, especially in its eastern and southern part where the pyramids stood. It seems far more plausible that the idea behind these trenches that surrounded the burial shaft was inspired by a purely religious concept, namely the 'Tomb of Osiris'.[423] This possibility was recently widely discussed by many authors, including M. Stammers,[424] and there is at present little to add to this discussion. In general I agree with Stammers' conclusions based on the development of the funerary architecture and the revitalisation of older underworld deities and symbols in both parts of Egypt, namely in the Memphite and Theban necropoleis.[425] The cult of Osiris and the worship of this age-old deity reached its peak during the Late Period and numerous assimilations of Osiris with other deities have been observed and documented. The best known example was certainly Ptah-Sokar-Osiris.

One more architectural component needs to be mentioned in the overview of the direct impact that the Step Pyramid had on the Late Period shaft tombs: the 'South Tomb'. Imhotep's design and layout of this particular tomb was not only copied by the Saite architects but in all probability also transposed into the building disposition of the shaft tombs whilst keeping in mind the religious significance of its particular architectural elements. These characteristics were executed on a significantly more modest scale and in a rather simpler fashion, all in accordance with the social status of its owners. This hypothesis is supported by the fact that this type of funerary architecture occurred almost solely in the Memphite necropolis.[426] The extensive Saite knowledge and re-edition of all available funerary texts, documented in extenso on the walls of many Saite burial chambers in the Memphite necropolis, provides ample reason to suppose that they most likely had a very good insight into the symbolism of the particular architectural components of the Step Pyramid complex, of which the 'South Tomb' formed a significant part.[427] The monument is situated in the south-west corner of the southern courtyard and it is – in respect of its burial chamber – very similar

---

[417] Smoláriková, in Bárta – Coppens – Krejčí, (eds.), *Abusir and Saqqara in the Year 2005*, pp. 42-49; Bareš, in Daoud – Abd el-Fattah (eds.), *The World of Ancient Egypt*, (Supplément aux Annales du Service des Antiquités de l'Egypte 35), pp. 31-33.

[418] N. Swelim,'The Dry Moat of the Netjerykhet Complex', in J. Baines – T.G.H. James – A. Leahy – A.F. Shore (eds.), *Pyramid Studies and Other Essays Presented to I.E.S. Edwards*, London 1988, pp. 12-22.

[419] For a detailed description of these elements, see Bareš, *Abusir IV*, p. 76. fig. 10.

[420] Firth, *ASAE* 29 (1929), p. 66.

[421] Barsanti, *ASAE* 2 (1901), pp. 244-256.

[422] K. Myśliwiec – T. Herbich, with a contribution by A. Niwinski, 'Polish Research at Saqqara in 1987', *EtTrav* 17 (1995), pp. 177-203.

[423] A short discussion of the development of this phenomenon, which is moreover supported by archaeological excavations, can also be found in Z. Hawass, 'The Discovery of the Osiris Shaft at Giza', in Z. Hawass – J. Richards (eds.), *The Archaeology and Art of Ancient Egypt. Essays in Honor of David B. O'Connor*, (CASAE 36), 2007, pp. 379-397, with further references.

[424] Stammers, *Elite Late Period Egyptian Tombs*, pp. 33-39. In general every sarcophagus/coffin or burial chamber lying on a mound of sand can be considered as a 'Tomb of Osiris' or a primordial mound. At Abusir numerous variants were used but mainly the stone burial chambers rested on 'top' of a mound of sand.

[425] D. Eigner, *Die monumentalen Grabbauten der Spätzeit in der thebanischen Nekropole*, (DÖAW 8), Wien 1984, pp. 163-183.

[426] Gestermann, in Moers – Behmler – Demuss and Widmaier (eds.), *jn.t ḏr.w*, pp. 195-206.

[427] Lauer, *Les Pyramides de Sakkarah*, pp. 14-15.

to the one located under the Step Pyramid proper, including the gallery decorated with faience tiles and the false doors on which King Djoser is depicted. The unusual affinity between two tombs within a single funerary complex has led since the moment of its discovery to numerous hypotheses regarding its function and religious significance.[428] Some theories are speculative, others are based on serious research. According to James E. Quibell the royal placenta was ritually buried here,[429] while Cecil M. Firth considered it a provisional tomb to be used in case the king dies suddenly.[430] Herbert Ricke suggested that the 'South Tomb' represented the Lower Egyptian tomb at Buto, but he also supposed that it could be the tomb of the king's ka.[431] Hartwig Altenmüller supported him and, similar to Gustave Jéquier,[432] recognised in the 'South Tomb' a predecessor of the cult pyramid.[433] Jean-Philippe Lauer supposed that it was a symbolic substitute for the burial in the royal cemetery at Abydos.[434] All in all, there does not seem to be much agreement among scholars and the question regarding the function of the 'South Tomb' still remains to be answered.

This structure situated in the south-west corner of Djoser's complex will keep our attention with respect to a very specific part of the shaft tombs: the embalmer's deposit as a possible aspirant to or symbolic heir of the 'South Tomb' in the Step Pyramid complex. This parallel was not so clear at the beginning of the excavations in Abusir, although we were aware of the report written by C.M. Firth on the embalmer's deposit in the south-west corner of the double tomb of Neferibra-sa-Neith and Wahibremen.[435] Such information is not available for the other large shaft tombs excavated in Saqqara. In Abusir the exact location of some caches was insufficiently marked and the remains of the unwanted materials from the embalming process were either spread throughout the extensive substructures or were not abundant enough to capture our attention. This seems to be the case of the funerary complex of Iufaa[436] and perhaps also of the tomb R3.[437] During the 2002–2003 season small but fully independent shafts leading to deep subterranean structures were discovered in the south-west corner of the shaft tombs of Udjahorresnet and Menekhibnekau.[438] Udjahorresnet's shaft (10 m deep) was situated about 4.20 m from the south-west corner of the tomb's limestone enclosure wall. The bulk of embalming materials located at its bottom was badly disturbed by thieves in antiquity. It still consisted of a remarkable assemblage of large storage jars, bottles, bowls, lids and stands. Some of these items bore short hieratic or demotic inscriptions which identified the materials stored inside that had been used during the mummification process. On several vessels traces were visible of a thin layer of sticky, cream-coloured remains of fine linen which had been used to seal the liquid content.[439]

---

[428] For an overview of the various theories consult for instance Verner, *The Pyramids*, pp. 127-128; R. Stadelmann, 'Pyramiden AR', in W. Helck – E. Otto (eds.), *Lexikon der Ägyptologie IV*, Wiesbaden 1982, pp. 1211-1212, and Stadelmann, *Die ägyptischen Pyramiden*, pp. 68-69.

[429] Quibell in Firth – Quibell, *The Step Pyramid* I, p. 57.

[430] Firth – Quibell, *The Step Pyramid* I, pp. 18-20. On the relation between the 'South Tomb' and the sed-festival, see C.M. Firth, 'Excavations of the Service des Antiquités at Saqqara (October 1927 – April 1928)', *ASAE* 28 (1928), pp. 85-87.

[431] H. Ricke, *Bemerkungen zur ägyptischen Baukunst des Alten Reiches* I, (Beiträge Bf 4), Zürich 1944, p. 106, and H. Ricke – S. Schott, *Bemerkungen zur ägyptischen Baukunst des Alten Reiches* II, (Beiträge Bf 5), Cairo 1950, pp. 105-106, and 127. See also H. Altenmüller, 'Bemerkungen zur frühen und späten Bauphase des Djoserbezirkes in Saqqara', *MDAIK* 28 (1972), pp. 4-5.

[432] G. Jéquier, 'Les pyramides non funéraires', *CRAIBL* 1927, pp. 188-193.

[433] Altenmüller, *MDAIK* 28 (1972), pp. 3-7.

[434] Lauer, *Pyramide à degrés* I, pp. 111-112.

[435] PM III 2^2, pp. 578-592, and J.-Ph. Lauer – Z. Iskander, 'Donnés nouvelles sur la momification dans l'Egypte ancienne', *ASAE* 53 (1956), pp. 167-195.

[436] K. Smoláriková, 'Some Remarks on Embalmers' Caches from the Saite-Persian Cemetery at Abusir', in H. Győry (ed.), *Aegyptus et Pannonia III. Acta Symposii anno 2004*, Budapest 2006, pp. 263-264.

[437] For details, see Chapter 2.3 in this volume.

[438] Smoláriková, in Győry (ed.), *Aegyptus et Pannonia III*, pp. 263-266, and Smoláriková, in P. Maříková Vlčková – J. Mynářová – M. Tomášek (eds.), *My Things Changed Things*, pp. 58-63.

[439] Ikram – Dodson, *The Mummy in Ancient Egypt*, p. 106.

The finds in the shaft in the south-west corner of the burial complex of the high-ranking Saite dignitary Menekhibnekau were much better preserved and left no doubt about their function.[440] About 330–350 well preserved Egyptian amphorae were discovered *in situ*. The find represents one of the most abundant deposits of ceramics dated to the second half of the 6th century BC ever discovered. The amphorae were deposited at the bottom of an 11.50 m deep shaft situated near the south-west corner of the enclosure wall. They were spread over two or three rows at the bottom of the shaft. Almost all amphorae had been packed or filled with embalming material and carefully sealed with plaster. A common feature was the deposition of both intact and broken smaller vessels inside the amphorae.[441] Many vessels were wrapped in very fine linen and contained embalming waste material: sand, whitish salt-like substances, fine black or brown powder, linen impregnated with oil, green and red paints, decayed straw and chaff and fragments of myrrh. A set of amphorae even contained gold sheets, tiny remnants of a gilded stucco mask and a beautiful net of faience beads which usually covered the mummy of the deceased.

Apparently the material used in the process of mummification was not employed again because of its strong ritual impurity and was ritually buried – as a whole – as close as possible to the deceased. A lavishly equipped deposit perfectly reflected the high social status of its owner, both during the Old Kingdom and the Saite Period. This embalmer's cache most likely had a special significance both religiously and architecturally. It can be considered a second tomb with carefully stored materials which had been in immediate contact with the body of the deceased. This symbolism is fully compatible with the religious importance of the 'South Tomb', whatever its exact function was, because it was directly connected with the interment in the burial chamber at the bottom of the deep shaft, situated in the centre of the funerary complex.

In conclusion, the huge Late Period shaft tombs perfectly united in their concept ideas and concepts from a respected royal mortuary complex (the Step pyramid), the tomb of Osiris and the private tomb. Due to many unfavourable political events they developed and lasted for only a limited period of time[442] and were realised only on the territory of the Memphite necropolis. Although they shared many common features, this did not exclude certain variability in the design. This is especially evident towards the end of the Saite Dynasty, to which the existence of the Saite-Persian cemetery at Abusir can be dated with certainty.

2.3. The Pottery

The detailed description of the archaeological situation and layout of this unique tomb in the previous sub-chapters suggests that its architects might have been strongly influenced by the intensive works that were going on at that time (i.e. the second half of the Saite Period) in the substructure of the nearby Step Pyramid. The unusual layout of tomb R3 – the extremely deep shaft without any underground corridors (compare with the building disposition of Padihor's and other shaft tombs) perhaps forced the tomb robbers to bring all items (including pottery vessels), originally deposited in the main shaft and in one of the two niches, to the desert surface. Limited quantities of ceramic material were uncovered during the excavation and what survived was in a fragmentary state and heavily weathered since, as was already mentioned, the majority of the shards were discovered in the upper layers or among the debris. Additionally, the easternmost part of the Saite-Persian cemetery at Abusir, where a series of smaller shaft tombs including R3 are located, severely suffered from being in the immediate

---

[440] Bareš – Janák – Landgráfová – Smoláriková, *ZÄS* 135 (2008), pp. 104-114.

[441] P. French, 'An Embalmer's Cache of the Late Dynastic Period', in U. Hartung – P. Ballet – F. Béguin – J. Bourriau – P. French – T. Herbich – P. Kapp – G. Lecuyot – A. Schmitt, 'Tell el-Fara'in-Buto. 8. Vorbericht', *MDAIK* 59 (2003), pp. 221-224, and D.A. Aston, 'The Theban West Bank from the Twenty-fifth Dynasty to the Ptolemaic Period', in N. Strudwick – J.H. Taylor (eds.), *The Theban Necropolis. Past, Present and Future*, London 2003, pp. 138-166, especially pp. 153-155.

[442] Bareš, in K. Daoud – S. Bedier – S. Adel Fattah (eds.), *Studies in Honour of Ali Radwan*, pp. 177-182.

Fig. 24
The large pit in front of the courtyard

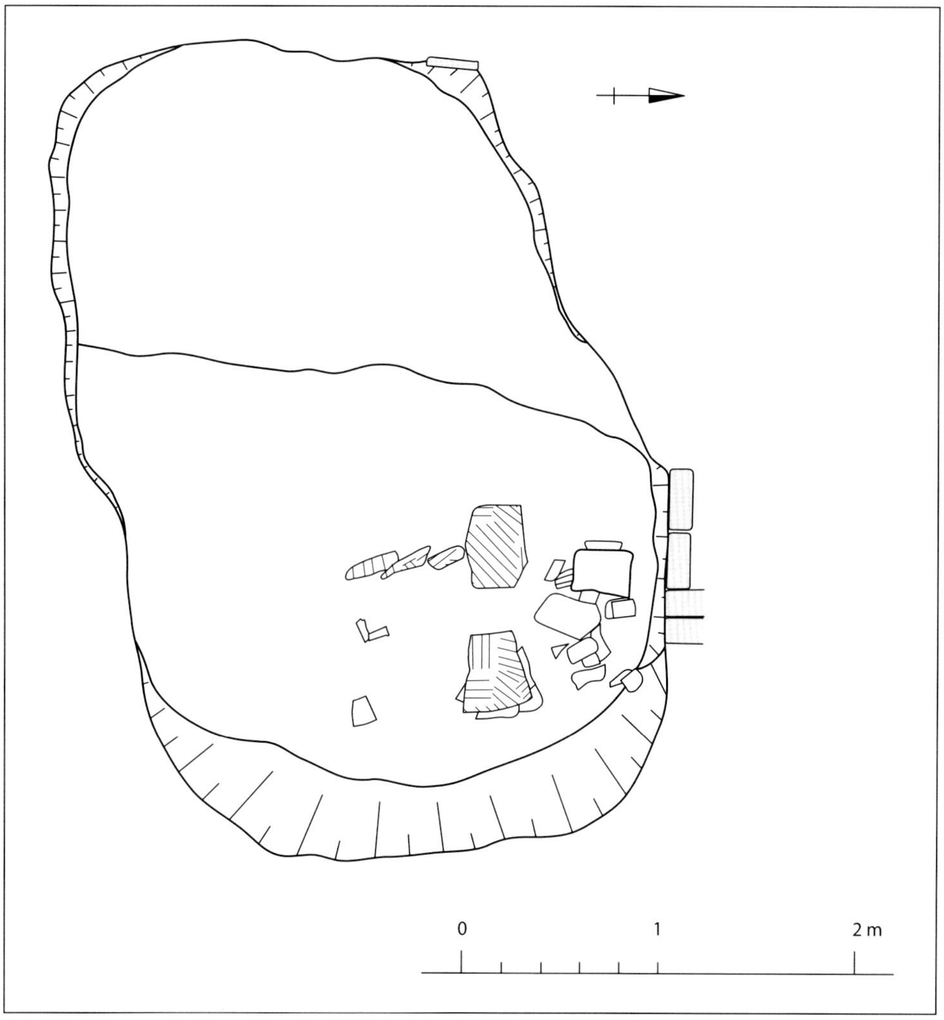

vicinity of a frequented desert road crossing the Abusir cemetery from the north-west to the south-east.[443] Despite all these unfavourable conditions, the gathered pottery assemblage is from a ceramological point of view not so small and can be divided into two significantly different groups.

The first group consists of the pottery obtained from the central shaft – mainly heavily weathered fragments of jugs and amphorae – which can be dated to the Late Roman/Coptic Period.[444] It testifies to intensive activities of the tomb robbers, who most likely brought the vessels with them.

The second group of pottery which casts more light on the date of this tomb comes in its entirety from a rather wide but not so deep pit located in the immediate vicinity of the tomb entrance. More precisely, it is situated along the south wall of the small courtyard and extends further to the south-west (Fig. 24, Pl. 13a). The filling of this pit is more or less homogenous and contained a large amount of shards that can be generally dated to the second half of the 6th century and the beginning of the 5th century BC. Although the material must be treated as a single group coming from one spot, a remarkable variety exists in the provenance of the pottery. The absolute majority of the ceramic material consists of imported East Greek archaic amphorae (coastal Ionian territory) with some coming from the Syro-Palestinian territory. All vessels unfortunately survived only in a fragmentary state, but a large portion of the shards could be joined together again.

443 Bareš – Bárta – Smoláriková – Strouhal, *ZÄS* 130 (2003), p. 148, fig. 1.

444 These fragments have not been drawn or described in detail because it was impossible to reconstruct a single significant profile. Many similar pieces are known from the Saite-Persian cemetery at Abusir, cf. Bareš, *Abusir IV*, pp. 98-103, and Bareš – Smoláriková, *Abusir XVII*, pp. 175-202.

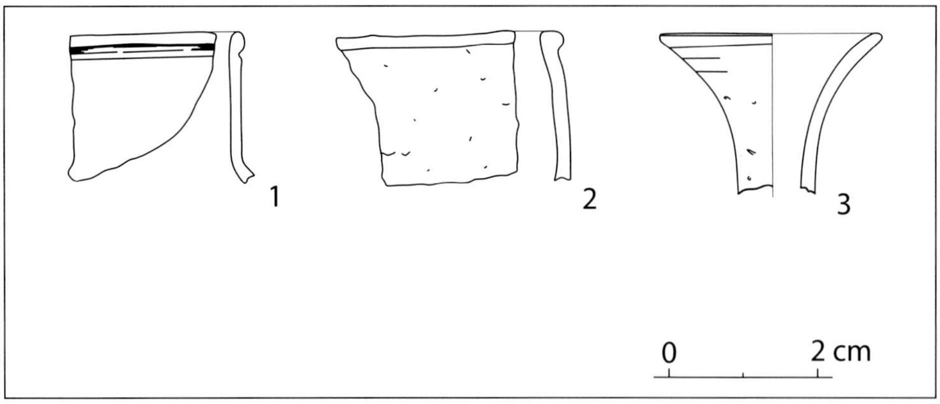

Fig. 25/1-3
A series of Egyptian pottery of various quality and surface treatment

The imports from the Eastern Mediterranean area are complemented by local vessels which are also highly fragmented. The pottery of Egyptian origin constitutes a minority among the finds, but the recovered types follow the shapes that are characteristic of the Saite-Persian Period, evolving precisely during the last decades of the 6th century BC and the beginning of the Persian occupation of Egypt. A wide range of vessels was identified typologically: from a large storage jar (only a few eroded body shards remaining) to numerous small or medium-sized jars, cups and dishes.[445] As was usual for the pottery of this period, the surface was covered with a thick layer of fine polished red slip. This is especially true for jars/bottles[446] with a long cylindrical neck and a shallow groove below the rims; the thickness of their walls varies considerably (Fig. 25/1). A cooking pot with an ovoid body represents another very popular shape (Fig. 25/2). It occurs in Late Period localities all over Egypt. Its exterior is frequently red slipped and sometimes polished. The torches (Fig. 25/3) were presumably used to provide light for the funerary and/or building activities in the tomb substructure. Torches generally belong to the so-called coarse ware with a self-slipped surface treatment. The texture of the vessels is heavily tempered with straw and mineral inclusions.[447] The low quality of the texture of the Egyptian vessels (especially in the case of large storage jars) is a well known fact, and it is all the more obvious in comparison with the Eastern imports.

The aforementioned assemblage of Phoenician import is represented by ample fragments of – most likely two – torpedo-shaped jars – in addition to the body shards, some diagnostic rims, necks and handles were also found (Fig. 26/1-3, Pl. 25c). This type of jar is similar to those known from Saqqara, Migdol and other sites, mainly from the Nile Delta, which range in date from the second half of the 6th century BC to the beginning of the 5th century BC.[448] On the almost completely reconstructed upper part of one specimen, with massive handles[449] on the shoulders, a short, almost invisible Aramaic inscription in black ink was identified (Fig. 30, Pl. 25d).[450]

---

[445] Close parallels for these vessels can be found among the pottery from the shaft tomb of Udjahorresnet, see K. Smoláriková, 'The Pottery', in Bareš, *Abusir IV*, pp. 90-98, and fig. 16/1-13. Similar vessels are also found in nearby Saqqara: P. French, 'The Pottery', in L. Giddy, *The Anubieion at Saqqara II: Cemeteries*, London 1992, pp. 79-85, pl. 62/12, 16, and 17; P. French – H. Ghaly, 'Pottery of the Late Period at Saqqara', *CCE* 2 (1987), pp. 93-124, figs. 61, 83, 87-89, 110, and 112; J. Bourriau – D. Aston, 'The Pottery', in G.T. Martin, *The Tomb Chapels of Paser and Ra'ia at Saqqara*, (Excavation Memoir 52), London 1985, pp. 51-55, pl. 37/106, 111, and 112, p. 120, and B. Aston-Green, 'The Pottery', in M.J. Raven, *The Tomb of Pay and Raia at Saqqara*, London 2005, pl. 132/163-165.

[446] P. French, 'Distinctive Pottery from the Second Half of the 6th Century B.C.', *CCE* 5 (2004), p. 92, pl. I/type 2. For a very inspiring discussion on certain types of pottery dated to the Saite-Persian Period, see pp. 91-97.

[447] For comparison see Bareš, *Abusir IV*, fig. 16/11.

[448] E.D. Oren, 'Migdol: A New Fortress on the Edge of the Eastern Delta', *BASOR* 256 (1984), p. 17, and fig. 21/7, and J.S. Holladay, *Cities of the Delta, Part III: Tell el-Maskhuta*, Malibu 1982, pls. 14/5 and 27/4.

[449] B. Aston-Green, in M.J. Raven, *The Tomb of Pay and Raia at Saqqara*, pl. 133/171 – dated to the 5th century BC.

[450] The Aramaic inscriptions from the Abusir necropolis are being studied by Dr. Jana Mynářová of the Czech Institute of Egyptology, Charles University in Prague.

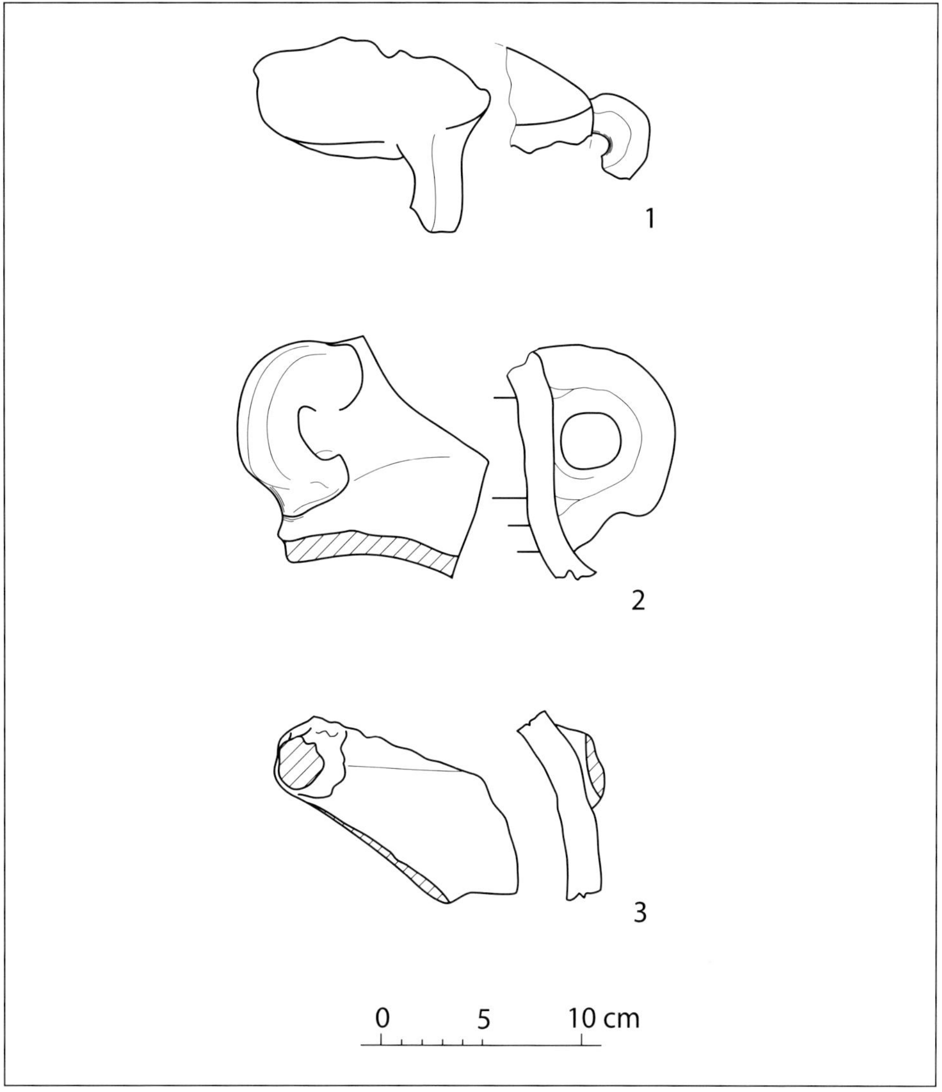

Fig. 26/1-3
Selected collection of diagnostic shards from imported Phoenician vessels

The pit yielded predominantly fragments of East Greek transport amphorae (approximately five pieces) and a large number of shards from which it was possible to reconstruct only a Chian amphora of Lambrino's A1 type,[451] dated to ca. 560-530 BC. This amphora has a slender neck, long handles, ovoid belly, and hollow foot. Its surface is without the white slip and the decoration consists of a red double band around the shoulder and a single band applied to the lower part of the belly. A single wide red band runs down from each handle along the body and joins the horizontal band on the belly. The red bands are on average 1 cm wide (Fig. 27/1, Pl. 24a-b). The lower section of another amphora,[452] with a more sandy texture but very probably of the same provenance, was partly reconstructed from several joining body shards with old breaks (Figs. 27/2, 28/1-2, Pl. 24c). Another Chian amphora (Fig. 29/2-3, Pl. 25a) dates doubtlessly to an earlier period in time.[453] A very fine, thick white slip

[451] R.M. Cook – P. Dupont, *East Greek Pottery*, London 1998, p. 150, fig. 23.2a. With respect to its provenance I am not entirely sure whether it represents a Clazomenian specimen (cf. fig. 23.3f) from the end of the 6th century BC, since both types of amphorae are almost identical – see K. Myśliwiec, *Keramik und Kleinfunde aus der Grabung im Tempel Sethos' I. in Gurna*, (AV 57), Mainz 1987, nos. 833-841.

[452] At first glance all obtained shards seem to come from a single amphora, but the large amount of body shards recovered indicates that it is not the case and that at least two amphorae were thrown into this pit.

[453] Only a very small part survived of the amphora, making it difficult to date it precisely, but the second half of the 6th century BC seems plausible, cf. Cook – Dupont, *East Greek Pottery*, p. 147, fig. 23.1g-h.

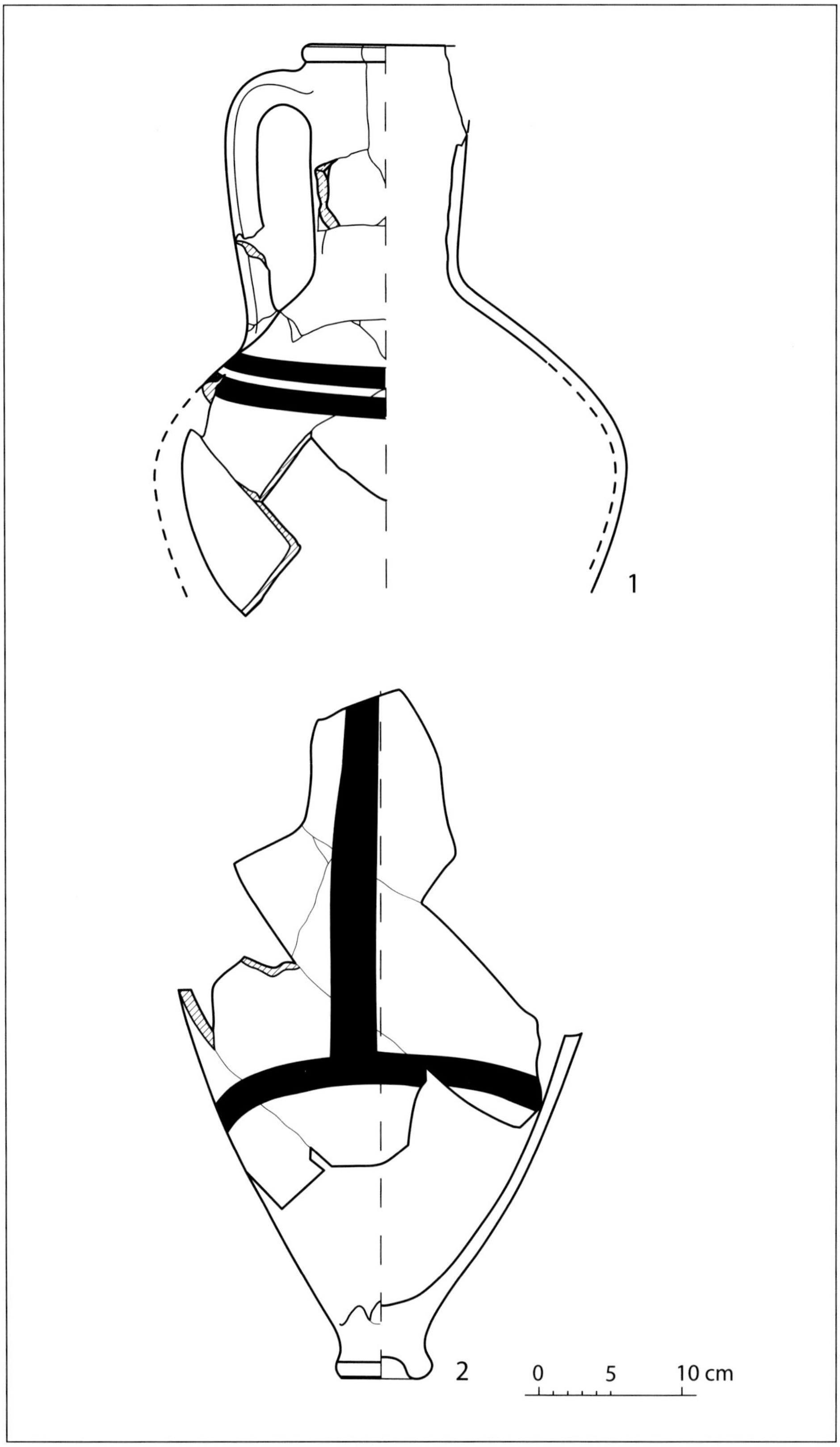

Fig. 27/1-2
Partly reconstructed archaic Greek amphorae

still survived on the neck, and red colour was applied to the lip and the outer part of the handle.

Numerous fragments, mostly body shards, of Lesbian provenance (Pl. 25b) were too damaged to be used for a reconstruction, but the fragments of the rather slender neck suggest that they derived from the 'en-phi' type.[454] This type is very well-known

[454] Cook – Dupont, *East Greek Pottery*, p. 157, fig. 23.4h-i.

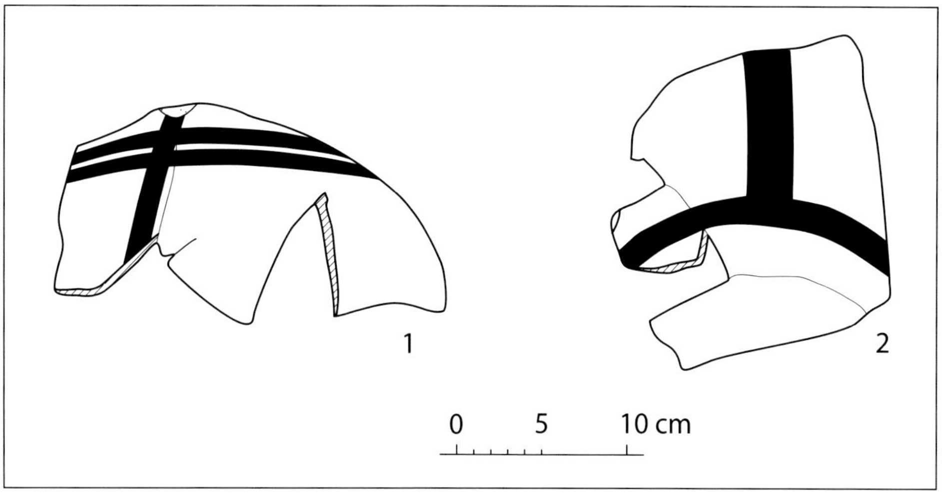

Fig. 28/1-2
Fragments of painted shards of the body of an imported amphora

from the already published assemblages of imports retrieved from Iufaa's shaft tomb.[455] This type is interesting from a chronological point of view. According to P. Dupont, its manufacture started only during the last quarter of the 6th century BC. Taking into consideration the time needed for these amphorae to reach the Egyptian markets; to find their way to the Greek community in Memphis; to be emptied and then used by the Greeks and the Egyptians likewise as a common container for liquids, and finally broken and left in the pit next to tomb R3, one can tentatively date the pit to around 510-500 BC. The rims and body shards of other amphorae discovered in the pit were extremely damaged and covered with a thick layer of sinter, and could not be identified with certainty (Fig. 29/1, 4). Surprisingly, the content of the pit was not contaminated with later intrusive specimens, hence it appears to be strongly related solely to the building and funerary activities in and around the anonymous tomb R3.[456]

One can only speculate about the function of this shallow pit filled with fragments of large vessels, blocks of stone, and some remains of baskets and reed matting. It is very tempting to identify it with a provisional small embalming edifice,[457] the *wꜥb.t n.t wt* that was usually built in the immediate vicinity of the tomb.[458] The dimensions of the pit, 8×10 m, are more than sufficient for the construction of a tent or reed hut used for the embalming of the anonymous occupant of the largely unfinished sarcophagus deposited at the bottom of the 22 m deep shaft and/or the wooden coffin placed in the north niche. Nothing resembling an embalming structure was, however, unearthed on the territory of the Saite-Persian cemetery in Abusir up until the present day, and it remains uncertain whether these structures were ever present here.

It seems much more likely, and more acceptable given its contents, that the pit was simply used to deposit rubbish. The solid Greek and Syro-Palestinian transport amphorae can be considered containers for liquids which were used by the builders during their activities in the tomb. A quite significant number of pottery vessels was also found by J.-Ph. Lauer in the vast substructure of the Step Pyramid in Saqqara. He was convinced that these vessels had been used by the Saite Egyptians exploring the

---

[455] K. Smoláriková, *Abusir VII. Greek Imports in Egypt. Graeco-Egyptian Relations during the First Millennium BC*, Prague 2002, p. 39, pl. II.

[456] This is the right place to mention the recent, very accurate statement of F.S. Frick: '...*The value, however, of these often rather unattractive relicts (potshards) lies precisely in their lack of attraction. People throw their broken pots away, they are not picked up, yet as potshards they are almost imperishable, and remain where they fell, to be covered by layer of dirt until some archaeologist excavated and interpreted them, thereby determining the precise date of a site by examining its pottery*...' – F.S. Frick, 'Pottery at Taanach', in S. Kreuzer (ed.), *Taanach/Tell Ta'annek. 100 Jahre Forschungen zur Archäologie, zur Geschichte, zu den Fundobjekten und zu den Keilschrifttexten*, (Wiener Alttestamentliche Studien 5), Frankfurt 2006, p. 35.

[457] Smoláriková, in Györy (ed.), *Aegyptus et Pannonia III*, pp. 261-268, especially p. 266 (n. 14).

[458] See for instance the reconstructions in A. Badawy, *A History of Egyptian Architecture I. From the Earliest Times to the End of the Old Kingdom*, Giza 1954, pp. 65-67. See also Coppens, *The Wabet*, pp. 57-60.

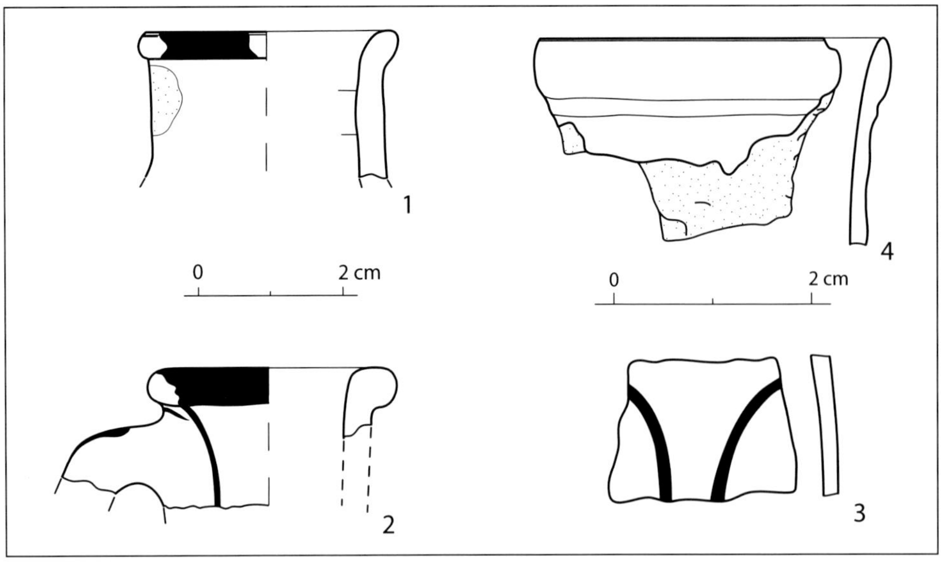

Fig. 29/1-4
A series of heavily eroded necks and shard(s) of the body of an imported Greek amphorae

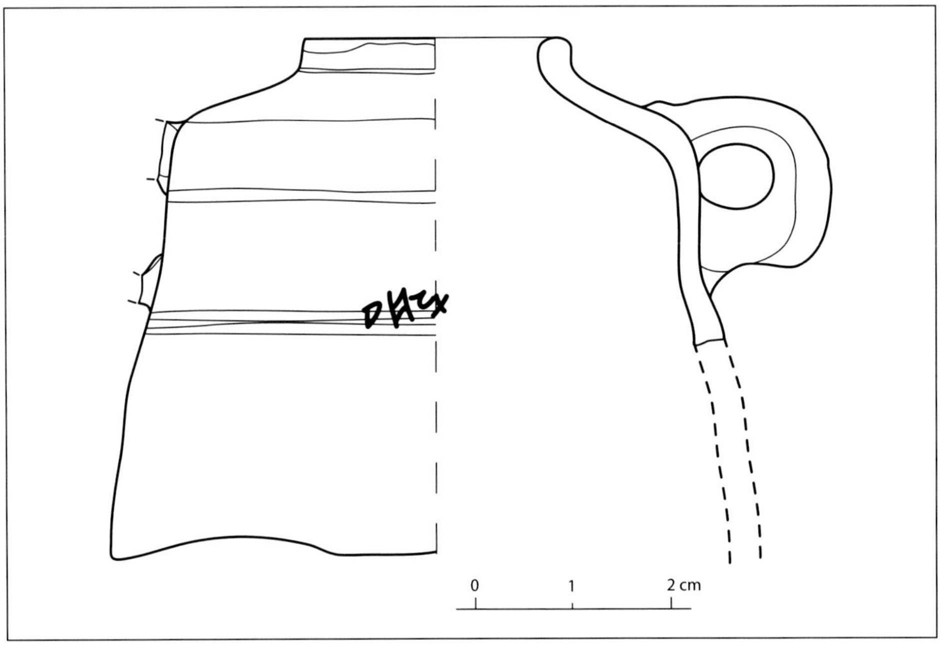

Fig. 30
The upper part of a Phoenician amphora with a short Aramaic inscription

substructure and excavating the south gallery.[459] In Abusir, the broken vessels seem to have been simply thrown behind the walls of the small courtyard that bordered the area on that side of the tomb. On almost all fragments of pottery old breaks could be observed in the sections. The habit of throwing out broken vessels is well known from many other ancient Egyptian cemeteries and from all periods of Egyptian history.[460] In light of this and in the absence of other sources, the content of the pit and consequently the works carried out on this spot can be dated, with caution, to the end of the 6th century BC and the very beginning of the 5th century BC or the time of the reign of the Persian king Darius I (522-486 BC).[461]

---

[459] Lauer, *La pyramide à degrés I*, p. 45 also mentions some other utensils used by the Egyptian builders that were simply left behind after the work was finished.

[460] J.M. Galan – M. el-Bialy, 'An apprentice's board from Dra Abu el-Naga', *EA* 25 (2004), p. 38; A. Dunsmore, 'Pottery from the Tomb of Meryneith', *JEOL* 40 (2006-2007), p. 18, and P. Wilson – G. Gilbert, 'Sais and its Trading Relations with the Eastern Mediterranean', in P. Kousoulis – K. Magliveras (eds.), *Moving Across Borders. Foreign Relations, Religion and Cultural Interactions in the Ancient Mediterranean*, (OLA 159), Leuven 2007, pp. 251-265.

[461] N. Grimal, *Histoire de l'Egypte ancienne*, Paris 1988, p. 473, fig. 167, and P. Briant, *Historie de l'Empire Perse, de Cyrus à Alexandre*, Paris 1996, pp. 488-500.

Chapter 3

Anthropological report on the burials from inside and outside the anonymous shaft tomb R3.

Eugen Strouhal

3.1. Introduction

A small anonymous shaft tomb (dubbed 'R3') was excavated at a distance of 60 m from the north-east corner of the monumental burial complex of Iufaa during the spring season of 2002 of the Czech Institute of Egyptology (Fig. 16, Pl. 11a). The burial complex was dated by means of indirect evidence to the end of the Twenty-Sixth Dynasty - beginning of the Twenty-Seventh Dynasty.[462] A heap of human bones was discovered at the foot of the east wall of its superstructure, and remains of human bones, which might have come from the original burial, were found discarded in the sand of the burial chamber at about the level of the lid of the sarcophagus.[463] These two groups of human remains are analysed in the following report.

Abbreviations

L = left	R = right	T = thoracic vertebra
L = lumbal vertebra	S = sacral vertebra	I = incisor
C = canine	P = premolar	M = molar

3.2. The adults from the mixed up bones near the surface

Archaeological background: A heap of scattered human bones without skulls was found mixed up in the sand, only 0.20-0.30 m under the surface, to the east of the superstructure of tomb R3, in the immediate vicinity of its east wall. Following the cleaning and sorting of the bones according to their age and sex it turned out that the bones belonged to three adult individuals; two males and a female. About seven fragments of ribs and four metacarpals could not be attributed to any of these individuals. The bones were found without any burial offerings that could be used for their dating. Not a single trace of resin was found on the bones. They are most probably the remains of three burials, removed from their original place of burial and heaped together near the east wall of tomb R3. They were poor class burials, undoubtedly part of the large secondary cemetery that flourished during the first millennium B.C. in the Abusir necropolis.[464] The anthropological study was performed on February 27, 2002 using the usual anthropological techniques based on K. Saller and R. Martin's methods and a few other procedures cited further below.[465]

a. The adult male 146/R/02

Preservation: No skull survived. Spine is represented by vertebrae T_{12} to L_3 and arches of L_{4-5}. Fragments of the head and distal end of the humerus and the mid-third of the ulna from the L upper extremity. Of the hip bones, fragments of both lower quarters of the acetabulum survived. Of the lower extremities, partly defective left femur and tibia, R tibial head and R fibula without its distal end have been preserved. All bones are ochre coloured except for the brownish to grey humerus, indicating the remaining traces of the soft tissues.

---

[462] Bareš – Bárta – Smoláriková – Strouhal, *ZÄS* 130 (2003), pp. 149-151. See also Chapters 2.2 and 2.3 in this volume.

[463] Bareš – Bárta – Smoláriková – Strouhal, *ZÄS* 130 (2003), pp. 150, and 154. See also Chapter 2.1.

[464] In general: Strouhal – Bareš, *Secondary Cemetery*. See also Bareš, in Daoud – Bedier – Abdel Fattah (eds.), *Studies in Honor of Ali Radwan*, pp. 177-182, and Krejčí, – Verner – Callender, *Abusir XII*.

[465] R. Martin – K. Saller, *Lehrbuch der Anthropologie in systematischer Darstellung* II, 3. Auflage, Stuttgart 1959.

Sex and age: The big robusticity of the bones, the well developed muscular relief and the large head of the L femur indicates that the remains are decisively of a male. Degenerative arthritis and osteophytosis of the spine – together with the uneven, wavy and partly concave facies auricularis of the ilium – point to an age in the range of 30-40 years at the time of death.

Osteoscopy: All preserved postcranial bones are robust, the crista iliaca massive, and the femur has a high pilaster (Martin-Saller's grade 4). The crista ulnaris protrudes considerably, the tuberositas glutea and the linea musculi solei are medium, while the fibula possesses medium to strong grooves. This suggests a medium to strong developed muscularity.

Pathology: There is a medium-progressed osteophytosis in the lumbal section of the spine (see Table 2). The lipping on the femoral head reaches up to 4 mm, in the foveola capitis 2 mm and on the talocrural joint 1 mm. An osteophyte (7 mm long) protrudes from the tuberositas tibiae. In the centre of the fibular edge of the L patella a healed compressive fracture (height 9 mm, breadth 6 mm, depression of 2 mm) can be recognised.

Osteometry: Available data are in Table 1. Using the tables for Afro-American males by Trotter and Gleser,[466] which are better suited for reconstructing the body proportions of the ancient Egyptians than the tables for Americans of European origin,[467] the stature of the deceased male, reconstructed according to the length of the L femur, was about 166.4 cm. This is near to the ancient Egyptian male average.

b. The adult female 147/R/02

Preservation: From the spine three defective lower thoracic and one lumbar vertebrae were identified. Only the R arm yielded the distal quarter of the humerus and the proximal ends of the radius and ulna. From the L hip bone the upper anterior part and lower quarter of the ilium survived. From the L femur the proximal quarter and from the R one the medial condyle have been preserved, while the anterior half of the R calcaneus also survived. All bones are ochre coloured with brown or grey spots, except for the entirely dark vertebrae.

Sex and age: The body build and bone dimensions (see further) betray the female sex, while the attachments of the muscles did not survive. The apophysis of the L crista iliaca still has a fissure after the recent fusion with the body of the ilium. The traces of the fusion are faintly marked on the proximal end of the radius. No pathological change could be found in any of the available bones. The age at death falls into the range of 20-25 years.

Osteoscopy: All preserved bones are slender, except for a slightly more robust fragment of the hip bone.

Osteometry: Only a few measurements could be taken: (4) the circumference of the R humerus 50 mm, the diameter of the head of R radius 21 mm, the breadth of the R ulnar trochlea 28 mm, (9) the upper transversal diaphysis diameter of the L femur 31 mm, (10) the upper sagittal diaphysis diameter of the L femur 21 mm, (20) the circumference of the L femur 120 mm, (21) the condylar breadth 76 mm, (3) the minimum breadth of the R calcaneus 26 mm, and (4) the height of the same 38 mm.[468]

Pathology: The joints of the distal humerus, the proximal radius and the ulna, and the proximal and the distal femur are still devoid of any signs of degenerative osteorthritis.

c. The adult male 148/R/02

Preservation: From the spine, all lumbal vertebrae with some defects, from the sacrum S_1 and the posterior wall of $S_{2\text{-}3}$, from the L hip bone the lower quarter of the

[466] M. Trotter – G.C. Gleser, 'Estimation of Stature from Long Bones of American Whites and Negroes', *AJPA* 10 (1952), pp. 463-514.

[467] Strouhal – Bareš, *Secondary Cemetery*, pp. 90, and 162.

[468] The numbers in brackets follow Martin – Saller, *Anthropologie in systematischer Darstellung*.

Table 1
Postcranial measurements (mm) of the two males found outside and inside the anonymous shaft tomb R3. No measurable bone survived of the male 148/R/02.

Abbreviations:
diam. = diameter, for. = foramen, L = left, max. = maximum, R = right, and transv. = transversal.

No.	Bone/Individual	146/R/02		186/R/02	
	Side	L	R	L	R
	Humerus				
4	Lower epiphyseal breadth	62	–	–	–
7	Minimum circumference	65	–	61	–
8	Circumference of the head	143?	–	138	–
	Radius				
3	Minimum circumference	–	–	–	41
	Os coxae				
22	Maximum diameter of acetabulum	53	–	–	–
	Femur				
1	Maximum length	455	–	491?	–
2	Length in natural position	453	–	–	–
6	Sagittal mid-diaphysis diam.	32	–	33	33
7	Transv. mid-diaphysis diam.	27	–	27	27
9	Upper transv. diaphysis diam.	33	–	30	30
10	Upper sagittal diaphysis diam.	27	–	28	26
20	Circumference of the head	154	–	–	147
21	Condylar breadth	79	–	–	–
	Tibia				
1	Total length	346	–	388?	–
8a	Max. diam. at for. nutricium	35	–	37	–
9a	Transv. diam. at for. nutricium	26	–	28	26
10b	Minimum circumference	82	–	80	–
	Fibula				
4a	Minimum circumference	–	–	29	–
	Patella				
1	Maximum height	46	–	–	–
2	Maximum breadth	42	–	–	–
3	Maximum thickness	23	–	–	–
	Calcaneus				
1	Maximum length	–	–	–	75
3	Minimum breadth	–	–	–	26
4	Height	–	–	–	40

ilium and from the L femur the distal third of the posterior compact bone with both condyles have been preserved.

Sex and age: The bones are medium robust and the attachments of the muscles did not survive. The shape of the incisura ischiadica major is definitely of a male. Traces of epiphyseal fusion are still visible on the lumbal vertebrae, bodies S_{1-2} did not yet fuse. The facies auricularis of the ilium is sharply delimited and billowed. The age falls into the range of 20-25 years.

Osteoscopy: The humerus, hip bone and crista iliaca are medium to robust, the sacrum medium robust, the pilaster medium to strong (Martin-Saller's stage 2-3).

Pathology: Slight beginnings of lipping can be recognised on the distal joint surfaces of the humerus and femur. The osteophytosis of the spine did not yet start.

Osteometry: No measurable bone was available except for the vertebrae.

Spine: The high values of the vertebral heights are an indication of the probably higher than average stature of the person (Table 2).

Vertebra	146/R/02		148/R/02	
	Height	Osteophytosis	Height	Osteophytosis
12th thoracic	25	0	–	–
1st lumbal	27	2	27	0
2nd lumbal	27	1	28	0
3rd lumbal	26	2	28	0
4th lumbal	–	–	28	0
5th lumbal	–	–	29	0

Table 2.
The anterior heights (mm) and the degree of osteophytosis of the spine of the two males found near the anonymous shaft tomb R3.

3.3. The original burial from the sarcophagus of the anonymous tomb R3

Archaeological background: The human skeletal remains were found in the burial chamber of tomb R3 lying beside the sarcophagus and mixed up in the sand at the level of the lid of the sarcophagus.[469] They were obviously lifted from the sarcophagus by tomb robbers, who by throwing them out and treading on them damaged some of the bones and even destroyed several others. These bones were studied on February 26, 2002 by the common anthropological methods as noted above.

Mummification: The nasal cavity did not survive, but the entire external side of the calva shows large areas stained black. This is a result of the resin applied to the original wrappings. The brain removal and its replacement by hot resin is documented by the black resinous coating of the inner surface of the lower half of the occipital scale, and it continues on the posterior half of the R parietal bone and onwards as a 1.0-1.5 cm band in a semicircle across the midline back to the occipital stain. Another small spot of resin (4×2 cm) is visible around the lambda point. All postcranial bones are ochre coloured with brown spots indicating the remaining traces of the soft tissues. On these black spots patches of resin can occasionally be found.

Preservation: The calva could be reconstructed from 15 fitting fragments. A few bones of the cranial base and almost the entire maxilla also survived. Only a single mid-thoracic vertebra, the L humerus without the distal quarter, the distal third of the L radius, the medium thirds of both ulnae, one proximal phalanx, both defective femurs and the tibiae, fragments of both fibulae and a defective R calcaneus have been preserved. All bones proved to belong to a single individual.

Sex and age: The cranial features are prevalently male in nature (see further). The postcranial bones are medium robust, the muscular relief is medium, the heads of the humerus and the femur are large. The long extremity bones – in spite of being partly defective – reveal a high stature, fitting to a male. The sagittal and coronal sutures are closed from the inside and are starting to close from the outside. The abrasion of dentition is medium progressed. There are no traces of epiphyseal lines. The joint surfaces show only the incipient stage of degenerative arthritis. The age at death falls into the range of 30-40 years.[470]

Cranioscopy: The skull vault is medium robust (5-6 mm thick), the glabella protruding (Broca),[471] the arcus superciliares medium,[472] the tubera frontalia developed slightly, the tubera parietalia medium, the lineae temporales feeble (marked only on the frontale), the cristae supramastoidae low and obtuse, the profile of the forehead regularly arched (starting from a postglabellar depression), the protuberance occipitalis externa medium (Broca),[473] the nuchal muscular relief medium to strong, the processi mastoidei medium thick (L 12 mm, R 10 mm), and the incisura mastoidea small.

[469] Excavation no. 186/R/02.
[470] In the preliminary report it was assessed as five years higher: Bareš – Bárta – Smoláriková – Strouhal, *ZÄS* 130 (2003), p. 154.
[471] Grade 4 according to Martin – Saller, *Anthropologie in systematischer Darstellung*.
[472] Grade 2-3 according to E. Eickstedt, *Die Forschung am Menschen. Teil 2. Physiologische und morphologische Anthropologie*, Stuttgart 1944.
[473] Grade 2 according to Martin – Saller, *Anthropologie in systematischer Darstellung*.

Craniometry: (1) Cranial length 185 mm, (8) cranial breadth 136 mm, (9) minimum frontal breadth 92 mm, (10) maximum frontal breadth 120 mm, (48.1) maxilloalveolar height 20 mm, (50) anterior interorbital breadth 23? mm, (60) maxilloalveolar length 57 mm, (61) maxilloalveolar breadth 60? mm,[474] mastoid height L 32? mm and R 30 mm.[475]

Dentition: Only the upper tooth row from R M_1 to L M_3 has been preserved. Abrasion is medium progressed: mostly on L I_1 with grade 6 (dentine entirely exposed), L M_1 has grade 5 (dentine exposed except for islets of enamel), R C, R P_1 and L $M_{2\text{-}3}$ have grade 4 (large islets of dentine in enamel), and L C and L P_1 grade 3 (beginning exposure of dentine). An isolated crown of one of the upper P shows abrasion of grade 4. L P_2 revealed sequels of tooth caries which destroyed the crown, leaving only roots in its alveoli, around which tips on buccal side a fistula evacuated pus of an abscess. R M_1 was intravitally lost, most probably also due to caries, and its alveolus was closing.

Osteoscopy: The robusticity of the upper extremity bones was medium, while of the lower extremity bones medium to strong (except for the feeble to medium fibula). Muscular attachments were developed slightly on the humerus, and medium on the femur and tibia. Tuberositas deltoidea was almost absent, cristae of the radius and ulna feeble, while the femur possessed a strong pilaster (of Martin's grade 4) and the grooving of the fibula was extremely deep. Age changes on the proximal humerus and femur were only beginning. The lipping on the humeral head was only 1-2 mm broad, while on the femoral head 2-10 mm with beginning erosion, and in the foveola 4 mm. There was no indication of lipping at the knee joint, but 1 mm at the talocrural joint. At the distal end of tibiae outstanding facies orientales (13×8 mm) were noted.

Osteometry: All extremity bones are long or high, but slender (Table 1). According to the tables for Afro-Americans by Trotter and Gleser[476] the reconstructed stature proved to be high (around 172.5 cm). The body build was leptomorphic.

Spine: Only a single mid-thoracic vertebra ($T_{7\text{-}8?}$) was found (anterior height 21 mm) with only incipient osteophytosis.

Pathology or pseudo-pathology: A largely gaping, straight cut broke through the skull vault. It starts on the right parietal bone, 3.0 cm in front of the point lambda and 1.5 cm right of the sutura sagittalis, and runs in an oblique direction to the left across the mid-line, ending near the middle of the left parietale (length 5.5 mm). The V-shaped gap (up to 13 mm wide at the level of the surface of the outer compact bone) has anteriorly obliquely sloping sides, changing into more perpendicular ones posteriorly. The upper half of the diploe was blackened by resin, and the lower half retained its ochre colour. The calva was most probably broken into 15 fragments due to this stroke and not even a slight trace of healing could be found. If the stroke was inflicted during the lifetime (probably by an axe) the wound would have been mortal, killing the victim immediately. We cannot, however, fully exclude the possibility that the cut was inflicted post mortem, probably during the looting or excavation of the burial.

3.4. Conclusion

The mixed up human remains belong to three adults: a 30-40 year old male and a 20-25 year old female and a male of identical age. Since no trace of mummification has been preserved on the bones, they can be considered as belonging to the large secondary cemetery that flourished in the first millennium BC in Abusir.[477] The three bodies were either not very carefully assembled from their original locations by workmen in order to provide space to build tomb R3, or they were discarded by the activities of the tomb robbers or the stone masons later on. The extant bones are scanty but eloquent enough to enable their distinction and sexing, and partly measurements. The latter fit

---

[474] The numbers in brackets follow Martin – Saller, *Anthropologie in systematischer Darstellung*.

[475] Following E. Giles – O. Elliot, 'Sex Determination by Discriminant Function Analysis of Crania', *AJPA* 21 (1963), pp. 53-68.

[476] Trotter – Gleser, *AJPA* 10 (1952).

[477] Strouhal – Bareš, *Secondary Cemetery*.

perfectly within the ranges of the Late Period to Ptolemaic and Roman Period series established during the study of the secondary burials within the Ptahshepses mastaba.[478] Only banal palaeo-pathological changes could be revealed.

The remains of a 30-40 year old male from the burial chamber of tomb R3 proved to be mummified by the use of resin. His brain was removed and replaced by filling the braincase with hot liquid resin. Judging from the bone robusticity, the development of the muscle attachments and the stage of degenerative arthritis, the man used more intensively his lower rather than upper extremities. In this perspective he fits among the 'white collar' professionals – scribes, officials, priests – to which he must have belonged also according to the layout of his sumptuous tomb. His high stature (around 172.5 cm) and leptomorphic body build are in harmony with the external length of 2.5 m (hence about 2 m of internal length) of his rather large rectangular sarcophagus of white limestone.[479] The severe cut in the top of his skull might have been the result of post mortem damage. If it occurred, however, in vitam by a blow of an axe (in a fight or murder attempt) it would most definitely have been mortal.

---

[478] Strouhal – Bareš, *Secondary Cemetery*, pp. 159-160. The only exception was the male 148/R/02 with not measurable bones.

[479] Bareš – Bárta – Smoláriková – Strouhal, *ZÄS* 130 (2003), p. 150.

Index

Plates

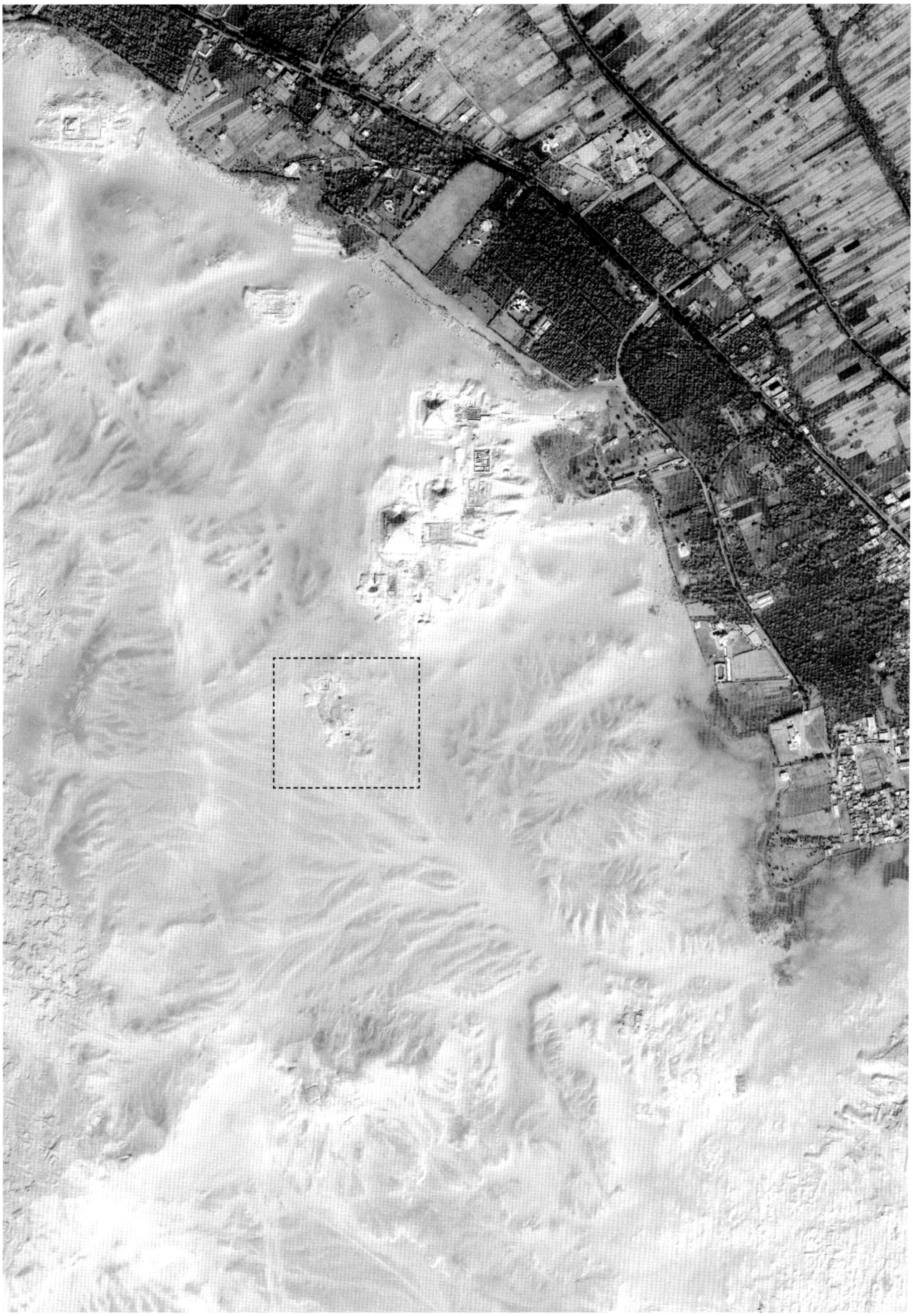

Plate 1 The Saite-Persian necropolis of Abusir (courtesy of M. Bárta – V. Brůna, *Satellite Atlas of the Pyramid Fields of Abusir, Saqqara and Dahshur*, Prague 2006, plate I)

Plate 2a The cult structure situated in front of the eastern facade of Iufaa's central shaft, with the excavation of the tomb of Padihor in the background (KV); **2b** Remains of the mud brick wall that connects the corridor with the burial chamber - south side (CIE)

Plate 3a The entrance into the burial chamber of Padihor (CIE); **3b** The burial chamber of Padihor (FC)

Plate 4a The north wall of the burial chamber (west section) (CIE); **4b** The north wall of the burial chamber (east section) (CIE)

Plate 5a The south wall of the burial chamber (west section) (CIE); **5b** The south wall of the burial chamber (east section) (CIE)

Plate 6a The lintel above the entrance into the burial chamber (east wall) (FC); **6b** The west or rear wall of the burial chamber (CIE)

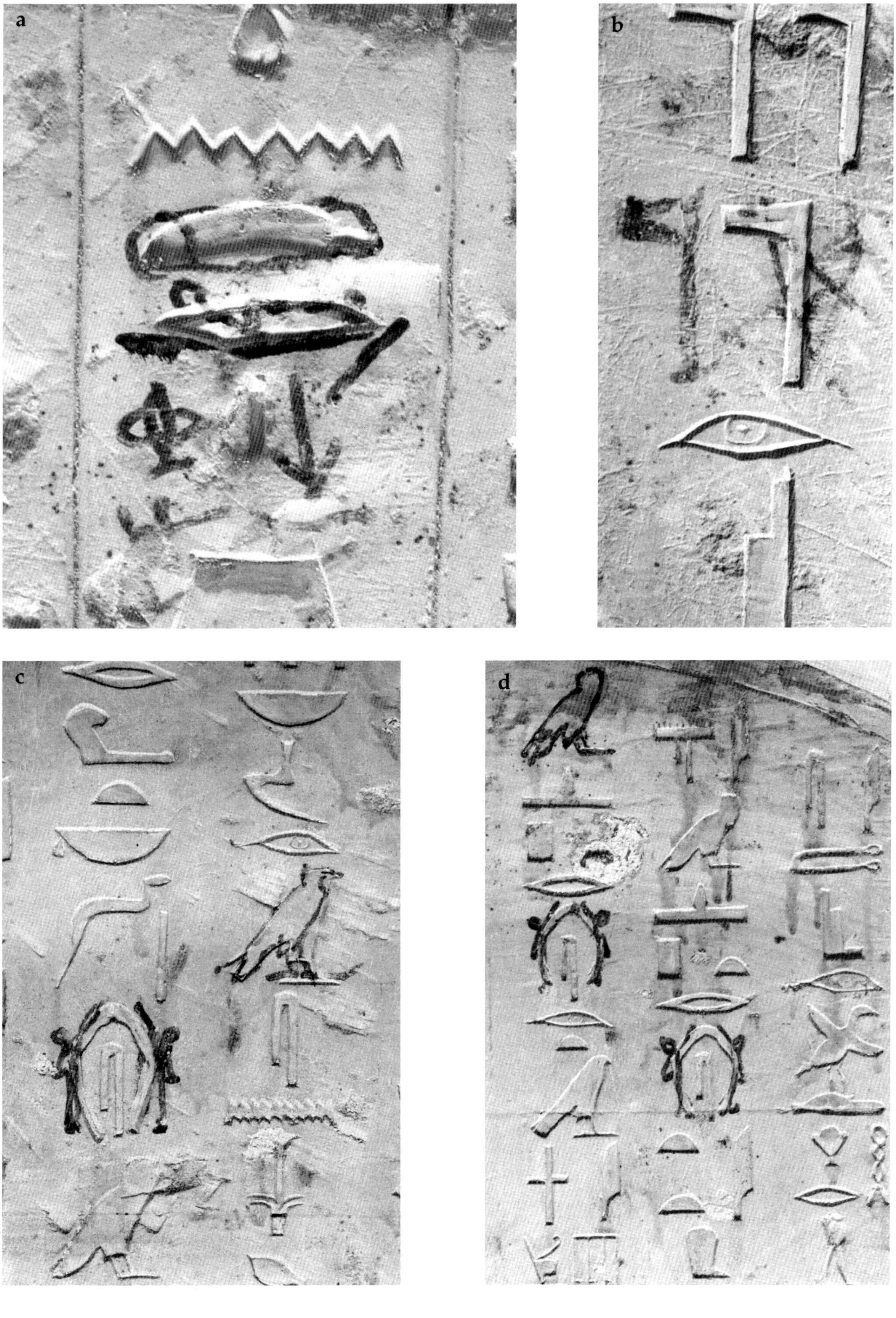

Plate 7a Correction on the east wall (CIE); **7b** Correction on the north wall (CIE); **7c** Corrections on the west wall (CIE); **7d** Corrections on the west wall (CIE)

a

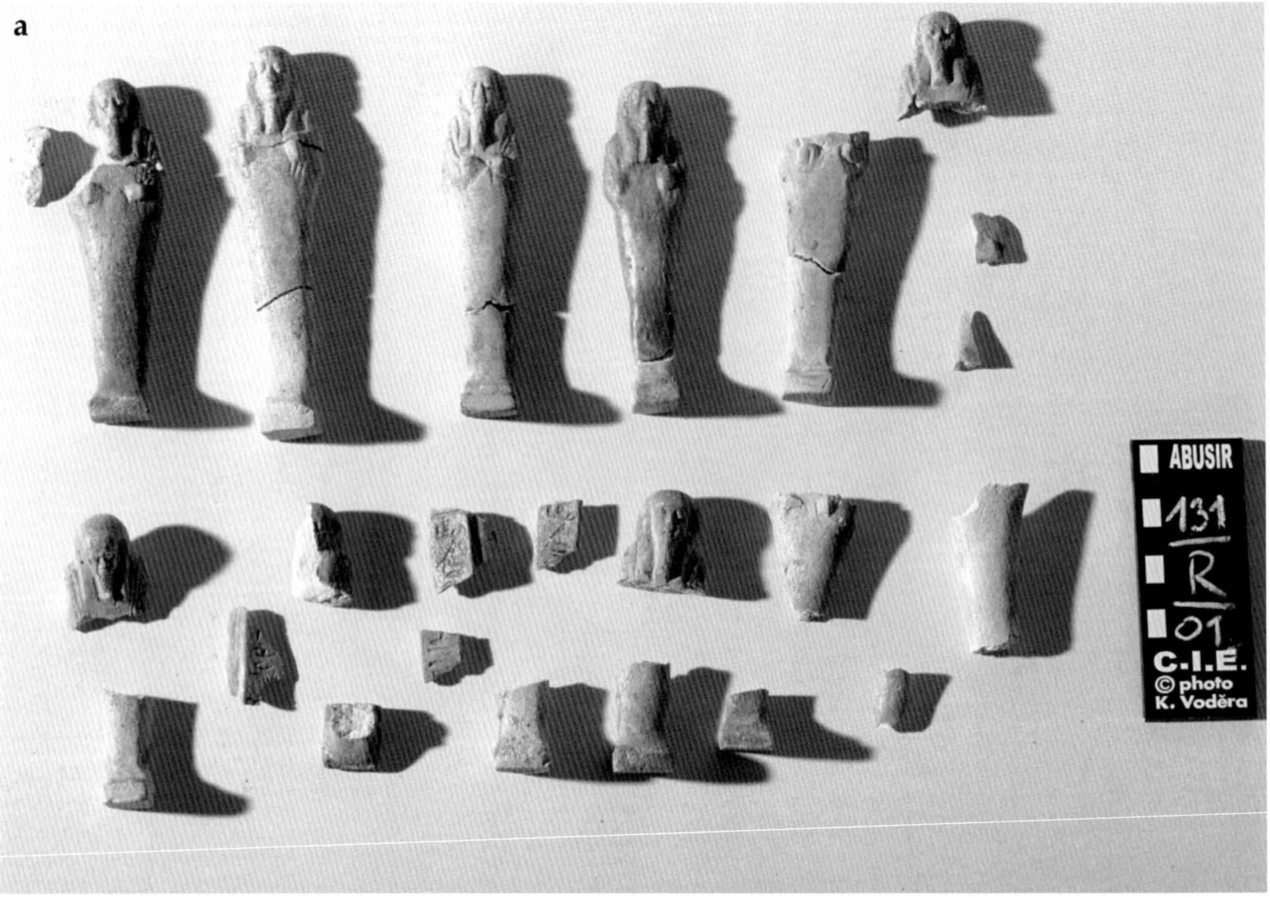

b

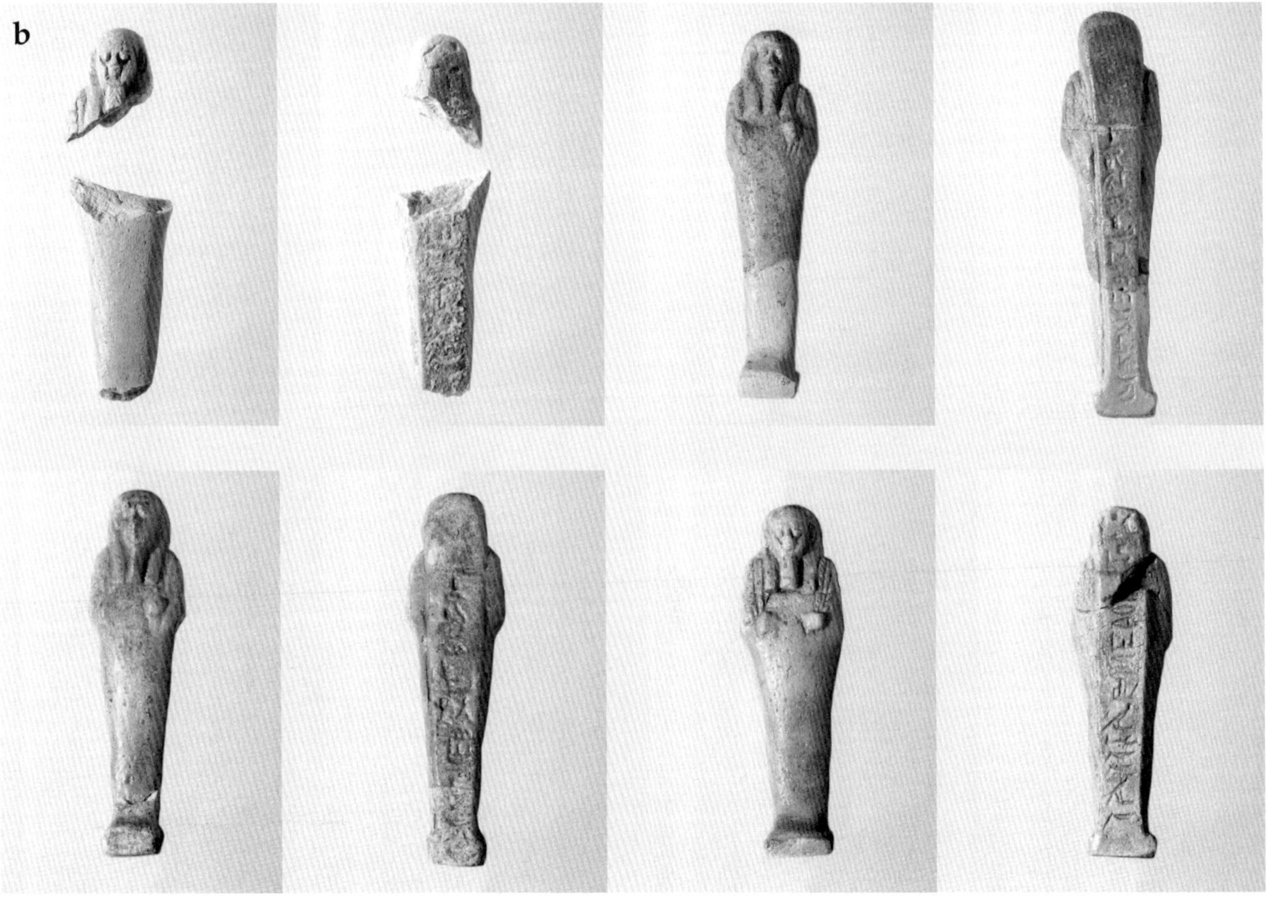

Plate 8a Overview of all shabtis and fragments of shabtis discovered during the excavation of the burial complex of Padihor (CIE); **8b** Shabtis a) 99/R/01, b) 131/R/01a, c) 131/R/01b, and d) 131/R/01c (clockwise) (CIE)

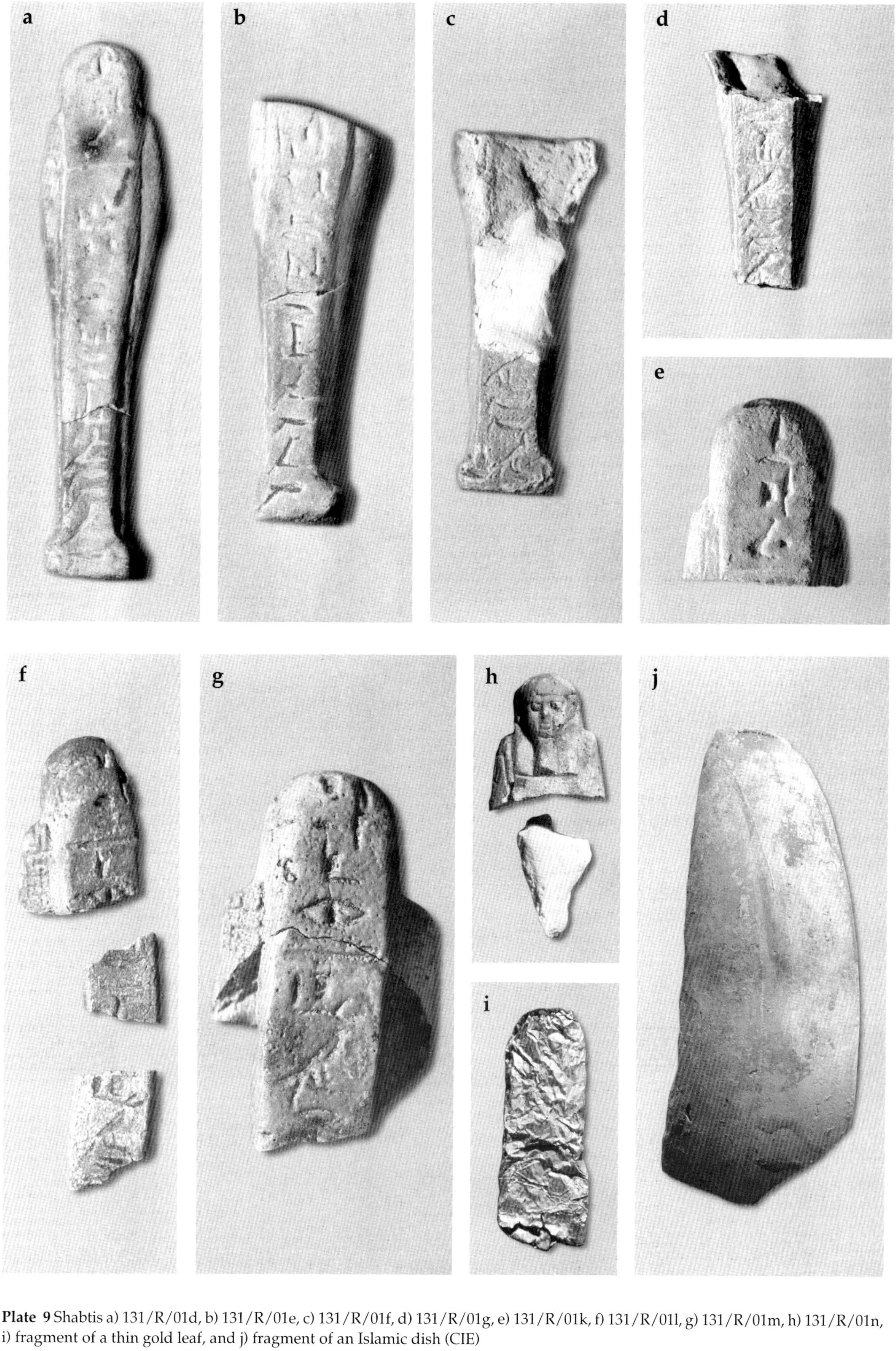

Plate 9 Shabtis a) 131/R/01d, b) 131/R/01e, c) 131/R/01f, d) 131/R/01g, e) 131/R/01k, f) 131/R/01l, g) 131/R/01m, h) 131/R/01n, i) fragment of a thin gold leaf, and j) fragment of an Islamic dish (CIE)

Plate 10a/b The Arabic inscription in the corridor leading from the subsidiary shaft to the burial chamber (CIE)

Plate 11a The superstructure of the anonymous tomb R3 (KS); **11b** The entrance passage to the inner space of the tomb (KS)

Plate 12a A detailed view of the outer and inner blocked entrances (KS); **12b** Three mudbrick steps leading to the small courtyard (KS)

Plate 13a A large pit located in the vicinity of the south-west corner of the courtyard (KS); **13b** A blocked niche in the south wall of the central shaft (KS); **13c** A view of the entrance passage towards the south (KS)

Plate 14a A view of the preserved parts of the superstructure – north-south direction (KS); **14b** The mudbrick superstructure from the south-west corner (KS); **14c** A large pit dug into the body of the mud brick superstructure (KS)

Plate 15a A detailed view of the destroyed east section of the superstructure (KS); **15b** The cleared mouth of the central shaft (KS)

Plate 16a The anonymous tomb R3 from the south (KS); **16b** The entrance corridor from the north (KS)

b

Plate 17a Secondary destruction of the mass of mud bricks in the north-west corner (KS); **17b** The blocked inner entrance, a view from the north (KS)

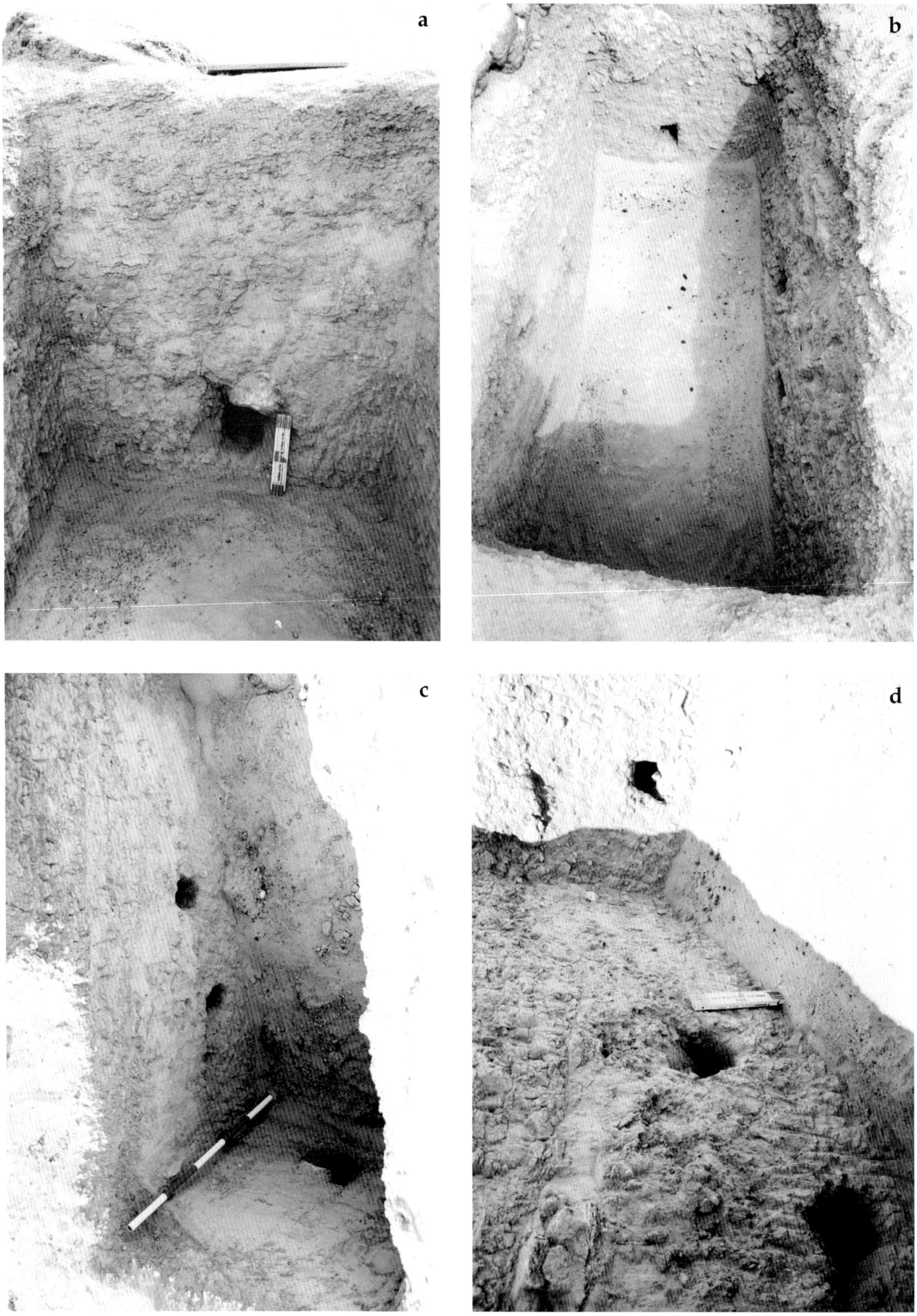

Plate 18a A large trench cut into the *tafla* bedrock to the east of the central shaft (KS); **18b** A hole cut into the north wall of the trench (KS); **18c** The south-west corner of the trench (KS); **18d** The north-west corner of the trench (KS)

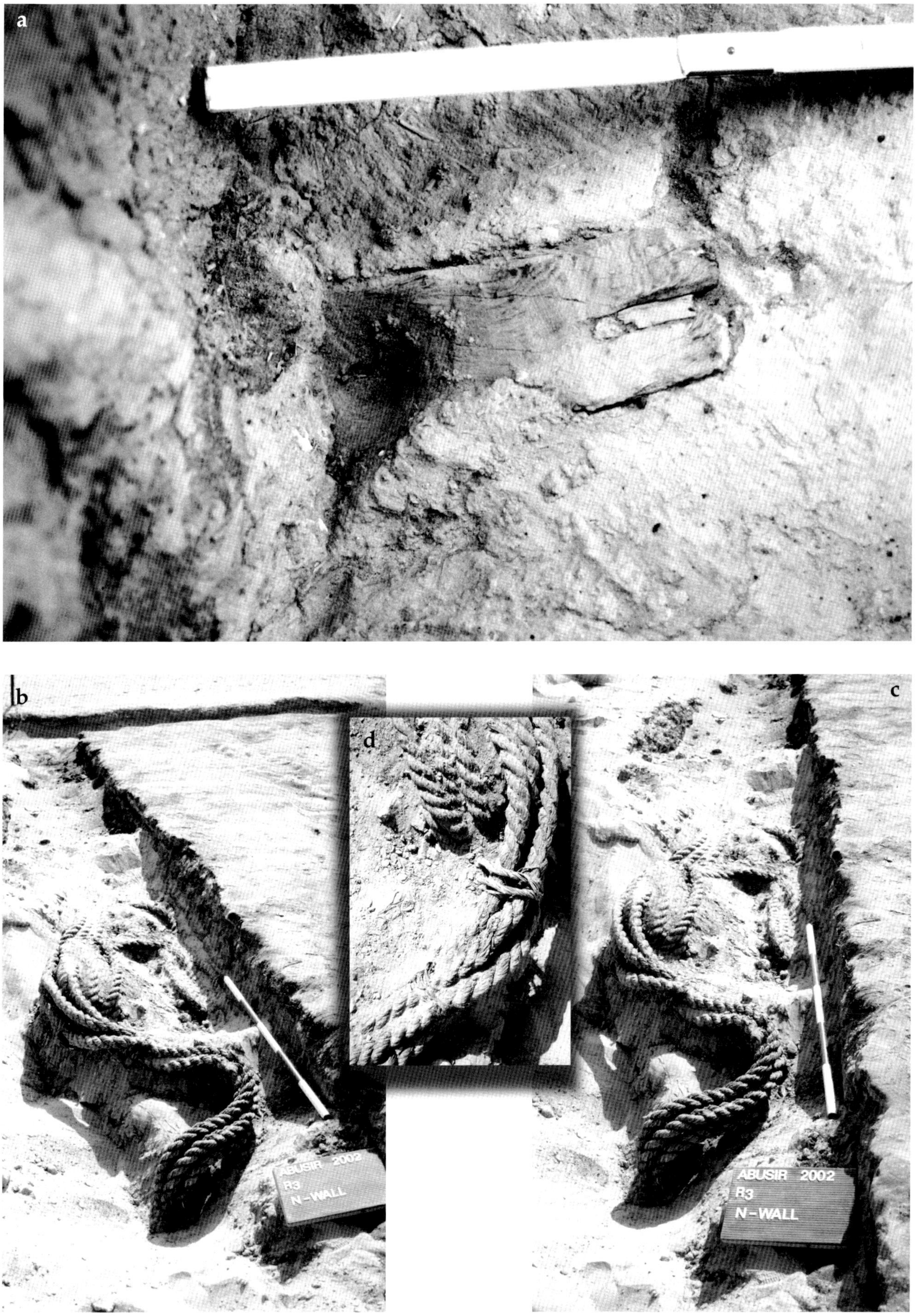

Plate 19a The wooden door pivot located just behind the inner entrance (KS); **19b** Remnants of huge ropes abutting the northern side of the superstructure (KS); **19c/d** Detailed views of the ropes (KS)

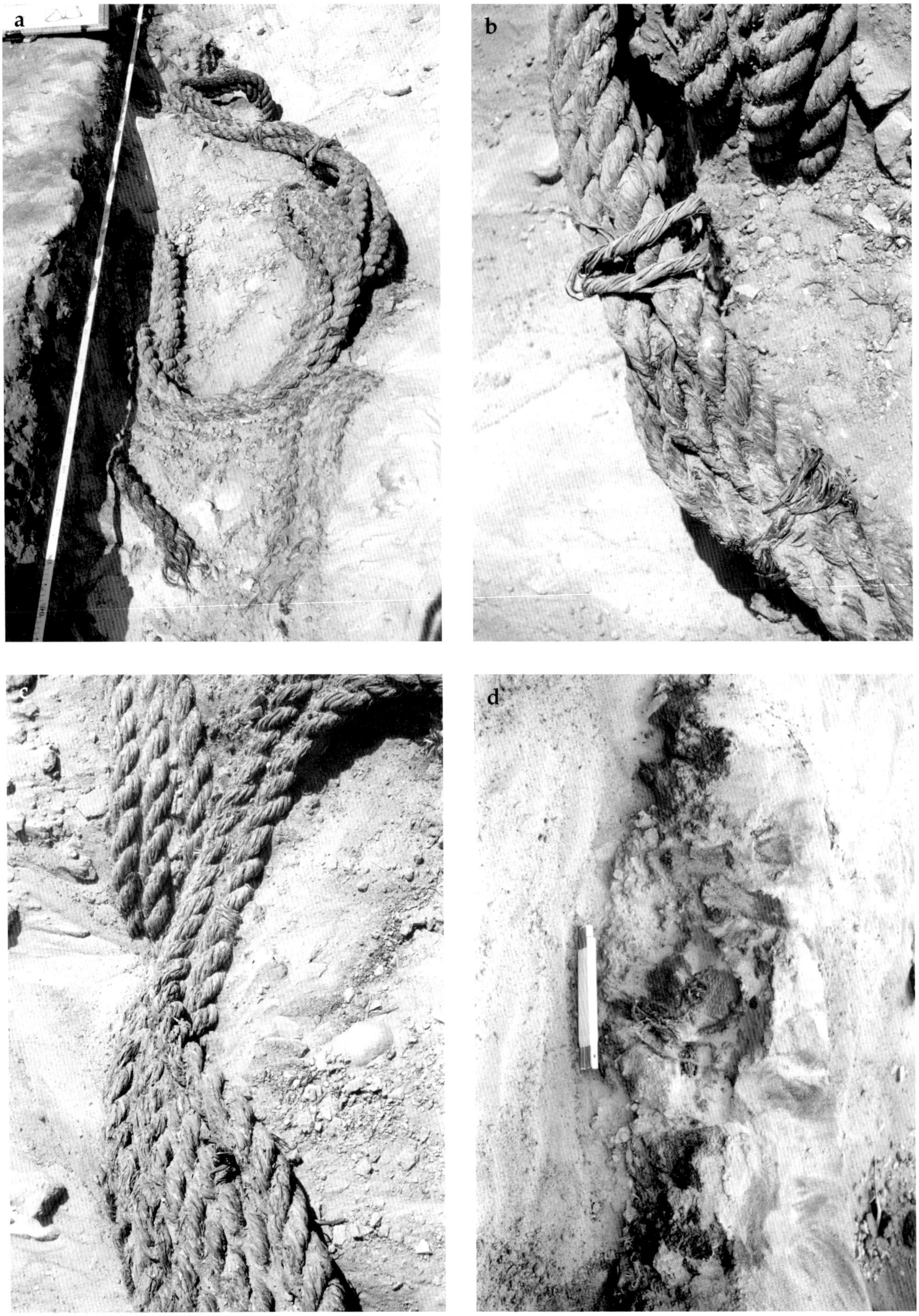

Plate 20a Ropes at the west side of the superstructure (KS); **20b** A detailed view of the ropes tied up with twisted plant stalks (KS); **20c** A mass of ropes at the west side of the superstructure (KS); **20d** Poor remains of a basket from the layers to the east of the superstructure (KS)

Plate 21a The narrow corridor between the east wall of the shaft and sarcophagus (KS); **21b** An *Udjat*-eye painted on the east side of the limestone sarcophagus (KS)

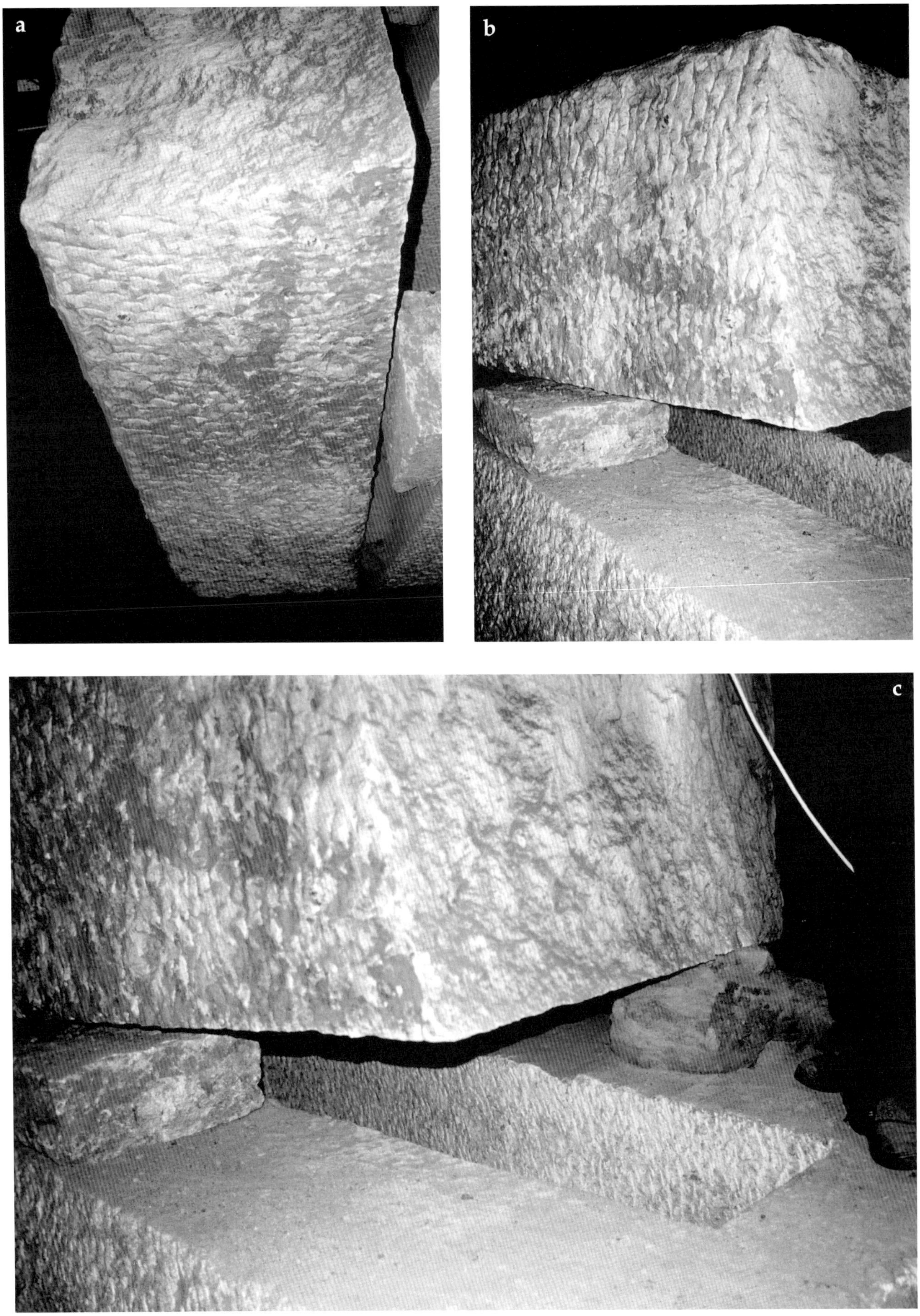

Plate 22a The south-east corner of the limestone sarcophagus (KS); **22b** The broken east part of the lid (KS); **22c** Small pieces of a limestone block and *tafla*, keeping the sarcophagus open (KS)

Plate 23a A view towards the west side of the sarcophagus cavity (KS); **23b** The nearly finished cavity of the anthropoid limestone sarcophagus (KS)

Plate 24a A partly reconstructed upper part of a Chian amphora (KS); **24b** The same Chian amphora (KS); **24c** Fragments of another Chian amphora (KS)

Plate 25 The neck of a Chian amphora covered with white slip (KS); **25b** A set of shards from a Lesbian amphora (KS); **25c** A selected collection of diagnostic shards from Phoenician amphorae (KS); **25d** The upper part of a Phoenician amphora with a short Aramaic inscription (KS)